Entangled Evolutions

Entangled Evolutions

Media and Democratization

in Eastern Europe

PETER GROSS

WOODROW WILSON CENTER PRESS
Washington, D.C.

THE JOHNS HOPKINS UNIVERSITY PRESS
Baltimore and London

EDITORIAL OFFICES

Woodrow Wilson Center Press
One Woodrow Wilson Plaza
1300 Pennsylvania Avenue, N.W.
Washington, D.C. 20004-3027
Telephone 202-691-4010
www.wilsoncenter.org

ORDER FROM:

The Johns Hopkins University Press
P.O. Box 50370
Baltimore, Maryland 21211
Telephone 1-800-537-5487
www.press.jhu.edu

2 4 6 8 9 7 5 3 1

Library of Congress Cataloging-in-Publication Data

Gross, Peter.
    Entangled evolutions : media and democratization in Eastern Europe
/ Peter Gross.
        p.   cm.
    Includes bibliographical references and index.
    ISBN 0-8018-6850-5 (hbk.) — ISBN 0-8018-6852-1 (pbk.)
    1. Mass media—Political aspects—Europe, Eastern.   2. Europe,
Eastern—Politics and government—1989–   I. Title.
P95.82.E852 G76 2002
302.23'0947—dc21
                                                                2002000309

ABOUT THE CENTER

The Center is the living memorial of the United States of America to the nation's twenty-eighth president, Woodrow Wilson. Congress established the Woodrow Wilson Center in 1968 as an international institute for advanced study, "symbolizing and strengthening the fruitful relationship between the world of learning and the world of public affairs." The Center opened in 1970 under its own board of trustees.

In all its activities the Woodrow Wilson Center is a nonprofit, nonpartisan organization, supported financially by annual appropriations from the Congress, and by the contributions of foundations, corporations, and individuals. Conclusions or opinions expressed in Center publications and programs are those of the authors and speakers and do not necessarily reflect the views of the Center staff, fellows, trustees, advisory groups, or any individuals or organizations that provide financial support to the Center.

*To Vera, Eric,
Nicholas, Katrina,
and Sonya*

Contents

Preface

That the events of 1989 in Eastern Europe were labeled "momentous" and "surprising" is testimony to the West's failure to detect the advanced moribundity of Communism in the region. Actually, what happened there was less like the first moon landing and more like the final melting of very thin ice. Communism's death came with a whimper (the sole exception being Romania, where the violent circumstances surrounding the fall of Communism remain a mystery). What followed was a traumatic, still-to-be-completed transition and transformation to what some hope will be liberal democracy.

The events of 1989 allowed me to continue my academic interests in the region where I was born and raised, and to do so during the region's transformation to democracy, an era with even greater challenges, it would seem, than those of its transition from Communism. The focus of my research was the evolution of the Eastern European news media, at once glorified as vehicles of democratization and vilified as the Devil's own weapons against it.

In an age of instant, omnipresent mass communications, the real and imagined centrality of the news media to societal developments dominates discussions of democratization. Indeed, media studies provide a glimpse both into a society's culture, politics, social and economic life, and into how and why they may be changing. Yet there are no models or theories to explain how the media change in the transition and transformation from an authoritarian or totalitarian regime to a democratic one, and what or how they can contribute to these processes. What I offer here is not a conclusive work but one that examines the first eleven years of Eastern Europe's transition and transformation, the beginning of a long process of democratization.

In large measure, this work constitutes a rethinking of conclusions reached during the first post-Communist years, when I intently followed the building of new media systems, the practice of unprofessional journalism, and the relationship between the media, journalists, and journalism, on the one hand, and society at large, with all its reforming institutions, on the other. In several of my works on the media in Eastern European nations, I fell into the trap of measuring the media's evolution and role in—and their contributions and importance to—the transition and transformation against expectations that were far too wishful, idealizing a process of democratization that is neither certain, rapid, nor predictable. In retrospect, my initial conclusions were far more negative than warranted

Work on this manuscript allowed me to reconsider bits and pieces of the larger puzzle that constitutes the Eastern European news media. I am grateful to the Woodrow Wilson International Center for Scholars for giving me the opportunity to begin doing so during my tenure as a research fellow and to the Joan Shorenstein Center for Media and Politics at Harvard University and the International Research and Exchanges Board (IREX) for grants that enabled me to continue my research in Eastern Europe.

My heartfelt thanks go first of all to my family for their support. My wife, Vera, has my eternal gratitude for her encouragement and constructive criticism. I am also deeply grateful to Vladimir Tismaneanu and Kenneth Starck for their careful reading of the manuscript and for their sage advice, which greatly improved it, and to Karol Jakubowicz, Oleg Manaev, Mihai Coman, Colin Sparks, Slavko Splichal, Ray Hiebert, Jerome Aumente, Dean Mills, and Owen Johnson, and others, whose work on Eastern European media was invaluable in formulating many of the ideas in this book and in strengthening its theoretical underpinnings, and with many of whom I have spent countless hours in fruitful conversation over the last dozen years. I also want to thank the Woodrow Wilson Center Press's reviewers, whose concise and well-reasoned suggestions increased the clarity and cogency of the manuscript. Finally, I owe a debt of gratitude to Joseph Brinley, Jr., director of the Woodrow Wilson Center Press, for supporting the project and to Carol Belkin Walker and Jeffrey H. Lockridge for their attention to detail and expert editing.

December 2001

1

Political Culture, Civil Society, the Media, and Democracy

How are the news media shaped by other societal institutions in the post-Communist era? How and what do they contribute to change in other institutions and in the political cultures of former Communist societies—and with what effect? Can a nation democratize without autonomous and professional media and journalism? These are the questions that frame the main theme of this book: the nature and role of the news media and their journalism as defined by their relationships with contemporary political culture, civil society, democratization, and all the institutions associated with them. In addressing these questions, this work is meant to help readers understand what Andrew Arato calls the "reconstruction," Ernest Gellner the "rebirth," and Adam Seligman the "revival" of civil society as a concept.[1] It is also meant to shed light on what Gabriel Almond has called the "return of political culture" in democracy and democratization, emphasized in a number of recent works.[2]

During their approximately forty-year reign, Vladimir Tismaneanu wrote in 1992, the Eastern European Communist parties "engineered the methodical destruction of the traditional political cultures" of their respective nations, although, as he would later recognize, they did not destroy all aspects of traditional society.[3] Indeed, Marxism-Leninism adopted and further warped many of the cultural characteristics most detrimental to a democratic society that had been established over centuries of Eastern European history; to these it added new antagonistic elements.[4] A veritable bouillabaisse of attitudes, behaviors, beliefs, habits, and values inimical to democratization and democracy persists in Eastern Europe to this day.[5]

The Marxist-Leninist system and its culture, by no means homogeneous, were studied in their minutest details and analyzed by innumerable schol-

1

ars and social critics on both sides of the Atlantic before and after the "year of miracles," 1989.[6] Even before Eastern Europe was walled off by the Iron Curtain, a significant body of work accurately predicted the effects of Marxism-Leninism on the economy, political culture, society, and the individual.[7] Max Weber, for example, foresaw that, far from making society more decent and egalitarian, it would instead result in an overbureaucratization that would increase the alienation of individuals.[8]

In a century marked by rapid growth in media technologies, literacy, and access to a plethora of mass media outlets, the depth and breadth of Communism's deceit, its barbarism, its destructiveness to society and to the very soul of man were fertile ground for writers and journalists alike. In their novels, literary giants from Milan Kundera to George Orwell and Aleksandr Solzhenitsyn vividly, precisely, and chillingly caught the very essence of the "progressive" Marxist-Leninist political culture in its various permutations. A rich journalistic record in the West and the East documented the world of Communism to millions of daily readers, listeners, and viewers. Journalism also recorded the effects of Marxism-Leninism on the daily lives of Eastern Europeans, and their reactions. Now that former Soviet and Eastern European archives are available and the former Communist societies are more accessible to scholars, a host of Western and Eastern European and American works have further documented the world created by Communism.[9]

To be sure, there were differences among Communist regimes and between the political cultures they helped establish, but these were differences between varieties of apples, not between apples and oranges. Thus, even though the "sultanistic regimes" of Albania, Bulgaria, and Romania might be distinguished from the regimes of Hungary, Poland, and Czechoslovakia by their greater patronage, nepotism, cronyism, and corruption, everywhere in the region political culture was "ghettoized," with acceptable behavior being defined as obedience rather than participation.[10] In any case, political participation had been unevenly and poorly developed in Eastern Europe even before the Communist takeovers.

The Communist political cultures were expressions both of the unworkable, centralized, command economy and of the social, political, and economic repression intrinsic to a Marxist-Leninist society. As expressions of all the institutions established by the Communist ideology and its flag bearers, the Communist parties, they combined with these to bring about the ignominious end of Communist rule in 1989.[11]

Although the Communist systems were quickly replaced and the party systems, interest groups, media, legislative and executive institutions, and laws altered or reinvented, the speed of the changeovers does not speak to the completion or success of the transitions. Indeed, given the myriad of vicissitudes experienced by all societies in transition from authoritarianism or totalitarianism, it could take generations for the political, social, economic, and professional cultures of Eastern Europe to be transformed. All the more so because democratic success "may be traced not only to the growth of democratic values but also to their roots in a country's historical and cultural traditions."[12] In Eastern Europe, pre-Communist and Communist traditions run on tracks that, more often than not, intersect: both traditions are inimical to democracy, with the Communist tradition wholly destructive to democracy in its own right.

Ultimately, as Karl Popper has convincingly argued, and the application of Marxism-Leninism has proven, there are no set laws for social development or progress.[13] Although some preconditions for democratization do exist even in contemporary Eastern European societies lacking prior experience with liberal democracy—birthrates are low, literacy is high, European Enlightenment ideas are at least familiar, and bourgeois traditions are long-standing—none of this is sufficient for a democratic future. To become stable democracies, the nations of Eastern Europe must transform themselves by adopting certain beliefs, attitudes, habits, behaviors, and values universally essential to the birth and sustenance of democracy, namely,

> belief in the legitimacy of democracy; tolerance for opposing parties, beliefs, and preferences; a willingness to compromise with political opponents, and, underlying this, pragmatism and flexibility; some minimum of trust in the political environment, and cooperation, particularly among political competitors; moderation in political positions and partisan identifications; civility of political discourse; and political efficacy and participation—tempered by the addition of two other roles—the subject (which gives allegiance to political authority) and the primordial (which involves the individual in traditional, nonpolitical pursuits).[14]

Among the systemic changes accomplished in Eastern Europe by the end of 2000 were the establishment of multiparty political systems, mostly fair and regular elections, progress toward a market economy, and the establishment of private, commercial media. The blooming of free news media does not necessarily mean, however, that these media are appropriate to democratization or to a democratic society—or that they bring with them a fitting professional culture and journalism. In its most idealistic form, media freedom means not only freedom from governmental involvement but also a significant distancing both from political influence and partisanship and from exclusionary commercial goals.[15] News media should be "structurally free of directly inhibiting economic, political, social, and cultural entanglements," as well as independent of "parties, classes, regions, and religious groups."[16]

Democracies need accurate, fact-based journalism because, without it, the decision-making process is "itself falsified."[17] Information is the fuel of public discourse, and a plurality of opinion, expressed in commentaries and editorials, gives rise to heated, healthy, and productive debates on the issues concerning a free society and free, self-governing individuals. Simply put, a free media offer the citizens of a democracy the means, in Tocqueville's words, "to converse every day without seeing each other, and to take steps in common without having met."[18] Modern mass media in democracies must first and foremost provide information. Without free, unbiased news media, a democracy could hardly be informed or have an appropriate political culture reinforced.

This chapter discusses a series of issues as background to the study of the media and democratization in Eastern Europe. First, it explores the relationship between culture and institutions—does culture produce institutions or can institutions create a culture?—an issue especially relevant to studying Eastern Europe because of the unclear role played by pre-1989 groups opposing Communist political culture. Second, it briefly considers theories relating to political culture, civil society, and democracy, giving short overviews on Eastern European political culture and civil society. Finally, it presents media theories and models for societies in transition and transformation from Communism to democracy. Although most issues will be left unresolved, they serve to frame this study of the media in Eastern Europe.

Chapter 2 focuses on the relationships between the media and the political systems established after 1989. Current politics and political parties in Eastern Europe are "vehicles for personal promotion and influence in the name of privatization," and an antagonistic, combative politics prevails.[19] Media independence and the evolution of independent, professional journalism have been co-opted by this type of politics and its relationship to media outlets, publishers, editors, news directors, and journalists. Nevertheless, because there is a plurality of media outlets, and a pluralism of opinions and news constructions, media independence needs to be redefined.

Chapter 3 explores the relationship between the media and government and state institutions, extending the examination of the media's relationship with political systems, politics, political parties, and politicians. It looks at media privatization, distribution, and production, as well as media access to governmental and legislative bodies, the laws governing the media, and the councils and boards established to apply those laws. In doing so, it concludes that paternalism and state control are not generally reasserting themselves, despite the claims of some scholars.

Chapter 4 examines journalism and its professional culture, arguing chiefly that the current political culture affects the professional culture of journalists more than the new possibilities offered them under media freedom. Until the news media define for themselves a shared role and professional standards, little will change.

Chapter 5 investigates the media's interrelationship with civil society and political culture. It analyzes issues of media autonomy, pluralism and diversity, specialized versus mass media, the media and citizen participation, and the media and the free market in Eastern Europe.

Finally, in considering the role of the media and journalism in democratization, chapter 6 offers a critical summary of the post-1989 Eastern European media's failures, successes, and contributions. It concludes with some thoughts on the future evolution of the media, journalism, and their role in democratizing the countries in the region, focusing on what should not and must not happen from a liberal perspective. It specifically addresses the almost universal call by the most vociferous of American and European academics for "democratization through the media" and "democratization of the media."

Cultural Determinism and Institutional Determinism

Before we can define the role and nature of the post-Communist media, we need to consider what drives the transformation of a society from Communism to a free-market, liberal democracy; which fundamental elements of a society promote societal change, and which slow or prevent it.[20]

"Political culture" is a valid and important element of any equation that endeavors to explain what it takes to successfully transform post-Communist societies into Western-style liberal democracies, even though its use is still a controversial matter among "transitologists," as well as among the "consolidologists," who focus on consolidating democracy. Some scholars emphasize the role of institutions as central to the transition from Communism to democracy.[21] With Francis Fukuyama, they think it a "common mistake . . . to view cultural factors as *necessary* conditions for the establishment of democracy" (emphasis original).[22] They argue that the state can create new habits, customs, and cultures. For example, Attila Agh maintains that "institutions must be created and then the proper political culture to behave in," assigning the former to the "transition" stage and the latter to the "consolidation" stage.[23] Fukuyama also considers political culture to be secondary in the transition to democracy:

> Cultures are not static phenomena like the laws of nature; they are human creations that undergo a continuous process of evolution. They can be modified by economic development, wars and other national traumas, immigration or by conscious choice. Hence cultural "prerequisites" for democracy, while definitely important, need to be treated with some skepticism.[24]

Others, however, especially longtime students of Eastern Europe, consider political culture to be a key element of the transition to and the maintenance of democracy.[25] Their work buttresses Robert Putnam's and Ronald Inglehart's claims that cultural norms do not substantially change in the short run but help shape societal transitions.[26] Tismaneanu, for example, illustrates "the role of political traditions, memories, and deeply entrenched attitudes" in studying the evolution of post-1989 Eastern Europe.[27]

These fundamental disagreements between institutional and cultural determinists go to the heart of the events that have unfolded in Eastern Europe since 1989. The systemic transition from Communism to democracy was achieved in a relatively short period of time, even as the political, social, and economic cultures of the region's nations began a transformation, one still not completed, and one moving along faster in some nations than in others. Eastern European nations are still battling to transform the mentalities, values, and behaviors of their citizens and elites into forms consonant with democracy, and with the institutions, politics, civic involvement, and ethos that serve it. This work addresses the evolution of the news media and journalism in both the transition and consolidation phases of the transformation.

The existing political cultures in the region, with their Marxist-Leninist and pre-Communist legacies, have a great bearing on the organization, nature, role, and effects of the institutions built in the post-Communist era, including the media. Yet, reconfigured and functioning under new rules, the media are seen by those who believe "institutions bring about change" as capable of shaping "behavior by creating incentives."[28] Such a view presupposes that institutional change also renews the opportunities political actors have, in turn changing their behavior.[29] Of course, this presupposition in turn assumes a positive, democratic-oriented change in behavior, something that could happen only if the institutions were liberal. For example, Beverly Crawford and Arend Lijphart stress that "liberal institutions can structure preferences and constrain choices in ways that create new political and economic cultures."[30] But if institutions are not liberal, they can actually prevent, or at the very least slow, liberal change. And it is highly questionable whether the post-1989 institutions of Eastern Europe, including the media, are liberal.

Thus the basic question remains unsettled: what does political culture mean to the post-Communist transition and transformation?[31] Even if political culture is not crucial, its establishment is an important and complex process, one that must forever remain incomplete, and such culture is at least somewhat malleable.[32] Cultural change is gradual and cumulative; in the context of profound social changes such as are developing in Eastern Europe, it is "prolonged and socially costly."[33] With Bruce Parrott, some argue that it comes about "primarily through the generational turnover of citizens."[34] Others take a more encompassing and complex approach.[35] Still others, in a compromise of sorts between the institutional and cultural determinists, propose a reciprocally promoting relationship between democratic institutions and democratic political culture.[36] The question of which comes first, the chicken or the egg, remains unanswered and may be unanswerable.

It is, however, a particularly important question in examining the establishment or reestablishment of civil society in Eastern Europe after 1989 and the "antipolitics" of the opponents to Communism, who were intimately involved in journalism and the media, that led up to it, at least in Poland, Hungary, and Czechoslovakia.

Democracy and democratization are not possible without civil society, so the argument goes.[37] I am speaking here of a type of civil society that, according to Gellner, "excludes both stifling communalism and centralized authoritarianism" and that requires an independent economy, one free enough, he argues, to provide foundations for plural institutions, but not so powerful as to damage society.[38]

Most scholars see civil society as having been at the core of opposition to Communism in Poland, Hungary, and Czechoslovakia, and palpably absent in Romania, Bulgaria, and Albania.[39] Others claim that civil society did not emerge and played no role in the overthrow of Communism, as in

Hungary, where the civil rights opposition was more an intellectual subculture than a social movement. The protest movements of the 1980s, for instance, occurred mainly in the student and youth subcultures.[40] Assuming that civil society did exist in 1989, it was not bereft of the tensions between liberal and illiberal notions of democracy that now also plague the democratic opposition in Eastern Europe.[41] Scholars further confused the meanings of civil society by counterposing "the notion of small oppositional movements under communist regimes to the notion of the macrostructure of entire societies in noncommunist or postcommunist states."[42]

Civil society is central to this work because the media are considered one of its key elements, part of an array of nongovernmental institutions making up the varied outlets through which citizenship is carried out. In Seligman's definition, civil society joins within itself the institutional or organizational system and the belief or values system, which are at the core of the examination of the post-Communist evolution of the nature, role, and effects of the media in democratization.[43] The mass media are part of the network of opinion-forming institutions that constitute what Jürgen Habermas calls the "public sphere."[44] Does an appropriate political culture need to exist to establish such media institutions? Can they be established without it? Can media institutions, lacking the appropriate democratic culture itself, affected by other institutions equally deficient in this culture, and functioning in a quasi-democratic society, contribute to a salutary change in political culture?

This is by no means the first attempt to explicate the evolution of the post-Communist media and their relationship with and reciprocal effects on political culture, politics, civil society, or democratization in general. Scores of journalistic and scholarly articles and a handful of books have been written since 1989–90 analyzing the evolution of the mass media and their journalism in one or more of the Eastern European nations in the context of existing theories and normative criteria, and examining the relationship of the media and society, politics, culture, economics, and overall democratization. They inform my work. After nearly eleven years of research in Eastern Europe, including interviews with journalists, editors, news directors, politicians, and media owners in Albania, Bulgaria, Hungary, the Czech and Slovak Republics, Poland, and Romania, I have come to subscribe to the basic view of how the media and journalism have evolved in the region expressed by the authors of these articles and books.

However, I do not subscribe to the normative, idealistic, even utopian assumptions of most analysts in the field.[45] Nor do I entirely agree with John

Downing's suggestion that, in studying the Eastern European media, we move "beyond the foreshortened perspectives redolent of U.S. or British media systems as the latter are experienced from relatively favored social circumstances."[46] Despite all their current problems, I still consider the American and British media and their journalism, or rather the liberal democratic ideals on which they are based, to be the models against which all others should be measured.

Political Culture, Civil Society, and Democracy

There is no consensus on what political culture is or which variables are to be assigned to it. Neither is there a consensus on the theory or practice of democracy. Furthermore, how political culture arises and whether it ought to be analytically separated from political structures are matters of ongoing debate.

One view of political culture, which clearly distinguishes between elite and mass political cultures, sees it as a set of predominant beliefs, attitudes, values, ideals, sentiments, and evaluations regarding the political system in which a group of people live and the role of the individual in that system.[47] In this view, as Gabriel Almond and Samuel Huntington point out, the political culture of a nation is made up of political subcultures, which are found in various cohabiting groups, whether ethnic, racial, religious, or regional, in groups belonging to different institutions within a society, such as the military, the university, the professions, and the media, and in groups such as city dwellers, peasants, and intellectuals.[48]

Definitions of political culture have been directly predicated on the variables assumed to be important to democracy, itself a term open to a variety of interpretations and definitions. Thus, in Gabriel Almond and Sidney Verba's original work, *The Civic Culture,* political knowledge and skills, value orientations toward the political system, the self as participant, political parties and elections, and the bureaucracy were the main variables examined.[49] Verba later included attitudes toward fellow citizens, attitudes and expectations regarding governmental performance, knowledge about and attitudes toward the process of political decision making, and a sense of national identity in his definition of political culture.[50] Robert Dahl added two more variables: attitudes toward cooperation and individuality and orientation toward problem solving.[51]

Huntington outlines a democratic political culture in terms of five considerations:

1. how political and other elites and the public respond to the plethora of problems in a non-Communist society in transition or transformation;
2. how political elites cooperate to deal with societal problems;
3. whether they "refrain from exploiting those problems for their own immediate material or political advantage";
4. whether the public can "distinguish between the regime and the government or rulers" and, when dissatisfaction sets in, "change the rulers, not the regime"; and
5. when "people learn that democracy is a solution to the problem of tyranny, but not necessarily to anything else."[52]

Cultural determinists such as Lucian Pye, Aaron Wildavsky, and Harry Eckstein subscribe to the notion that political behavior represents coherent patterns, although, in 1985, Pye cautioned that "logically coherent views do not necessarily prevail and that people, in their collective moods and inclinations, are quite capable of adhering to contradictory positions."[53] Whatever the case may be, political culture is "durable and persistent" because it is rooted in distinctive national histories and in individual personalities, which suggests that quick and meaningful changes in the political culture of Eastern European societies are highly unlikely.[54] Support for this deterministic view is provided in a number of studies of democracy's prospects in Latin America and Africa, as well as in the work of Inglehart, whose data show the relative influence of political attitudes on democratization.[55]

Eckstein, Almond and Verba, and Almond writing on his own, have broken down the concept of political culture into related subjective and objective dimensions. The subjective dimension consists of

1. cognitive orientation (knowledge of and beliefs about the political system);
2. affective orientation (feelings about the political system); and
3. evaluational orientation (commitments to political values and judgments about the functioning of the political system relative to those values).

The subjective dimension of political culture in turn bears on its objective dimension, which consists of

1. the political system (the regime—legislatures, executives, bureaucracies, courts, political parties, interest groups, mass media, their incumbents);
2. the political process (the actions, conflicts, alliances, and behavior of parties, interest groups, movements, and individuals); and
3. political policy (the policies and decisions of the political system).[56]

With Robert Tucker, other scholars differentiate between the psychological characteristics and beliefs of a society's political culture and the conduct of its people.[57] Tucker raises the possibility that the conception of an autonomous political culture "may itself reflect a cultural bias."[58]

In their totality, the subjective and objective dimensions of political culture address the very premises of democracy. Built upon classical theory incorporating concepts such as "will of the people" and "the common good," modern democracy is essentially a procedural concept.[59] According to Dahl, it involves two dimensions: competition (contestation) and participation.[60] These dimensions in turn involve open, free, and fair elections, limitations on power, the "nation of laws" concept, stability, and freedom of the press. There are more sweeping and idealistic connotations of democracy ("fuzzy norms") that address the subjective, more direct aspects of political culture. Huntington lists unspecified civic virtues, "*liberté, égalité, fraternité,* effective citizen control over policy, responsible government, honesty and openness in politics, informed and rational deliberation, equal participation and power."[61]

To sum up, there are economic, institutional, cultural, and social preconditions to democracy. Whether all have to be present in equal measure for democratization to proceed is debatable. Yet they set the stage for how elites and ordinary citizens act, react, and coact in and to their situation and to changes, and for how the public and private realms of citizenship, those individual and social concerns in a society, are combined, that is, for civil society.

Edmund Burke and James Madison laid the groundwork for defining democratic society as civil society, a partnership between citizens from whom all authority is derived and a collection of different groups, interests, and classes whose very number precludes any perils to the individual or minority groups and interests.[62] Checks and balances are thus established by the existence of a multiplicity of groups, organizations, and associations with active memberships. The words "active memberships" are the operative ones in this definition of civil society, as they are in contemporary theoretical formulations. Individuals have to take on the attributes of citizenship and create these elements of civil society and participate in them. Civil society cannot be created by state decree or by any type of diktat, but only by citizenship.

Contemporary definitions of civil society retain these underlying sine qua nons. For instance, John Keane defines civil society as

> an arena in which modern man legitimately gratifies his self-interest and develops his individuality, but also learns the value of group action, social solidarity and the dependence of his welfare on others, which educate him for citizenship and prepare him for participation in the political arena of the state.[63]

Seligman, however, questions the adequacy of a civil society based on the "synthesis of public and private, individual and social concerns and desiderata."[64] He dismisses what he views as the three main uses of the idea of civil society: as a slogan and critique of government policies, as an analytic concept, and as a philosophical normative concept.

In a similar vein, Gellner writes that civil society *is* democracy, rather than being contained by democracy: "What distinguishes Civil Society (using the term to describe the entire society), or a society *containing* Civil Society (in the narrower sense) from others is that it is *not* clear who is the boss" (emphasis original).[65] Civil society or democracy is meant to ensure pluralism, the absence of ideological monopoly, the separation of polity from the economy and social life, a mutual checking and balancing between political centralism and economic autonomy, with individual interests being given expression, but with their most extreme manifestations held in check. This is classic liberalism, the marriage of libertarianism and social responsibility. It closely matches Ralf Dahrendorf's and Karl Popper's notions of an "open society."[66] An open society, as Dahrendorf defines it, is not a system but constitutes "the open spaces of infinite possible futures" in which all "systems," which he labels "illiberal," are to be fought.[67] His definition by no means suggests a perfect society, but one whose imperfections are at least not dictated by ideological fiat, as most people on the Left and Right hold to be necessary. Although "democratization" is still a requisite of this open society, it is not as a process establishing a democratic system, but rather as an element that allows for varied views, lifestyles, and the absence of or continuous resistance to the potential tyranny of the marketplace, the majority, a minority, raw government power, an ideology, or political demagogues.

Civil society has most commonly been defined as a myriad of nongovernmental associations and groups that allow individuals to freely pursue socioeconomic interests and hold in check the state and the monopolization of political power. Civil society is a separate realm between the state and individual. Its features include, among others, autonomy, associationism, pluralism, legality, and mediation.[68] These associations and groups may include "religious confessions, charitable organizations, business lobbies, professional associations, labor unions, universities, and non-institutionalized movements for various social causes."[69]

Independent media are both elements and facilitators of civil society. In fact, if civil society can be viewed as "both the cause and the effect of freedom to inform and to inform oneself," then truly independent media (whose definition itself is still contested) *are* civil society (see chapter 5 for an elaboration of this issue).[70] Or, as Jürgen Habermas, Peter Dahlgren, and Nicholas Garnham, among others, have defined them, the media are part of an independent public sphere alongside other opinion-forming institutions.[71] More specifically, Habermas's theory of communicative action places civil society as an intermediary sphere between economic action and the state.[72] (More will be said about the media's nature, role, and effects in democracy in the last part of this chapter.)

Whether civil society also includes political parties is a contested proposition. The argument can be made that if civil society is, indeed, a form of political society, then political parties are part and parcel of civil society.[73] Political parties, even if they do not represent all possible segments of the polity, do carry out the functions assigned to civil society by Gellner.[74] Richard Rose, William Mishler, and Christian Haerpfer are even more specific categorizing political parties as representatives of civil society by pointing to the creation of competitive political parties in Western Europe: "the representatives of pre-existing organized interests in civil society."[75] Furthermore, parties offer one avenue by which the individual can participate in the political arena outside of voting.

Václav Havel and others, however, tend to deny that participation through political parties acts as a substitute for civil society. If political society is a freestanding sphere between civil society and the state, as in Jean Cohen and Andrew Arato's formulation of political society, Havel may be right.[76] Still others say political society may not be a substitute for civil society, but it is part of it.[77]

Whether we consider civil society to be democracy or only part of it, citizens in a democracy must be willing and able (capable of reason, informed, and somewhat articulate) to assume responsibility for public life, that is, to be involved in it in some capacity, extent, and manner of their choosing. They must be free, social, ethical, and moral beings.[78] The ethical and moral dimensions of citizenship are the core of a civil society, creating "the generalization and universalization of trust," that makes a civil society possible.[79]

Liberal democracy, whether participatory or representative, requires citizens to share certain public virtues that commit them to values, attitudes, and behavior, and the establishment of certain types of institutions consonant with its meaning and intent.[80] Both participatory and representative types are tied to the Lockean democratic ideal that governments must have their citizens' consent to act and that the citizens must define what they want their government to do.[81] An open society and the market have a common core, as Jacques Attali aptly puts it, choice and the freedom to make a choice, which presents its own problems, specifically regarding the media.[82]

Political Culture in Pre- and Post-1989 Eastern Europe

Thanks in part to anti-Communist uprisings and organized dissident movements, Hungary, Poland, and the former Czechoslovakia experienced a form of post-Communism even before 1989, one that in itself created two political cultures that existed side by side: an official and an unofficial one.[83] The unofficial political culture was predominantly a culture of opposition, which united various political and ideological orientations in passively or actively resisting the Communist system and its culture. In Hungary, Poland, and Czechoslovakia, these orientations constituted a small but significant "parallel polis" whose task, as articulated by Havel, was to resist "the irrational momentum of anonymous, impersonal and inhuman power—the power of ideologies, systems, apparat, bureaucracy, artificial languages, and political slogans."[84] Hungary and Poland's opposition mirrored Czechoslovakia's, where Charter 77 members included "radical democrats, democratic socialists, reform Communists, independent Trotskyists, liberals, religious conservatives."[85] The very heterogeneous makeup of the opposition helps define the various unresolved tensions and social, political, cultural, and economic problems in post-Communist societies. Yet, even in those nations where post-Communism, in any format, did not take hold until after 1989, such as Albania, Bulgaria, and Romania, official and unofficial political cultures coexisted, just as the official and unofficial economies did.[86] If nothing else, there was a marked difference between the official "Socialist culture," authoritatively espoused as an ideal achieved, and the real system and its creations, together with the beliefs of those who served it and of those who tacitly went along with it.[87]

The side-by-side existence of two political cultures until 1989 did not provide any discernible positive elements in the 1989–2000 transition and transformation period. Indeed, the conflict between the official and unofficial, the ideal and real political cultures of the Eastern European nations created a questionable platform for launching a new post-Communist political culture. After all, anti-Communism is not a prescription for democratization, and, unfortunately, other than anti-Communism there is little understanding of democracy as a living concept among Eastern Europeans and their elites, for most of whom democracy and a market economy mean "a better life, perhaps, but without content," according to Gale Stokes.[88] Jean-François Revel points out that it is not sufficient for a post-Communist nation to free itself from Communist rule in order to escape Communism; it must also free itself from all the *consequences* of Communism.[89]

These pernicious consequences are also, to a great extent, the legacy of pre-Communist days. Indeed, that Communist culture is a continuation and exacerbation of pre-Communist culture makes it harder to uproot. Stjepan Mestrovic, in his superb work on the political culture of the Balkans, points out that the vacuum left in post-Communist Slavic nations has been filled by "nationalism, religion, the family, and other centripetal forces that bespeak the power of habits of the heart" present for hundreds of years.[90] His observation is equally true for the non-Slavic nations of the region. That is, Eastern Europe has embarked on ridding itself of not simply a political culture forty-plus years old, but one that has taken root and grown over hundreds of years, spreading, deepening, and becoming, by design, more pernicious in the Communist era. Centuries of pre-Communist culture created societies with feeble traditions of the rule of law and with deliberately separated public and private domains; they gave rise to constitutionally constrained governments, on the one hand, and robust tendencies toward "illiberal 'ethnic' nationalism," on the other.[91] This regionwide pre-Communist culture was not only predominantly illiberal, it was antiliberal, including among other elements, "anti-Westernism, feudal romanticism, anti-capitalism, and even anti-industrialism."[92] The one glaring, short-lived exception was Czechoslovakia, that idealistic creation of the Versailles treaty.

There have always been cultural differences between Eastern European countries with a more Western cultural bent and those with Eastern cultural underpinnings, as is suggested by the dissimilarities between the general cultures of the Czech Republic, Poland, and Hungary and those of the Slovak Republic, Bulgaria, Romania, and Albania. Each has been greatly affected and shaped by the nature of its Christianity: Orthodox in Romania and Bulgaria; Catholic in Poland, Hungary, and the Czech Republic. In Albania, both Islam and Christianity (the Albanian Orthodox Church and the Catholic Church) contributed to its cultural evolution. Other influencing factors included the lengthy occupation by or vassalage to the Ottoman, Russian, and Austro-Hungarian Empires.

Ken Jowitt, among other students of the region, convincingly argues that Communism reinforced the pre-Communist separation between the rulers and the ruled, and the "exclusive distinction and dichotom[ous] antagonisms between the official and private realms."[93] These divisions persisted despite the zealous and sometimes brutal attempts by Communists to unite social and political life, public and private realms, in what Leszek Kolakowski has called a "soteriological myth."[94] The central features of the political culture under Communism reflected the fears and avoidance responses of the ruled, the very nature of their interactions with the regime, the absence of "shared public identity." They also reflected the "explicit and authoritative status differences" between the rulers and the ruled, the "insular privatized quality of social life, the regimes' employment of violence, and the ethos and structure of the 'mobilization regime.'"[95] They included dissimulation, rumor as "covert political discourse," bribery, and the overall reinforcement of "covert, personalized, hierarchical relationships involving complicity rather than public agreement."[96]

The dominant Communist political cultures were made up of different and conflicting subcultures of the Communist ultranationalists, reformers, quasi-liberals, and dissidents, among others.[97] They fostered "an individual hostility to risk, to fair competition, to pluralist values,"[98] as well as cynicism, contempt for the law, a forced, tribal collectivism, general suspicion, fear, double-thinking and -speaking, endemic hypocrisy, general irresponsibility, and distrust of intellectual freethinkers. And they played on the national chauvinism and anti-Semitism already well entrenched in the region before the Communist takeovers. Zbigniew Brzezinski notes that Communism produced a political culture imbued with intolerance, self-righteousness, rejection of social compromise and massive inclination toward self-glorifying oversimplification. On the level of belief, dogmatic communism thus fused with and even reinforced intolerant nationalism; on the level of practice, the destruction of such relatively internationalist classes as the aristocracy or the business elite further reinforced the populist inclination toward nationalistic chauvinism. Nationalism was therefore nurtured, rather than diluted.[99]

The political realm was viewed by the inhabitants of the region as something to be shunned because it was dangerous. Political activity was strictly choreographed by the Communist regimes, with the attendant effect of increasing the people's psychological and political alienation.[100] Ultimately, the political culture established in the Communist states, the control of party and state over all institutions, the co-optation of the public sphere, meant that civil society did not exist. Its reappearance in Hungary, Czechoslovakia, and Poland as resistance to Communism gave it specific parameters, form, and meaning.[101]

The anomie created by Communism, which spilled over into the post-Communist period, was consciously and subconsciously inculcated into the population by, among other means, the mass media. The Communist leadership, the party, the state, and the government controlled information flow in a number of ways, most overtly through their monopoly over the mass media. The party served as the "supreme board of directors" of what amounted to a "gigantic multi-media" corporation.[102] To a greater or lesser extent, depending on which Eastern European nation's media one scrutinized, journalists were "public officials."[103]

Censorship and self-censorship dominated the region's media.[104] With minor differences from country to country, journalism was carried out in accordance with the functional necessities and the methodologies of the Communist Party and ideology, the media systems in general functioning as described in Wilbur Schramm's Communist press theory.[105] Mobilization, proselytizing, indoctrination, and persuasion were all part of the party-directed functions of the Communist mass media and mass communication. They were "part of a larger project, that of assimilation of the totality of culture."[106] Professionalism did not exist in the Western sense of the word, being defined in terms of the Marxist-Leninist ethos, a sort of community journalism, with what was best for the community being defined by the Communist Party and its goals and having an effect opposite to Havel's notion of "living in truth."[107] Orwell's Newspeak was firmly entrenched through the substance and presentation of themes and the language used. Controlling language was most important for maintaining totalitarian power, as Czeslaw Milosz points out.[108] Language became "wooden."[109] "Deprived of semantic contact with reality and transformed into a system of ritual signs that replace reality with pseudo-reality," it helped to destroy elements of the pre-Communist culture that did not dovetail with the Marxist-Leninist conception of society; it helped install the new "Socialist culture" and, with it, molded the new *Homo sovieticus.*[110]

The Communist monopoly of the media was broken, however, both by the indigenous non-Communist media (more on this in chapter 5) and by the foreign media, which increasingly penetrated the Iron Curtain, reaching even the most isolated of the Communists' inmates.[111] Indeed, this form of early demonopolization would constitute "the key to the breakdown of Communist totalitarianism."[112] Nevertheless, the breakdown of Communist totalitarianism in 1989 did not represent a break with the past. Some or all of the central features of the Communist political culture, to include the media's professional culture as well as the elements that gave them birth and sustenance, would remain in all post-Communist Eastern European nations. Bronislaw Geremek was mistaken when he claimed in 1990 that the "weakness of democracy in the post-communist countries does not originate" in their pre-Communist societies, although he was correct in identifying as a fundamental obstacle to democratization: "the [Communists'] suffocation of the market economy, a suffocation that destroyed relations between people," and in pointing out that Communism was anchored in the psychological passivity of pre-Communist society.[113] This passivity was coupled with what Stephen Holmes calls "learned helplessness," a fatalism well illustrated by and most acutely present among the Romanians, for example.[114]

In its effects, Communism differed little from fascism, except that it infected its societies more deeply and festered for much longer.[115] In its aftermath, with the regimes overthrown and the ideology disowned, what remained was "a way of thinking and feeling, a group of cultural habits, of obscure instincts and unfathomable drives"—the "us" versus "them" mentality, cynicism, and a persistent collectivist "nostalgia for the benefits of the socialist welfare state"—essential to the Communist regimes and their ideology.[116] Cronyism, contempt for law, fragmentation, populism, and divisiveness survived the demise of Communism, as did corruption, yet another "continuation of communist clientelism, double thinking, hypocrisy, and second economy."[117] The post-Communist societal instability and the unemployment brought about by economic restructuring, among other elements of the transition and transformation, have exacerbated a political culture of fear, panic, anguish, and suspicion, giving further impetus to the ethnic particularism in the region and the resulting nationalism, racism, and anti-Semitism.[118] As Jowitt so aptly puts it:

> The Leninist legacy, understood as the impact of party organization, practice and ethos, and the initial charismatic ethical opposition to it favor an authoritarian, not a liberal democratic capitalist, way of life, the obstacles to which are not simply how to privatize and marketize the economy, or organize an electoral campaign but rather *how to institutionalize public virtues* (emphasis added).[119]

A good deal of dissatisfaction with "democracy" was discernible in the 1990s. It was created by social, political, and economic instability; the cultural legacies of Communism and pre-Communism; the general vacuum of liberal democratic leadership; and the failure of mass media to purposefully and directly explain the reform process and aid the overall transition/transformation to democracy. This dissatisfaction may also be a by-product of one or more of the national, religious, and moralistic "fundamentalisms" identified by Adam Michnik, to which some people in the anti-Communist movements, where they existed, succumbed.[120] The freedom that was gained by ending Communism "has certain aspects of mob rule, and is associated with "disorder and corruption," bringing with it "disillusionment and fatigue."[121] There is a danger the freedom made possible by democracy will also be associated with a reduced quality of life and a growing sense of insecurity.[122] Only in the Czech Republic does there seem to be any significant satisfaction with the development of democracy.[123]

In the other six nations under consideration here, satisfaction with the meaning and the reality of democracy in the first post-1989 decade appears to have been ethereal and volatile. Surveys and polls in the 1990s show support for democracy, but also dissatisfaction with it, and almost a quarter of the population of the region appears to opt for a "paternalistic leader who would presumably look after their welfare."[124] Some Eastern Europeans still have nostalgia for the alchemy of utopia promised by the Communist welfare state because "even if they hated their cage," it provided some stability and predictability.[125]

Despite all the negatives, the first decade of post-Communism does not bode ill for the eventual establishment of democracy and a democratic culture in most countries in the region. The Churchillian hypothesis that people will prefer democracy to all other forms of government may prove accurate for Eastern Europeans in the long run, provided they rid themselves of the legacy left them by pre-Communism and Communism.[126]

This is a tall task, indeed, in a region whose political elites are derived mostly from the ranks of former Communists or from opposition groups one would be hard put to call "unambiguously liberal democratic."[127] Indeed, George Schopflin considers the political cultures of Eastern Europe to be both intolerant of political competition and hostile to criticism.[128] Self-interest, the view that political power can be parlayed into economic power, with a few notable exceptions, is present at every level of the new Eastern European political system, from mayors, to parliamentarians, to presidents. It shapes the elites' perceptions and actions as much as do the political, social, and economic cultures in which they live and work. The new social and economic elites are mostly derived from the old political elites; moreover, the bureaucrats are still in place, as this description of the Hungarian situation indicates:

> A disturbing political legacy of the Communist regime is the survival of its *nomenklatura* in the administrative and economic spheres. Particularly among the middle-ranking echelons of political officialdom, thousands of former Communist bureaucrats remain, partly owing to the dexterity in holding onto power and partly because there are few qualified to replace them.[129]

It is not the presence of an elite that is problematic in a democratic nation, however. Rather, as Schumpeter suggested back in 1943, the problem in a would-be democracy is the absence of several vigorous elites vying with each other for votes and influence.[130] The truly new elites, political, social, and economic, are few, still in the process of establishing themselves, and often ill equipped to lead and compete with the better connected and more savvy old elites. The rule of man, or of the elite, now exists side by side with the rule of law, so necessary for the survival of a democracy: to a greater extent in the Czech Republic Hungary, and Poland, and to a lesser extent in Albania, Bulgaria, Romania, and the Slovak Republic.[131] It is unclear where one ends and the other begins—or which is to dominate. The nations of Eastern Europe thus find themselves in limbo. Their tendencies toward democracy, on the one hand, and toward authoritarianism, on the other, hang in the balance, and the slightest reversal could derail their quest to become fully and truly democratic. Indeed, some seem frozen between democracy and "creeping authoritarianism."[132]

While there are marked differences between the political cultures of the Czech Republic and Albania, Poland and Romania, or Hungary and Bulgaria and the Slovak Republic, all lack to some degree the beliefs and values of democratic culture.[133] More important, all share in the cultural and institutional dimensions of the transition and transformation they are undergoing, summarized by Wojciech Lamentowicz as

- short-term adaptive shock, which is natural in conditions of such far-reaching change,
- the heritage of the past, with the legacy of the Communist past weighing heavily on the present,
- the revolution of rising expectations,
- arrogant elites,
- uncompleted institutional transitions, [and]
- the crisis of legitimization.[134]

Trust in political institutions is low or nonexistent; membership and participation in political groups and parties have fallen rather than grown since 1989.[135] The very essence of a liberal, democratic political culture appears to be missing, namely, citizenship beyond the formal existence of civil, political, and social rights.[136] In theory, every Eastern European citizen now has these rights. In practice, few citizens exercise their rights, at least not according to ideal prescriptions. Nevertheless, there are other forms of citizen involvement in the public affairs of Eastern Europe, as I point out in chapter 5. Such involvement has a great deal to do with establishing a liberal, democratically constructed civil society there.

Civil Society in Pre- and Post-1989 Eastern Europe

In the years before 1989, a form of civil society diametrically opposed to the Marxist-Leninist "rule of coercion in the name of collectivism" appeared in Eastern Europe.[137] Only a small fraction of the population in each nation was involved in this form of public affairs, which was almost singularly defined as anti-Communism. Some observers of the Eastern European scene saw the anti-Communist movement less at the center of what might have been civil society in the pre-1989 era and more as "a product of individuals' needs to carve out private space in a system that controlled everything."[138] Indeed, at least part of the movement was detached from both the political and the public world; while it did not collaborate with the Communist political or public world, neither did it actively seek to defeat it.[139] Suffice it to say, individuals and groups in this inchoate anti-Communist civil society adopted a political culture that contained only selected aspects of democratic tendencies. Their beliefs, attitudes, values, ideals, sentiments, and evaluations about the political system and the role of the individual in this system were neither Marxist-Leninist nor necessarily liberal-democratic.

However one defines pre-1989 civil society in the region, one cannot argue that it was built on the notion of democratic citizenship or that it developed or created citizens. Political and civil citizenship in the liberal-individualist tradition "never existed," even in pre-Communist days, with the limited exception of Czechoslovakia.[140] Consequently, after 1989 there is no question of reconstructing or reestablishing whatever pre-Communist civil society existed, nor of establishing one on the basis of what evolved during the Communist years. Rather, establishing civil society is part of the fundamental process of democratization, now free to take place.

Depending on whose analysis one chooses, civil society in post-1989 Eastern Europe is

1. nonexistent, such as in Bulgaria, where it "is an imaginary construct";[141]
2. underdeveloped and weak, that is, the space between the individual and the state and the range of free associations, groups, organizations, and institutions that allow individuals to participate in making decisions or be represented in decision making are not fully functional;[142]
3. expressed in nationalist movements or in local organizations;[143]
4. a bona fide presence, contributing substantially to the transformation of a formerly Communist society into a democracy, first and foremost by the "invention of a democratic tradition";[144]
5. largely a political society, one with political pluralism and political polarization, in which everything is politicized, and, as Cohen and Arato see it, one standing between civil society and the state.[145] In this case, the main actors are not the citizens but political parties and politicians, who, observers of Eastern Europe's evolution generally agree, have done little or nothing to represent any particular con-

stituencies and have been much more inclined to pursue their own power-related interests (see chapter 2).

In the economic realm, the private sector organizations, groups, associations, and institutions (e.g., companies, banks, and private shops) have made a comeback, thus creating one aspect of civil society, a private sector power base. The outward, structural signs of civil society are present: a plethora of nongovernmental organizations, associations, and institutions such as trade unions, professional organizations, consumer associations, religious and charitable groups. "Tens of thousands of civil associations have been organized in each country from the early 1990s onwards, which have been very active at the level of civil society and have facilitated its efficient workings."[146] The extent of their development and power, however, and of the actual civic involvement on their part and that of their members is at the crux of the critique of civil society in post-Communist Eastern Europe. Specifically, it is argued that the cultural and institutional dimensions of post-Communism have served to endanger rather than to promote civil society by creating a "collapse of hope, trust and confidence."[147] Yet, as the Polish case illustrates, grassroots protests in the region have somewhat offset their negative effects.[148]

Missing from the political culture of the region are well-developed participation and assumption of responsibility by citizens, social influence and consensus, and "a mutuality of purpose, a shared frame of reference."[149] A "robust civil society," as Habermas points out, can

develop only in the context of a liberal political culture and the corresponding patterns of socialization, and on the basis of an integral private sphere; it can blossom only in an already rationalized lifeworld [*sic*]. Otherwise, populist movements arise that blindly defend the frozen traditions of a lifeworld endangered by capitalist modernization. In their forms of mobilization, these fundamentalist movements are as modern as they are antidemocratic.[150]

First, in Eastern Europe a liberal political culture is missing and can only slowly be introduced and adopted over the course of generations (see "Cultural Determinism and Institutional Determinism" and "Political Culture, Civil Society, and Democracy" above). Second, the "corresponding patterns of socialization" are for the most part missing, as is the "integral private sphere." And third, the "lifeworld," which includes all the sources of interpreting information reproduced through communication, is restricted, incoherent, and without any rules to govern it. Establishing civil society, democratization, takes time. Ultimately, civil society as a concept "must advance an idea of the individual as an autonomous social actor and as an ethical and moral entity, an idea that is in a sense foreign to [Eastern Europe's] traditions."[151]

Regardless of how civil society was perceived, the main philosophical and theoretical battles in the 1990s raged between those who had a liberal-individualist vision of democracy and those who had a socialistic or communitarian one. Indeed, contemporary conceptual differences in the meaning of civil society "are rooted in the abiding differences that characterized the liberal-individualist and socialist traditions in their respective relationship to the conflicting demands" and tensions between "private and public, individual and social demands and desiderata," between liberty and equality.[152]

Disagreement and confusion about what constitutes civil society reduce the citizens' lack of awareness, argues Jiri Pehe, leaving the transition and transformation to be directed from above, that is, by the state and government, with little input from individual citizens, save perhaps for periodic trips to the voting polls, by political parties in what Adolph Bibic calls "excessive partification," and by the political and economic elites.[153] The state still has overwhelming power and everything is still politicized, albeit in a far more heterogeneous form than before 1989. But if transition and transformation require a civil society to be aware of its autonomy from the state, then the state is hardly the "best equipped body to act as midwife."[154]

The microcosm of the debate over civil society was embodied in the 1994 tug-of-war between Czech President Václav Havel and Prime Minister Václav Klaus.[155] Havel argued that citizens should be involved in society beyond membership in political parties and voting: their collective conscience should be expressed through a commitment to society. Klaus, on the other hand, said, "We are interested in a market without attributes, in a standard system of political parties without national fronts and civic movements."[156]

Echoing other observers, Schopflin describes post-Communism as a unique system in which political and economic competition are present, and democratic practices with "stronger or weaker commitments to pluralism" coexist with persistent antidemocratic ideas and practices having deep historical roots. The latter are kept alive by legitimating discourses, which include statements and actions by certain politicians, political parties, government officials, bureaucrats and business people, as well as certain editorials and news stories. [157]

In the aggregate, some argue, the Communist order of Eastern Europe has been modified but not eliminated; there has been a "reformative" rather than "transformative" change that would have resulted in new societies emerging.[158] Regardless of their differing interpretations, scholars are agreed that democratic tendencies are weak among Eastern European citizens and elites alike and that the structural traits of their societies are controlled from above rather than from below. Consequently, it is argued, this situation will not "give rise to healthy institutional structures for the public sphere. Such structural features translate into mechanisms whereby the basic patterns of power and social hierarchy detrimentally shape the character of the public sphere."[159]

Can this reality give birth to or sustain news media and a public sphere that could have a salutary effect on democratization? After all, the basis of the "legitimating discourses" are provided and informed by, and embodied in, the post-Communist media as an institution. Moreover, the "dynamics of democracy are intimately linked to the practices of communication, and societal communication increasingly takes place within the mass media."[160]

The Media and Democracy

The media as an institution bore the quickest and most overt witness to the fall of Communism. In each country, media outlets quickly doubled, tripled, or quadrupled in number.[161] Economics, special interests, and audience likes and dislikes created a revolving media door with scores of newspapers, radio stations, and even television stations (albeit local) appearing and quickly disappearing from the new media world. When the media monopoly of the Communist Party evaporated, a battle for control or influence over the new media outlets was joined by governments, states, political parties, politicians, ethnic and civic organizations, organized religions, and businesses, among others.

Although thousands of new journalists joined the media's ranks, linking up with former Communist journalists and, in some of the countries, with those who worked in the underground opposition media, their newfound freedom was not matched by a professional ethos or practices resembling those found in Western democracies. The "new journalism" disseminated a plethora of opinions, rumors, incomplete and biased information, and sensationalized accounts of everything from crime to politics. On the whole, European notions of an activist, political media system were adopted in the extreme, with every journalist wanting "to influence politics and audiences according to his own political beliefs."[162] And although clearly there are differences among East Europe's media, their journalists and journalism, just as clearly there are many more similarities, including setbacks, delays, and the variety of challenges they encountered in professionalizing and democratizing the political and civic cultures of their nations.

Can the media contribute to remaking political culture? Do Eastern European institutions have a salutary effect on the media as an institution? How is the extant political culture affecting the Eastern European journalists' professional culture and their journalism? Do the media reinforce the extant political culture or are they helping to shape a new culture? If freedom does not necessarily bring democracy, does freedom of the press necessarily bring independence for the media or a professional journalistic culture and ethos that can help reshape political culture and foster the democratization process?

Media studies can reveal the potential of mass communication to affect change, the constraints or opportunities of the sociopolitical reality, and the nature of the social culture. In the Eastern European case, media studies reflect a process of political, social, economic, cultural, and individual transition, transformation, and adjustment. They provide data and intelligence concerning the possibilities and realities of the media's roles in advancing social, political, and economic goals, in helping to form and sustain groups and associations that represent varied interests, and in helping to educate individuals struggling to understand their new circumstances and to participate in the future of their societies. When examined as expressions of these post-Communist societies, the media may even suggest the directions the Eastern European transition and transformation are taking.

Media typologies attempt to explain the relationship between the media and the economic, political, and ideological realities of a society. The four major media system types first proposed—libertarian, social responsibility, Communist, and authoritarian—reflected the sociopolitical structures of a society, with freedom versus control being the core notion.[163] Albert Namurois categorized broadcasting as private enterprises, public interest partnerships, public corporations, and state-operated organizations; his typology anticipated the introduction of other dimensions for press or broadcasting classifications: ownership, media dependence on capital, levels of economic development in society, and the very nature of the economy itself.[164]

By 1969, the pure media-political structure relationship, the free versus controlled dichotomy, was disputed, and the authoritarian, paternalistic, commercial, and democratic media system types were advanced, followed in the 1970s and 1980s by the transitional, revolutionary, and developmental system types.[165] All of them ran along a libertarian-authoritarian continuum, with consideration being given to media economics and economic development in general.[166] Richard Picard put forth the proposition that media systems could be (1) libertarian, socially responsible, or democratically socialistic; (2) duodirectional, that is, either developmental or revolutionary; or (3) authoritarian-tending.[167] John Merrill and Ralph Lowenstein, and later J. Herbert Altschull, used economics, media sponsorship, media dependence on capital, and the market as the main criteria for describing media systems, arguing, mistakenly from my point of view, that there were major similarities between the media in democratic countries and those in the then-Communist ones.[168]

The political role of the media was observed to depend in large measure on where they were placed on the subordination-autonomy continuum.[169] Depending on the stability of society, the media were seen as serving either to strengthen the status quo (mirror the existing order) or to oppose it (mold and help reshape it).[170] Recognizing that societies change, Karl Erik Rosengren posited that media either mirrored society, were agents of social change, affected and were affected by society, or had no influence on society.[171]

Walter Lippmann characterized the media as a "fourth estate," or a "watchdog" providing checks and balances vis-à-vis established power, both political and economic.[172] Arguing that the media were dependent on the power structure for access, laws, and even legitimization, others have characterized them as a "guard dog."[173] Indeed, media dependency theory seeks to address the relationship between the media and other institutions, as well as their more functionalist role, through which, among other adaptive and integrative functions, the media resolve all problems connected to the "ambiguity threat and social change," although the theory is insufficiently specific and comprehensive to have any exceptional applicability to Eastern Europe.[174]

Merrill and Lowenstein added a new twist to the classification game, proposing a three-stage classification based on media audiences.[175] No matter the nature of society, they argued, the media evolved through three stages, from elitist (primarily appealing to and consumed by elites), to popular (primarily appealing to and consumed by the masses), to specialized (appealing to and consumed by fragmented, specialized segments of the population).

Four general concepts have been used to describe the central role of the news media in society. Let us briefly consider which of these concepts, if any, applies to post-1989 Eastern Europe.

According to the revolutionary concept, the media are composed of "people who believe strongly that the government they live under does not serve their interests and should be overthrown"; this is exemplified to some small degree by the underground or samizdat press in Czechoslovakia, Hungary, and Poland.[176] But there are no revolutions in the making in Eastern Europe today, despite the persistence of authoritarian mentalities there. Indeed, the so-called revolutions of 1989 were themselves less a matter of classical revolutions (which Machiavelli characterized as the forcible overthrow of rulers and change of forms of government) than of a negotiated transfer of powers.[177] The one possible exception is Romania, where the nature of the events of December 1989 that ended the Communist dictatorship of Nicolae Ceausescu is still hotly debated. Nevertheless, even here, the revolutionary concept seems out of place.

The second developmental concept holds that the mass media must serve a mobilization function in the task of nation building. Neither independent, commercial, private sector media nor public service media in the throes of their own transition and transformation are suitable: either kind may be unable or unwilling to carry out nation building, and may instead challenge authority at a time when criticism may heighten the danger of chaos. Furthermore, under the developmental concept "information or news is a scarce national resource," which should therefore support the national goals spelled out by the state or government.[178] The developmental concept, whose chief architects are Western scholars, is almost exclusively focused on so-called Third World nations.[179] It holds no promise of even partially applying to the evolution of the media in Eastern Europe because it presupposes government control of or at least very strong government influence on the mass media. Such control or influence is inimical to the principles that underlie democratization and is generally rejected by Eastern Europeans because it reminds them of the Communists' control of the media.

Under the third, authoritarian concept, commercial or private media are permitted, but they must support the state or the powers that be; thus censorship or self-censorship is the order of the day. Some post-1989 Eastern European politicians, parties, and governments subscribe to such a concept of the media and have attempted to institute it. Their successes and their more numerous failures in the post-Communist years from 1990 to 2000 are examined in the chapters to come.

The fourth, social responsibility theory supports a diverse media system out of reach of state and government control. The media are responsible for providing essential and reliable information, as well as a variety of views, thus feeding the "marketplace of ideas" that underlies a liberal democracy. Whether this contemporary Western concept applies to post-1989 Eastern Europe is at the core of this work.

In the years since 1989, models of the evolution of the news media in the transition and transformation of Eastern Europe have been offered by scholars on both sides of the Atlantic. Of these, three convey a sense of the diversity of views and approaches. The transitional model accommodates "several antagonistic prescriptive press concepts, that is, the developmental, authoritarian, communist, libertarian, revolutionary, and social responsibility normative concepts" operating concurrently.[180] Taking his cues from Paolo Mancini, Slavko Splichal concludes that Eastern European media are developing along Italian lines. According to his model, they are under strong state control, they are strongly partisan, their elites are strongly integrated with the political elites, and their professional ethics are neither consolidated nor shared.[181] The great majority of articles on the Eastern European media written from 1990 to 2000 more or less support Splichal's conclusions.

By contrast, Marxists Colin Sparks and Anna Reading propose a variant of a more general Western European model, under which the media in post-1989 Eastern Europe quickly evolved into a "fiercely competitive," market-based system that benefited not civil society, but only the political elite.[182] And, finally, in Karol Jakubowicz's three-stage model of media development (an offshoot of Brzezinski's three-stage process of post-Communist transition and transformation), politics, economics, and legal issues predict the course and eventual outcome of the media's evolution.[183]

Michael Gurevitch and Jay Blumler's eight prescriptions for the media in a democratic society suggest a fourth media model, one that embraces the major concerns of autonomization, pluralism, and diversity, as well as the nature and meaning of journalistic professionalism. These prescriptions, crucial to most conceptions of civil society and democratic political culture, are central to the relationship between the media and various other institutions, and to whether political culture or institutions are more important in the transition and transformation of the media and societies:

1. surveillance of the sociopolitical environment, reporting developments likely to impinge, positively or negatively, on the welfare of citizens;

2. meaningful agenda setting, identifying the key issues of the day, including the forces that have formed and may resolve them;
3. platforms for an intelligible and illuminating advocacy by politicians and spokespersons of causes and interest groups;
4. dialogue across a diverse range of views, as well as between power holders (actual and prospective) and mass publics;
5. mechanisms for holding officials to account for how they have exercised power;
6. incentives for citizens to learn, choose, and become involved in, rather than merely to comment about, the political process;
7. principled resistance to efforts to subvert the media's independence, integrity, and ability to serve their audience; and
8. respect for the members of their audience as potentially concerned and able to make sense of their political environment.[184]

Taking the perspective of deliberative or participatory politics, Habermas translates the Gurevitch-Blumler prescriptions into media that

ought to understand themselves as the mandatary of an enlightened public whose willingness to learn and capacity for criticism they at once presuppose, demand, and reinforce . . . to preserve their independence from political and social pressure . . . to be receptive to the public's concerns and proposals, take up these issues and contributions impartially, augment criticisms, and confront the political process with articulate demands for legitimation.[185]

Habermas's vision for the news media goes well beyond the notion of media democratization (to be revisited in chapter 5) expressed by John Keane, who sees the media facilitating

a genuine commonwealth of forms of life, tastes and opinions, to empower a plurality of citizens who are governed neither by despotic states nor by market forces. [They] should circulate to them a wide variety of opinions. [They] should enable them to live democratically within the framework of multilayered constitutional states which are held accountable to their citizens, who work and consume, live and love, quarrel and compromise within independent, self-organizing civil societies which underpin and transcend the narrow boundaries of state institutions.[186]

Media pluralism, diversity, and autonomy affect the nature of journalism and the way news is gathered, selected, and reported. Todd Gitlin defines the journalistic paradigm as "persistent patterns of cognition, interpretation, and presentation, of selection, emphasis, and exclusion, by which journalists routinely organize discourse, whether visual or verbal."[187] What affects this paradigm? Michael Schudson, among others, argues that news is culture or a product of the culture of a particular society that in turn establishes the culture of organizations and institutions, inclusive of the media, as well as the culture of journalism.[188] Three other related determinants are offered by contemporary media scholars, two of them institutional and one cultural: the distribution of social power, market forces, and press ideology.[189] Bringing all of these approaches together, Denis McQuail points out that an examination of media roles and effects requires that a connection be made between "(1) the political, social and economic forces which shape media institutions, (2) the effect of media institutions on other institutions, (3) the effect of media institutions on messages they disseminate, (4) the effect of these messages on people and on institutions."[190]

McQuail's approach inspires my examination and analysis of the Eastern European media, political culture, civil society, and democratization from 1989 to 2000. One context for my work is an old, yet continuing American debate about the role and nature of journalism: fact-based journalism carried out by professionals, as espoused by Walter Lippmann, versus "town meeting" journalism from which information is derived, as espoused by John Dewey. That debate in great measure also served to define the dividing line between American and European journalism at least until the 1980s, when that line became increasingly thin.

2

The Media and the New Political World

The demise of Communism in Eastern Europe in 1989–90 had several immediate political consequences: changeovers to parliamentary political systems, the wild proliferation of political parties—and, driven chiefly by politics and expected financial gain, of media outlets as well—and the adoption of a fierce form of political combat. One other, essentially symbolic element served as impetus for establishing new media outlets at the outset of the post-Communist era: the freedom to do so.[1]

Political discourse, which revived in Albania, Bulgaria, and Romania almost simultaneously with the end of Communist rule, continues to be greatly affected by the nature of the political parties, political systems, politics, politicians, and extant political cultures, as are the media through and by which it is conducted.[2] As Pye noted already in 1963 about transitioning societies in the Third World, the media "in providing a new basis for understanding politics and for interpreting the realm of government, become involved in the most complex and psychologically intense problems of transitional societies."[3] This new political discourse, facilitated and enlarged by the freeing of the media from the Communist monopoly system, had in some respects begun in Czechoslovakia, Hungary, and Poland, even before the fall of Communism.[4] Three issues are thus of paramount importance to media scholars focused on the region: media autonomization and pluralism (see chapter 5) and the nature and practice of journalism (chapter 4).

Post-Communist media demonopolization and autonomization included, first and foremost, the separation of the media from Communist Party and state structures, of especial importance to the process of democratization. Gaining their independence from the state, the media could begin to help constitute civil society or to contribute significantly to it by virtue of their pluralism.[5] Additionally, and ideally, they could also begin the process of what Liana Giorgi has called "differentiation" or what Oleg Manaev has called "autonomization," one in which media structures become independent of the "inhibiting" market, political, and cultural forces.[6]

This chapter examines the relationship between the media, journalists, and journalism, on the one hand, and political parties, the political system, politics, and politicians, on the other, for the period 1990–2000. Because every aspect of Eastern European institutions and their relationships is in flux, it makes no predictions about what that might be ten, five, or even one year from the time this work is published.

Political Parties

Despite differences in the region regarding how rapidly the more stable political parties and competitive party systems are being molded, the citizens of the post-Communist societies share in their distrust of parties, partly a legacy of the Communist period, and in the difficulty they have amid socioeconomic upheavals "to assess their short- and long-term interests and to pick a party that will represent those interests."[7]

The proliferation of political parties and the post-1989 trend of over-politicization have "reinforced each other," turning politics once again into a "remote realm for people, but this time on a multi-party base."[8] As Habermas sees it, instead of directing their energies to "the opinion- and will-formation from the public's own perspective," political parties feel obliged to engage, through the media, in "extracting mass loyalty from the public sphere for the purposes of maintaining their own power," or more accurately, for the purposes of acquiring and retaining power.[9]

Agh is more specific in what made their relationship with the media so vital for political parties:

1. The new party leaders were intellectuals and they had an extreme sensitivity and vanity concerning the press. . . .
2. The new parties were engaged in a cultural war among themselves because of their vague and over-ideologized programmes and "tribal," sub-cultural political profiles. In this cultural war the media [were] crucially important to them.
3. Intensive media contacts compensated the party leaders for the organizational deficit and for the weakness of the national organization

with its missing communication channels within the party. In fact, the media messages (or "congressing") were substitutes for regular party meetings.[10]

In the first few post-Communist years, several elements conspired to politicize the media, now atomized and in the service of many parties and thus a pale reflection of the Communist media: (1) the perceived need of the political parties; (2) the legacy of the media relationship with the Communist parties and that of the underground media with the anti-Communist movement; (3) the absence of any other historical role for the media; (4) the economic limbo in which the media were suspended immediately after the demise of Communism; and finally, (5) the media's self-perception as expressed by their elites (discussed in chapter 4). As Agh sees it, political parties "have monopolized the public scene by securing privileged access to the media for themselves."[11] In short, the evolution of party politics and that of the media have become intimately conjoined. Nevertheless, by the end of the 1990s one could discern a "widening of politics" and an "opening of the national political scene."[12] The pressures brought on political parties by elements of the slowly growing civil society have begun to have an effect on the parties' decision making; the relationship between political parties and the media had changed by the second half of the 1990s, as had the nature of the media, their role, and their audiences.

What media did the new and old political parties have to work with in the immediate post-1989 period? There were two journalistic camps within Eastern Europe: one of states having authoritarian Communist regimes and underground media (Czechoslovakia, Hungary, and Poland) and a second of states having totalitarian Communist regimes and no underground media (Albania, Bulgaria, and Romania).[13] The presence of the underground press conferred a certain degree of added legitimacy on the media of the immediate post-1989 period.[14] States in the first camp, to varying degrees, experienced a bridging period between a Stalinist Communist society, with its cult of personality, and a pluralist society. This bridging "authoritarian Communist" period allowed for the emergence or reemergence of a highly limited civil society, the establishment of anti-Communist or alternative media, or both, and a political culture that was overtly anti-Communist among a small segment of each state's society, or a larger segment in the case of Poland, where anti-Communism was more open and widespread. Such a development did not bring with it, however, the evolution of professional, fact-based, independent media in any of the three states.[15] Nevertheless, these non-Communist media, having established their legitimacy in society during the Communist era, with larger or smaller audiences, took political and economic advantage of this legitimacy in 1989–90.

In the second journalistic camp, the media had the immediate task of seeking legitimacy. They were granted it quickly by virtue of their "newness" and their role as vehicles both for venting anti-Communism, giving audiences a chance to vicariously participate in a "revolution," and for individual and national catharsis. Yet they were to lose that legitimacy as rapidly as they had acquired it.[16] Thus the Romanian media and their journalists were first seen as heroes, martyrs, and revolutionaries. Within only a few months, their image quickly changed and most were viewed as liars, clowns, and moral bankrupts.[17]

In Czechoslovakia, Hungary, and Poland, the first camp, there were three major post-1989 media strands: (1) the former Communist media, which quickly changed their profile; (2) the old anti-Communist opposition media; and (3) the new media (private, commercial, noncommercial, party, religious, ethnic, etc.) launched after the end of Communist rule, including media outlets financed or owned in whole or part by foreigners.[18] By contrast, in Albania, Bulgaria, and Romania, the second camp, whose post-Communist media comprised chiefly leftover Communist news outlets and new mass communication outlets paralleling those in the first camp, foreign investment in or ownership of media was low or nonexistent (as I will show in chapter 3).

In this second camp, to an even greater extent than in the first, and contrary to the contention of some media observers, the success of the new electronic and print media outlets in the first few post-Communist years reflected not so much the "new marketization" of the media as the establishment of a pluralism of political parties, the return of participatory political life, and the emergence of a form of civil society.[19] Two of the most prominent examples of the latter two developments in Romania were the Free Timisoara Television, launched in December 1989 in the heated days of that city's revolt, and the respected news weekly *22* in Bucharest, published by the Group for Social Dialogue, made up of intellectuals ostensibly committed to a liberal democracy.[20] Although such examples had small audiences or circulations, others like them could be found elsewhere in Eastern Europe.[21]

In every nation of the region, the new political parties (some an outgrowth of the anti-Communist groups active prior to the overthrow of Communist regimes), the revived pre-Communist parties, and the Communist parties, which quickly regrouped and changed their names, established new publications and formally or informally took control of the press, once monopolized by the Communist Party or by the state.[22] The political parties that took over the reins of government and state (as will be discussed in chapter 3) sought to control the existing radio and television outlets and to influence the print media by whatever means they had at their disposal.

Only a handful of primarily commercial media outlets were initially established in Albania, Bulgaria, and Romania. By contrast, in Czechoslovakia, Hungary, and Poland, where foreign media companies quickly entered the race to acquire media outlets, profit was a primary motive, although, to achieve it, outlets had to be political and partisan.[23] While media outlets were also established that were neither solely commercial nor directly political, such as *Prace,* published by the Czech trade unions, the Roman Catholic newspapers in Poland, or the German-language newspaper *Banater Zeitung* in Romania, on balance Ekaterina Ognianova's description of the first stage of Bulgarian media transition holds true for all of Eastern Europe: the media changed "from tribunes of the Communist Party to tribunes of a diversity of political parties," even dailies and weeklies that were not formally party publications.[24]

The "oppositional media" in Czechoslovakia, Hungary, and Poland either "folded" or became "party affiliates with only a limited readership."[25] The primary goal of parties, individuals, ethnic and other groups in establishing or acquiring media outlets was to have communication platforms for political purposes. In Hungary, as elsewhere in the region, political parties "reasoned that the media were critical in conveying images and information to the masses. Media treatment was a matter of political life and death."[26] Consequently, aside from warring against each other, political parties were constantly warring against those elements of the media that opposed them. Charges by opposition parties that fair elections were hampered by government control of the national broadcast media reverberated across the region throughout the first nine post-Communist years.[27] The Polish reality, notes Slavko Splichal, was observed everywhere in Eastern Europe: "A new kind of media polyphony appeared, although to the ears of the many new politicians it sounded more like a cacophony. . . . All over Eastern Europe the media are being accused of irresponsibility and of being too 'liberal.'"[28] As Splichal goes on to say:

> In contrast to Western Europe, however, where media policymaking is strongly influenced by considerations of the economic and technological challenges presented by new media, East-Central European policies

are typically framed in party-political terms, and the media (particularly broadcasting) are largely used for political benefits rather than for commercial value.[29]

A brief review of the print media transition in the first two to three post-Communist years in the nations belonging to each of the two journalistic camps serves to prove the point. It also establishes that in Albania, Bulgaria, and Romania, the initial post-1989 stage brought a much greater affiliation of press with political parties than in Czechoslovakia, Hungary, and Poland, perhaps in part because the return of an open, free political life was more sudden, the search for political convictions more urgently pursued, and the need for disseminating views more strongly felt than in the nations that passed through an authoritarian Communist phase, with a clear, however heterogeneous, opposition already organized.

Albania

Almost all of the post-1989 newspapers were established by the new political parties. Only *Koha Jone, Albania,* and *Gazeta Shgipetare* (an Albanian-Italian coproduction) were not directly affiliated with a political party, although they were no less politicized, falling into one of two politically opposed categories: pro-government or anti-government.[30] The former Communist press was also taken over by various political parties.

Not surprisingly, the Albanian post-Communist press "has been highly partisan, more concerned with expounding the viewpoints of the respective parties than with factual news coverage."[31] Prec Zogaj, editor-in-chief of *Aleanca* in 1994, concluded that the Albanian press was simply an extension of the political parties and thus a "political battlefield."[32] Each of Albania's 250 newspapers espoused a particular party line: the opinions they expressed were tailored, and the facts they reported skewed, to advance that party viewpoint.[33] Albanian readers, explained Zogaj, "can rarely find a real debate in these Albanian party papers. Every party defends just one idea."[34]

Bulgaria

The Social Democratic Party launched *Svoboden Narod,* the Union of Democratic Forces, *Demokratsia,* and the Socialist Party (formerly, the Communist Party), its re-renamed newspaper *Duma.* Party political organs or newspapers informally tied to a political party outnumbered all others, prompting the remark that "newspapers in [Bulgaria's] early transition period were highly political copies of the old one-party newspaper system."[35] By the end of 1991, "practically all the major political organizations that existed under the communist regime had transferred their property rights to newly established, *legally* independent publishing firms" (emphasis added).[36] They did so without changing the political nature of their profiles. Additionally, the source of capital of some press groups remained a mystery, a situation that paralleled the one in Romania, for example. How many of Bulgaria's 1,700–2,700 publications in circulation by 1993 were owned, subsidized, or otherwise connected to the political parties is not known.[37]

Romania

Roughly half of all dailies and weeklies were party publications in the first three to five post-Communist years. The rest were quasi-commercial, quasi-independent newspapers, most of which were indirectly affiliated with a party by virtue of the personal relationship of owners, publishers, and editors with politicians and political parties. All the media were highly politicized and partisan, choosing sides in the wildly diverse political party scene.[38] The national press, mimicking its regional cousins, was quickly divided in two groups: (1) the press that supported the new government and represented, formally or informally, the parties in power or sympathetic to it; and (2) the "press of opposition," predominantly representing, again formally or informally, the various parties in opposition. Overall, the news media, "instead of being teamsters carrying information . . . to readers," transformed themselves "into political gunslingers."[39] The ownership or financial backing of media outlets in Romania was and still is a subject seldom openly discussed and is very difficult to ascertain for many, if not most, media organizations.

Poland

The most important daily, *Gazeta Wyborcza,* was the official organ of Solidarity until 1990, when Lech Walesa, angered at the newspaper's failure to support him, demanded that the newspaper remove "Solidarnosc" from its masthead.[40] The second most important daily, *Rzeczpospolita,* formerly a government newspaper and characterized by Tomasz Goban-Klas as "an almost independent, information-based paper," became a joint venture of the Polish government and a French company.[41] Other newspapers were not political organs per se but had a definite preference for or informal compacts with a particular political party, or at least a well-defined partisan political profile. With the breakup of the Prasa-Ksiazka-Ruch (RSW), the publishing conglomerate controlled by the Polish Communist Party, most of the country's 170 newspapers and periodicals were sold to "forces emerging out of 'Solidarity'" and to the Social Democratic Party, which grew out of the former Communist Party.[42] The process of demonopolizing the media from state control "was designed partly *to ensure a pluralistic press by selling newspapers to specified political parties*" (emphasis added).[43] Thus the Polish press, like its counterparts throughout the region, became free and pluralistic, but not really independent.[44] Polish readers continue to perceive the press as being highly political, and "it has widely been believed that each party or faction must have a newspaper as its mouthpiece and that every newspaper must have some affiliation with a party or a faction."[45] How many of Poland's 1,000–4,000 publications in circulation by 1993–94 were directly affiliated with political parties is difficult to ascertain.[46]

Czechoslovakia

After 1989 but before the 1993 "divorce" establishing the Czech and Slovak Republics, the former Communist Party flagship, *Rude Pravo,* became "an aggressive social democratic publication," and *Mlada Fronta Dnes,* a Communist newspaper directed at the young, became the "most prominent right-of-center publication."[47] Thus even the press not owned or subsidized by a political party offered readers content that was "politically from distinctive left to distinctive right."[48] So it was that the media in general supported the right-wing government of Václav Klaus in the initial phase of the Czech Republic's post-Communist transition.[49] In a pattern not unfamiliar in the other countries reviewed here, the Czech "national" press in the immediate post-1989 period consisted of, in Giorgi's words,

- party papers remaining with their original publishers but disengaging themselves from a party line . . . ;
- papers formerly published by political parties or associations passing into private hands . . . ;
- papers becoming independent from their original publishers via unilateral action on the part of the editors and employee associations.[50]

Judging by the correlation between readers' preferences in daily newspapers and their political sympathies and affiliations, it is clear that the Czech press, estimated to include about 2,500 publications by 1991, while not in general a party press per se, was highly partisan, with a well-established informal connection to the various political parties that had sprung up in the wake of 1989.[51] This politicization of the press brought about an overpowering inclination "to comment from the position of a certain political or interest group," an approach that predominated over unbiased reporting.[52]

In the Slovak Republic, as in the Czech Republic, political parties had a "common tendency" to establish their own daily or weekly publications, and even the nonparty press followed the regional pattern, being strongly influenced, if not actually controlled, by various political parties, politicians, or both.[53]

Hungary

Existing "media assets were privatized on the basis of ideological criteria," some remaining in the hands of the state, and new publications "although not directly state-owned, would back the ruling coalition."[54] Before the 1990 elections, new Hungarian parties started their own newspapers, "usually sad affairs, long on political bombast and short on professional journalism. Boring and demagogic, they contributed briefly to the boom in the number of newspapers available on the news stands."[55] Although, as with the other Eastern European countries, Hungary has no precise accounting, of the roughly 1,500–3,200 publications circulating in the 1990–93 period, 150 were published "by various party committees" on the local level and 650 were launched by associations or groups with varied political interests.[56] These numbers are in line with the post-1989 regional tendency of parties to acquire their own newspapers, in part to head off any attempts by other media outlets to portray them negatively. "In doing this, they reflect the old traditions, both those of the Communist press and those of the underground press, to which they have grown accustomed."[57]

National television in each Eastern European country remained almost universally in the hands of the state or government, that is, under the control or influence of the party or parties making up the government, despite pressure from Western governments and nongovernmental institutions, such as the Soros Foundation and the International Media Fund, to allow private national televisions stations to be established. The official state television stations' new designation as "public service" outlets (an issue to be further dealt with in chapter 3) did nothing to remove the stations from government control and manipulation. In Bulgaria, private broadcasting was not introduced until 1993; in Romania, it took until 1995 to establish a quasi-national, private challenge to Romanian Television (TVR), even though on the local level private, commercial television and radio were quickly launched beginning in December 1989; in Hungary, two years after the end of Communist rule, there were practically no commercial radio or television stations beside independent Radio Calypso and Radio Bridge; in Poland, private broadcast licenses for national outlets were not issued until early 1991, and private, mostly local television stations such as EL-GAZ shunned political programming; and in Czechoslovakia, authorization for private, commercial broadcast stations was also not given until 1991.

Media evolution halfway through the first post-Communist decade thus fits a media and development theory proposed by Wilbur Schramm in the 1960s for the developing countries of the Third World:

1. Ownership and control of the media and use of communications are mainly in the hands of political parties and commercial enterprises with a high level of political contacts, interests, and so on.
2. The content of communications reflects the struggle over social values in the only language that is understood: political language.
3. Communication networks are fragmented, mostly along political lines, but also along ethnic, educational, class, and religious lines.
4. Social communications are carried on mainly by a mixture of political, state, and commercial media enterprises, in that order.[58]

The one element of Schramm's old developmental formula that the Eastern European experience does not fit was his finding that, in developing societies, "the size of communication activity—the development of the mass media and their audiences . . . the stretching out and multiplying of communication chains—reflects the economic development of society."[59] The explanation for Eastern European media growth not reflecting economic developments in each country lies with the overpoliticization of these societies and the attendant proliferation of political parties, a developmental aspect not present to the same degree in the Third World countries Schramm studied in the 1960s. Thus the degree of media development in Eastern Europe had less to do with economic factors and more to do with perceived political exigencies on the part of political parties, politicians, and media enterprises operating in highly politicized societies (at least initially run almost exclusively by the old *nomenklatura* on the strength of their political contacts) and jockeying for position in the new political world after a prolonged absence of independent politics.[60]

The politicization and partisanship did not disappear by the second half of the first post-1989 decade, reflecting the continuing race for political and economic power, the opportunity to define values and the direction of the transition in the image of a particular interest or political goal and set of values. It remained a period of extremes: elation, hope, and an exuberant search for information and for varied opinions, countered by depression, despair, and a focus on entertainment and isolation from other views. In Bulgaria, as in the rest of Eastern Europe, the "fierce partisanship, aggressive propaganda and verbal dueling" of the young post-Communist press illustrated "John Milton's idea that 'where there is much desire to learn, there of necessity will be much arguing, much writing, many opinions.'"[61] The lifting of the Iron Curtain and the unfettering of once-captive societies gave freedom to the hunger for the greatest possible number and variety of media outlets. The race to find one's place in the new society, position one's political beliefs, ensure one's financial success, or have one's values dominate was run mainly by political parties, politicians, and the mass media.

By 1992–95, the party press began to fade away, thanks to disenchantment with its overt and aggressive pursuit of one-sided political party agendas. Throughout the region, its circulation fell, and it was attacked by the few "mainstream" media outlets and by other elements of society. On the local and regional levels, some outlets remained in the hands of "mainstream" political parties.[62] In general, however, the party press lost credibility and thus also its audiences. It became no longer feasible or politically profitable for political parties to own outright or to be overtly represented by one or more media outlets. In Bulgaria, for instance, because "party newspapers did not live up to the expectations of becoming professionally run publications that provided objective information to the readers," they all but vanished.[63]

In Romania after 1992, the party press suffered a similar loss of credibility and thus a similar fate: "Even a faithful and devoted reader [could not] read a text that endlessly repeats the same message," observed Mihai Coman.[64] The newspapers that managed to survive were reorganized as nonparty organs, even if they retained obvious political preferences.[65] In Poland, "few parties [could] afford to finance their own media and many openly party-oriented newspapers and periodicals have gone bankrupt."[66]

In Albania, all newspapers had "only limited appeal and distribution."[67] It is ironic that contradictory political views and beliefs, the very essence of a social dialogue, were considered by the post-Communist press to be inimical to that dialogue.

Because of the media's political partisanship, in their opinion pieces as well as in their so-called news reporting, readership was fragmented, splitting along party or political lines. And, as the political parties themselves split, further fragmenting the readership, any growth in party media outlets was no longer possible: some party newspapers were marginalized, while others simply folded.[68] Although the party press did not disappear altogether, either on the national or local level, many of the remaining party newspapers are associated with extremist parties, such as the anti-Semitic, anti-Hungarian *Romania Mare* serving the party by the same name in Romania.

Throughout Eastern Europe, save perhaps in Albania, the press achieved structural and financial autonomy from political parties by the end of the 1990s. Yet the two sides continued living together or, at the very least, dating even after their divorce. Consequently, what Colin Seymour-Ure calls "party-press parallelism," is far greater and deeper in the Eastern than in the Western European media world.[69] If we are to accept Ognianova's assessment, the Bulgarian media may constitute the unique exception to such parallelism in Eastern Europe, having become independent information and entertainment institutions in their own right.[70]

Goban-Klas's observation, that the Polish media "mainly perform an advocacy role, [being] still connected to government (electronic broadcasting) or political parties or factions (the press), rather than being truly independent," holds for their counterparts in the region.[71] Despite assurances by almost all Eastern European editors, publishers, and television directors, they and their media outlets are far from completely "independent" of political parties; their drive for greater autonomy, which began only in the late 1990s, has yet to run its course.

That, by the end of the first post-Communist decade, political parties had, for the most part, become better organized, that they had developed intra-party communication channels and clearer party profiles, did not make the media less important to them, although their effects on the media and their relationship with them had changed substantially. Still, the region's political parties and the mass media continue to relate and coordinate their actions along shared beliefs and interests. Both contribute to societies that are something less than "media democracies" and as France Vreg observes

New political parties in Eastern Europe are confronted with the dilemma of how to use the democratic model of communication or to apply some elements of the authoritarian models as well. Some mass media are using manipulative forms and methods of dissimulation and political marketing. Therefore, it is difficult to say that in the new democracies a democratic model of communication is prevailing.[72]

The print media's formal divorce from political parties did not mean the end of their relationship with them, as I already pointed out. That many newspapers continue, in the words of Dean Murphy, to "have uncompromising allegiances to political parties or political figures" does not denote a symbiotic relationship, however, but rather one in which the actions, words, stances, and philosophies of political parties and the media simply coincide.[73] Few if any newspapers in the region pay attention to Adam Michnik's admonition that "an independent daily should not become party in a political struggle."[74] Choosing to reject pure independence throughout the 1990s, and sometimes forced to by economic necessity, the media of Eastern Europe continue to serve as adjuncts to or platforms for elements of the political system, with a very small handful of exceptions in each of the now seven countries.

By the end of the 1990s, media outlets in the region were owned by a mixture of private or commercial interests, political parties, and elements of civil society, such as trade unions, religious denominations, and ethnic minority organizations. What all of the news media continue to have in common is an extreme politicization, even if overt political partisanship has subsided at least to some degree. There is a marked contrast between what happened in the transitional societies of the Third World during the 1960s and what is happening in post-Communist Eastern Europe. In the Third World, a scarcity of media outlets had the attendant effect of audiences not developing attitudes of selectivity and, therefore, the media played a more potent role.[75] In contrast, in Eastern Europe, where media outlets were abundant, audiences became exceedingly selective: hundreds of publications sprouted up and died away in the first few post-Communist years, with circulation for surviving publications plummeting, and with few having any consequential influence. Denis McQuail's conclusion that "we cannot assume that ownership and control of the means of mass communication [must] confer power over others in any straightforward or predictable way" may prove true for Eastern Europe, despite the perception, particularly in political circles, that, without the media, political power cannot be achieved.[76]

John Dewey, who preferred the deliberative model of democracy, bemoaned the disappearance of the party press in the United States of the 1920s.[77] Almost seventy years later, Christopher Lasch observed that "the decline of the partisan press and the rise of a new type of journalism professing rigorous standards of objectivity do not assure a steady supply of usable information."[78] Indeed, the decline of the party or partisan press in Eastern Europe has not given rise to any type of professional, neutral journalism. (Eastern European journalism and the utility of information disseminated by the postparty press of the1990s are discussed in chapter 5.)

Politicians and Political Elites

Eastern European political parties "have been the chief actors in democratic transition and they have played an almost monopolistic role in the creation of the new political elite, and beyond it, of the new political class."[79] This new elite, Dankwart Rustow asserts, "can create democracy," provided it can arrive at a "procedural consensus on the rules of the game."[80] Indeed, the power and influence of elites is such that if they wish to have democracy, they will produce and get democracy. The relationship between the Eastern European political elites and the media thus sheds light not only on the nature of media and journalism, but also on the dominant political culture they represent, reinforce, and thus propagate.

The political and economic elites of the new Eastern Europe are predominantly derivatives of the old Communist elites and of the anti-Communist elites in those countries where anti-Communist movements existed. They almost exclusively had the initial financial wherewithal and the connections to establish, control, or influence the news media. The new elites, who belonged to neither of the old elites, were and continue to be just as interested in controlling or influencing the media for political or economic benefit or both. Indeed, as Klaus von Beyme points outs, an "unholy alliance" quickly developed between old and new elites.[81] Agh breaks down these post-Communist political elites into

1. "politicians of morals," who played a role in opposing the Communist regime (predominantly in Hungary, Poland, and the former Czechoslovakia);
2. "politicians of historical vision," who represent a direct (e.g., Corneliu Coposu in Romania) or indirect (e.g., József Antall of Hungary)

continuity with the pre-Communist political past, and who have "a determined historical vision of . . . re-creating the past in the coming future";

3. "politicians by chance," who were catapulted to power by the chaos of the transition, and who are marked "by an aggressive exhibitionism and an emphasis on personal career" and by the absence of any political ability;

4. "old *nomenklatura*," who constitute a mixed bag of Communist Party members or leaders, halfhearted opponents of the Communist rules, Communist reformers, and die-hard Communists; and

5. "new professional political elites," old and new politicians, mostly from the younger generation, who emerged in the second half of the first post-Communist transition decade.[82]

There is much support for the conclusion that there were no established political elites in Eastern Europe in the first few post-Communist years.[83] Elemer Hankiss describes the new democratic forces as being divided, confused, without identities and "places in the political spectrum," without a sociopolitical model they want established.[84] By the end of the 1990s, however, though more in some of the region's countries than in others, the movement toward consolidation, organization, clarity of sociopolitical visions, and finding one's niche on the political spectrum had begun.[85] No one better summarizes the not-so-new political culture of the post-1989 political elites than Jowitt:

> The difficulty in creating a democratic established political elite with a tolerant culture is exacerbated by the "refolutionary" change that occurred in 1989. Leninist personnel still play a prominent role in administrative, economic (and, in the Balkans, political) life. In Eastern Europe, one sees a novel evolutionary phenomenon: *survival of the first*, not simply the fittest. Former party cadres are exceptionally well placed to successfully adapt themselves—and their families—to changes in the economic and administrative order (emphasis original).[86]

Intuitively comprehending the potential power of media, political elites did their best to bring the press, radio, and television under their control, or even, as Splichal would have it, to "monopolize" the media.[87] Sparks and Reading have gone so far as to assert that only politicians benefited from the new post-Communist media.[88] Neither conclusion is justified by the evidence. By the end of the 1990s, no one group "monopolized" the media; what is more, immediate appearances to the contrary, the transformation of Communist media systems and forms to non-Communist ones has benefited everyone. Post-1989 journalism, regardless of its quality, has taught "people participation . . . by depicting for them new and strange situations and by familiarizing them with a range of opinions among which they can choose."[89]

In every one of the Eastern European nations, Communist national dailies and weeklies passed into the hands of new political parties or, in the case of the local press, "into the hands of the old local *nomenklatura.*"[90] Furthermore, the political parties in control of the new governments view control of the so-called public broadcasting media, particularly television, "as a 'significant military position' to bolster [their] power."[91]

Sparks sees the new ruling class, largely a duplicate of the old-Communist ruling class, though "fragmented, atomized, constantly reshaping itself and its internal relations," striving for a "form of social power" based principally on private ownership of property and, through it, for political power.[92] But there is more to social or political power than simply private ownership of property. Power may be derived from an ideology, a political vision or program, from the public presence, moral stance, and credibility of an individual politician, or from the ability of a leader or party to provide people with what they need and want. Whatever the sources of or intent of this power, as Owen Johnson observes, "many government and political leaders do not think that a free and open press can be tolerated when the democracies and economies of their countries are still so fragile."[93] The Hungarian Democratic Forum, for example, holds the view that the media should serve the democratically elected government because it "represents the will of the majority of voters."[94] In Albania, "politicians consider journalists to be their servants."[95] In Poland, most politicians want the media to "serve as a political trumpet rather than an autonomous information agency."[96] All post-Communist political elites in Eastern Europe view the electronic media in particular as having "a critical role to play in creating a 'correct' view of reality through the reshaping of public opinion."[97]

Such widely held attitudes toward the media give "political competition" and "pluralism" a different tone than that found in established Western democracies: precisely because the new ruling class "speaks in many voices," there is an "enormous public struggle over who should control the media, and an enormous public struggle over what they should contain."[98]

For instance, the Slovak Television Council ruled in 1996 that news time for Slovak Television (STV) news was to be divided equally between the government, the ruling parliamentary coalition, and the parliamentary opposition. Yet, just before the fall elections of 1998, the government continued to receive 60 percent of air time on STV news, with the ruling parliamentary coalition and opposition each getting 20 percent.[99] Next door, in the Czech Republic, a society regarded by the West to be most advanced in its transformation to a democracy, in the fullest meaning of the word, the current affairs programs for Czech Television appear to be clearly tilted in favor of members of the Czech government.[100]

Eastern European politicians perceived the media "as being a magic wand regardless of public opinion [with] the power to mold and reshape public opinion," believing that "if they [controlled] the media—they should not [have to] worry about what people think."[101] Through the media outlets they owned, controlled, subsidized, or influenced, they helped create the highly partisan and politicized media and journalism of the first decade of post-Communism. The partisan wrangling of those years engendered "mutual distrust" and outright animosity between politicians and the journalists who worked for media outlets opposing them.[102] It led to an adversarial relationship between the media and politicians that was neither professional nor objective in nature, but rather political, even personal. Conflicts between politicians and journalists became commonplace, in part, because of a lack of cooperation between politicians in power and "opposition media" and between politicians out of power and government-supporting media.[103] Media outlets that were "critical and unsupportive" were "censured" in both the Czech and Slovak cases.[104] Indeed, throughout Eastern Europe politicians routinely classify the media into "friendly" and "hostile," "constructive" and "destructive," and "communicate with them accordingly."[105]

As already suggested, even media outlets divorced from political parties have links to the political elites. Many such connections and influences are at an individual level. For instance, Jerzy Urban, the former government spokesman during martial law in Poland, became editor of the pro-Communist, populist, anti-Catholic newspaper *Nie,* whose attacks against former dissidents run alongside its ribald photographs and stories of scandals.[106] Adam Michnik, the former Solidarity leader, edits the now-independent *Gazeta Wyborcza.* All across Eastern Europe, links between media owners and political elites evolved, yet were not always clearly discernible or overtly exhibited. In Romania, it is difficult if not impossible to establish who owns the media and whose subsidies influence the news they provide. By the end of the 1990s, the special relationship between the media outlets and particular political parties had changed to one between media outlets and particular politicians. It remains difficult to prove, but it exists.[107] In a work arguing there is even less independence than owners, subsidizers, or the state's attempts at controlling the Romanian media suggest, Richard Hall contends that the old Securitate, Romania's version of the KGB, now broken up into various factions and active on political and economic fronts, still has a significant influence "on political behavior . . . affecting all media sources regardless of ownership type (state or private), ideological orientation, or relationship to the regime."[108]

Although there is no way to conclusively prove it, the relationship between politicians, whether as parents, close relatives, mates, friends, or foes, and the post-Communist media has affected the way the media gather and report the news and continues to do so. Nevertheless, by the end of the 1990s media outlets once strongly manipulated if not actually controlled by politicians or political parties began to want more independence and to discover their own powers. As the century ended, a gradual separation took place between the media and the political elites, as the media sought to redefine their role and interests in society (see chapter 4). Far from united, these elites clearly do not fit the Italianization pattern posited by Slavko Splichal and Paolo Mancini.[109] The relationship between media owners and politicians, though still close, is not cabal-like; there is simply no evidence that it represents a form of state control.

Politics and Political Systems

Surveying world history from 1914 to 1991, Eric Hobsbawm concluded that, by century's end, it had "become evident that the media were a more important component of the political process than parties and the electoral systems, and likely to remain so."[110] It is doubtful, however, that this conclusion applies to Eastern Europe, where the political process of transition and transformation to democracy demands socialization or education in democratic political culture and the construction and use of new democratic institutions. Such education requires fact-based information as a basis for teaching citizens to assume their responsibilities for decision making in the new democracies. Yet, as Henry Carey observed in his study of post-Communist Romania, the media "more directly and effectively transmit political information than inculcate democratic values."[111] This may be particularly true in Hungary, where the news media have become instruments of political consolidation rather than models and teachers of democratic values.[112] What, then, can the nature of Eastern European politics and political systems tell us about the media's pluralism, autonomy, and the role and the character of their journalism?

If we accept the conclusion that political parties are "more diverse and more extreme in their approach" in partisan parliamentary systems than in majoritarian systems, then we can expect to find that their journalism is not only politicized but also highly partisan.[113] In Eastern Europe, political intensity and partisan extremism ranged in the 1990–2000 era from the party versus party struggles to the politician versus politician jousting that often goes beyond political and ideological antagonisms to deeply entrenched personal rivalries and animosities.[114] The result is a sharply combative rather than competitive politics, however slightly political systems may vary from country to country.[115]

It can be argued that such black-and-white politics is merely a continuation of the Communist versus anti-Communist combat carried on overtly before 1989 in Czechoslovakia, Hungary, and Poland, and covertly in Albania, Bulgaria, and Romania. Not only has the old *nomenklatura* perpetuated this type of politics, often from an ethnic nationalist perspective (e.g., Ion Iliescu in Romania or Vladimir Meciar in the Slovak Republic), but the democratic opposition, thanks in large measure to its leadership, has failed to reform it.

> The qualities and outlooks that had brought many former dissidents national and international acclaim and respect as dogged and unyielding opponents of the Communist regimes were not normally the ones that were needed in government, especially when the major issues and choices were no longer as black and white as they used to be.[116]

Indeed, the "all or nothing" mentality lingered in the recesses of Eastern European politicians' mentalities throughout the 1990s, as did the pro- and anti-government split in the media. Extreme partisanship among the media is not unique to Eastern Europe, however. Writing about the "transitional journalists" in Japan, Philippines, India, and Korea, Herbert Passin concluded in 1963 that "the result of the historical journalistic bias is that as the transitional states emerge . . . they have an oppositional, partisan press which finds it difficult to transform itself into the kind of responsible, non-partisan press that the new situation requires."[117] Passin is describing a stage of journalistic development in media that may have made a systemic transition, but whose journalism is still battling to transform itself into one that serves independent states. A similar situation was found in Latin America in the 1980s, where the media were in need less of systemic change and more of transformation.[118] In short, it is not the media that determine the nature of the political environment or the politics practiced, but the other way around and biased jornalism continues to be practiced in transitional societies.

Thus the messages transmitted by Eastern European political parties and politicians were not only one-sided but also highly prejudiced in their favor or against their opponents. And the media, at first owned or otherwise controlled by them, served as vehicles for and magnifying lenses of these messages. Given that news media, more so in the first than the second half of the first post-Communist decade, were not concentrated in a few hands, it was a case of widely competing propaganda outlets vying for attention and, ultimately, for the hearts if not the minds of the newly freed citizens. (I will explore the consequences of such competition for the media's role in democratization in chapter 5.)

That there was journalistic partisanship in a political milieu where opposition was anything but normal is again consonant with findings in other transitional or transforming nations. In an examination of early Japan, China, India, and Africa, states having little or no tradition of opposition tended to have partisan journalism, while "in states where opposition [was] more normal, the ideals of journalistic detachment [were] given more play."[119] In Eastern Europe, it was the universal perception, on the part of political parties, politicians, and media elites alike, that the only way to resist the politicization and partisanship of one's opponents was to answer in kind. Thus the transition from Communism having been completed, the politicized, partisan battle to transform society and its mentalities, values, and behaviors raged on throughout the 1990s.

There is little normality in the politics of Eastern Europe. Furthermore, the region's countries share Poland's predicament, finding themselves unable to "take advantage of new possibilities offered by the process of political democratization," and

still expect[ing] politicians to take [the] initiative and introduce regulations, also as regards change in particular segments and subsystems of society. Thus the political system still continues to play—at least so far as societal expectations are concerned—the role of the main force of modernization. Contrary to expectations, the emergence of post-

Communist societies does not galvanize other fields of social life to an extent conspicuous at the macro level.[120]

This description also points to another unique aspect of post-1989 Eastern European politics: it revolves around individual politicians, focusing on personalities instead of on political parties and their programs, thus adding to the combative nature of politics, the intensity of the personal fights, and their expression in the news media.[121]

The process of democratic institutionalization and political modernization or transformation is faster in the Czech Republic, Hungary, and Poland than in Albania, Bulgaria, Romania, and the Slovak Republic. It is argued that in the former group the process is one of "redemocratization" and in the latter, one of "beginning democratization."[122] However the process is defined, the media in both groups share more or the less the same nature, ethos, and practices, partly because the political culture of the actors involved (the political parties, politicians, and the citizens or audiences) is also much the same. Furthermore, the media, their elites, and their rank and file have been slow to separate themselves from the extant political culture (see chapter 4). That is, they have been slow or altogether remiss in defining professional standards and values for themselves, at least those in any way divorced from the predominant political culture and nature of politics.

By the end of the 1990s, the Eastern European media, even if no longer owned by political parties, were still not "more important components of the political process than parties and electoral systems," as Hobsbawm concluded for the rest of the world.[123] They choose to remain in great measure indirect extensions of political parties, politics, politicians, and political systems, and, more significant, of their political cultures. Beneath their identifications with culture and political institutions (as I will show in chapter 5), they are concurrently also extensions of social, cultural, civic, ethnic, labor, economic, and other institutions.

The news media are considered indispensable to the democratic process when democracy is defined by an appropriate, applied democratic political culture and by a degree of direct citizen involvement in civic and social matters based on information and views supplied by the media, and not simply in institutional terms, as having many political parties, periodic elections, and even substantial voter turnout on election day. The nations of Eastern Europe are, however, far less than "media-centered" democracies. That status would be a vast improvement because (as I argue in chapter 6) objective, neutral media are vital to the process of democratization.[124] For now, the concept of the media as elements of democracy, and not simply of partisan political battles, has not yet consciously taken root, neither among ordinary Eastern Europeans nor among the intellectual, social, business, or political elites.[125] Providing balanced analysis, and complete, accurate, verifiable, sourced information, undistorted by the journalists' judgments and views, is simply not a function carried out by the post-Communist media. Eastern Europeans, including the elites, do not yet understand the importance of such information to political self-expression and self-government. What they do understand, and what remains an instinctive part of their political culture, is the use of selected, and most often distorted, information for political purposes.

Responding to a culture of overpoliticization and partisanship, most of the region's media outlets allow demagoguery, biases, self-interest and even hate to undermine the mission of information gathering, reporting, and disseminating varied viewpoints. Sometimes, however, politicization and partisanship can be harnessed to combat lies, and demagoguery, as demonstrated by a handful of media outlets, such as Poland's *Gazeta Wyborcza,* which along with others, such as Hungary's *Nepszabadsag* and Romania's *Adevarul,* "are making efforts to separate commentary from the news columns at least part of the time."[126]

Nevertheless, recognition of the media's centrality to politicians, political parties, and politics was constantly juxtaposed with complaints of their biases, a pattern also exhibited in foreign coverage of election campaigns in the region for the period 1990–96. To illustrate the point, in Albania, where the Democratic Party of Sali Berisha overwhelmingly won the June 1996 election: "Opposition parties were restricted in campaign rallies. Media access was skewed for weeks before the vote."[127] In Hungary, "opposition parties cried foul during the [1994] parliamentary elections campaign, charging that state-owned television praised the government and attacked opponents."[128] In Poland, "government officials repeatedly have accused the new-found free press of vicious, constant attacks."[129] In Romania, during all three presidential and parliamentary elections (1990, 1992, 1996), politicians and political parties complained about the biases and unprofessionalism of the media that did not support them; the democratic opposition, in particular, was incensed at how national television, under the control of the incumbents, was dissimulating, biased, and unprofessional.[130] In the Slovak Republic, "supporters of former Prime Minister Vladimir Meciar—who was forced from office this spring [1994]—had an ongoing battle with the media, saying it was biased against him."[131]

These complaints of media biases in favor or against political parties and politicians were mostly justified, according to a variety of studies conducted by Western institutions in the 1990–95 period, many of them used in this work. By 1996–97, the general news coverage of elections had improved slightly, particularly in the print media, testimony that some progress in eliminating the most egregious aspects of partisanship and politicization had occurred.[132] The news programs of the public television and radio stations across the region, although financed by the state and thus expected to be above partisan interests, nevertheless remain problematic. Even when they manage not to be partisan, they display the reporting characteristics of Czech Television news: "passive, unimaginative and without independent critical thought. In fact [Czech Television] prides itself on mechanically and passively conveying information without placing it in context, questioning it or analyzing it."[133] Thus, even in the Czech Republic, supposedly the most advanced democracy in the region, politicians "have grown accustomed to using the weak news and current affairs team . . . as a docile instrument for the dissemination of their views and pronouncements."[134]

Such observations must not blind us to a simple political reality, however. The varied views available in the diverse media outlets, the predominantly one-sided information offered, and the presentation of candidates and their positions on issues provide a real and symbolic service to audiences. Thus the Romanian media, for example, serve voters, on the one hand, and the parties and their candidates, on the other, even if the balance decidedly tips in favor of the latter two. More important, as the region's media learn to separate themselves from dependence on political agents both in and out of government, they will have better opportunities to play a significantly unfluential, direct role in the political evolution of their societies. Indeed, they may have already become a "third force," exerting "a significant influence," in Poland.[135]

Just how far that separation, which slowly began in the second half of the 1990s, will go is unclear. For the time being, the media's penchant for "reporting" through the political lenses of owners, subsidizers, editors, news directors, and journalists, not to mention their inclination for sensationalizing, often also for political reasons, is likely to create an antipolitical climate and spectators to gladiatorial partisan contests, instead of participants in the building of democracy.

The current political cultures of Eastern Europe are thus a far cry from the antipolitical politics Havel had in mind when he was standing up to the Czech Communist system.[136] In time, this situation will change across the region and there is every reason to expect the nature of politics to also change, bringing about influences that will further alter the news media's overall role in politics and in how they practice journalism. The search, by way of political combat, for a media role and journalistic professionalism, it can be argued, is part of the democratization process. Last and not least, the nature of citizen participation in a transition or transformation is at best ill defined; the idealistic and utopian visions of participation are of no help in providing a yardstick for its measurement. Although it can be argued that the media, in not providing the offensive and defensive weapons represented by accurate and full information and the knowledge of new rules and objectives of post-1989 politics, create spectators instead of participants in the contemporary political combat being waged in Eastern Europe, there are other reasons for this seemingly passive role. They include ignorance on the part of almost all citizens, including journalists, about how to participate, the lack of time, energy, and interest to do so on the part of many, the absence of any vision of the results of such participation, and the abiding distrust of government, as well as intolerance and suspicion toward differing views. How the media can realistically help to alleviate, much less correct, these conditions is not clear.[137]

A Place for the Media in the New Political World

During the first five years of the post-Communist era, the control and influence exercised by political parties, politicians, political systems, and politics on the news media, particularly television, were greater than on any other institution. A combination of reasons can be posited for this: ownership and other sources of control and influence, the nature of politics and the political systems, the nature and behavior of political parties and of politicians, the overall political culture, the economic situation the media found themselves in after 1989, as well as the legacy of Communism and the absence of professional standards and modern journalistic traditions supportive of open, democratic societies.

The beginning of the post-Communist media is best characterized by their atomization, two consequences of which were clearly discernible. First, it served to define functions for the media that differed little from those of the Communist media: dissemination of selected information, partisan political indoctrination, mobilization, and propagandizing. Second, it served to define a gatekeeping role for the media, which was to decide what news items would be selected and the biases from which the items would be reported and presented, a process tied to the relationship between the media and the political powers and interests behind them. Significantly, the news media's predominantly political gatekeeping role provided for a diverse and pluralist presentation of the panoply of political, socio-cultural, and other (biased) information.

After 1992–95, the control and even influence of political parties and politicians over the media waned.[138] Economic survival and profit gained ascendancy as a motive driving media outlets, and, concurrently, the media, their elites and rank and file, established a modicum of intrinsic legitimacy, real or perceived power, and at least a sense that some degree of independence and professionalization was needed. Three fundamental changes occurred: (1) the number of institutions with which the media were interacting grew significantly, diluting the power of any one of these institutions; (2) the mechanisms governing the relationship between the media and political institutions, including their elites, became more nebulous and unpredictable; and as a result, (3) the gatekeeping role became less political.

The drive of the region's media to increase their control over resources and to minimize their dependency on other institutions has increased their power, although their dependency on the market—their audiences and advertisers—is increasing and creating its own problems. More important, however, the media have become less dependent on political parties, politicians, and political systems for their finances, for their legitimacy, and for their primary and exclusive news sources (more on this issue in chapter 4).

The power of the media has come into a degree of balance with and now even outweighs that of the political parties and politicians in some respects. Which is to say, the power of parties and politicians was greater when partisanship was high, when citizens believed in participation, were less cynical, and parties and politicians could rely more on party organization and a network of party workers and voters responsive to them for the dissemination of electoral messages. Their power was also greater when, to one degree or another, parties and politicians were able to control how reality was defined through media outlets they owned or influenced and for the audiences those outlets reached. In the second half of the 1990s, however, the media gained greater control over the presentation of news; politicians and political parties could no longer predict which "reality" was going to be presented, and how it was to be presented or interpreted, a situation that led Romanian parliamentarians, no longer assured coverage by "their" media, to demand in 1998 that a C-Span-like coverage by Romanian Television be initiated.[139]

Even though the media's divorce from political parties has not itself measurably improved their journalism, two things should be kept in mind:

1. While the media's dependence on political parties and politicians for financial support has lessened, their dependency on the market for such support has increased. Furthermore, the profit-making incentive of some owners has simply been married to the political use of the media, which is to say, some media owners are also politicians, members of a political party, politically engaged out of personal convictions, or all three.[140] When it comes to public service media, they are still dependent on the state or on the political party or parties in power and their largesse with the taxpayers' money.
2. Media power is derived from the trust their audiences put in them, from their ability to reach their audiences, and from media independence and societal respect for freedom of speech.[141] All three of these elements of media power (as will be discussed in chapters 3, 4, and 5) are missing or only partly present in the societies of post-Communist Eastern Europe.

To date, the nature of the media and their journalism appears to be affected to a much greater degree by the political culture in each of the region's countries than vice versa. The heated political contests, the politicians' frenzied hunt for votes not only increased media coverage of politics but also expanded freedom of the press, as Barbara Geddes suggested was happening in Latin America, itself in transformation from the legacies of its dictatorships.[142]

Last but not least, the fluid economic, political, and cultural situation in the region makes it difficult to pinpoint the relationships between the media and other institutions, the media and power structures, and the media and sociocultural changes, beyond recognizing that these relationships exist and continue to be altered by events, circumstances, and people. In this respect, the Eastern European media are similar to their counterparts in other societies that have transformed themselves after years of dictatorship, such as the media in post-Franco Spain.[143] Until the Eastern European political systems achieve full political stability and come of age, the media's relationship to them will continue to be uncertain and changeable. However, their power and influence will grow only if developments within the profession give them credibility and thus make them valuable to their audiences, not just to politicians and political parties.

3

State, Government, Laws, and the Media

Hungary's "media wars" in the early 1990s epitomized the attempts by Eastern European states to continue their ownership and control of the broadcast media and, at the very least, to influence the print media.[1] The underlying mentality, one shared by many Albanian, Bulgarian, Czech, Polish, Romanian, and Slovak public officials was best expressed by Istvan Csurka, vice president of the Hungarian Democratic Forum (MDF) just before the 1990 Hungarian elections: "Today . . . only those who control television can really say they are in power."[2]

As Splichal explains, the post-1989 Eastern European media, particularly the broadcast media, have been "organized in accordance with the former collectivist ideology and the dominant role of the party-state because [they] are considered the most appropriate means of getting public support for new political leaders."[3] The "deep conviction" that the media exist to serve the government or state (or the party or parties and politicians who control the government or the state) is slow to change.[4] Jane Curry clearly describes a common post-Communist phenomenon:

> Virtually all of the new East European leaders have struggled against the press's freedom to attack them and their policies. Parties fight to own their own newspapers and to bar the broadcast media from covering them negatively. In doing this, they reflect the old traditions (both those of the Communist press and those of the underground press) to which they have grown accustomed. . . . The new leaders fear that any negative information in the press will reduce their already weak standing.[5]

In its legacy of state and government ties to the media, Eastern Europe is joined by Western Europe, where state command over the broadcast media persisted into the 1980s, when their commercialization was given a green light. Western Europe retained its "public service" broadcasting, but it now has to compete with the market media. Eastern Europe's new democratic elites have repeatedly voiced their support of a strong state role in the media, ostensibly to safeguard democracy from "inimical forces," but in reality to safeguard themselves and their parties from the political opposition. Thus, in what appears to be a natural outgrowth of the notion that "if the state is too weak, it cannot foster democratization of civil society. If it is too strong, it becomes too interventionist." The absence of a strong civil society has created a situation in which media autonomy seems limited by the state.[6]

The result is the perception that, despite privatization, commercialization, and denationalization, the Eastern European media generally and public broadcasting specifically remain, at least in part, under state and government control. Or, as Patrick O'Neil sees the situation: "Between market and state, the media continue to run the risk that the power over information will be reconsolidated into the hands of a few [falling again under state control], to the detriment of civil society."[7] The lack of appropriate finances for quick and effective privatization, so the argument goes, creates fertile ground for "a monopolistic coalition between the state and media professionals."[8] It engenders an imbalance of power, one disfavoring the audience and either benefiting a minority or a majority, setting the groundwork for an authoritarian or a paternalistic system, respectively. On the other hand, to ensure a pluralism or diversity of media outlets, to ensure that each and every group within a society has an outlet for its views and receives news coverage (more on this in chapter 5), the use of state-subsidized media on the British or the Scandinavian models, or even the use of state-controlled media, may be appropriate.[9]

It cannot be denied that Eastern European states and governments attempted to influence and control the media throughout the 1990s. These attempts have taken several avenues, some made possible by slow systemic changes on both sides of the media–government or state equation, others by the very absence of such changes, and still others by a lack of change in mentalities. Indirect attempts by the states and governments to influence and control the media through the political parties and politicians in power show no signs of letting up. They include subtle and not-so-subtle campaigns on the part of government, state, and ruling party officials to lessen the media's credibility and influence and to intimidate their journalists by

1. Consistently deriding, demeaning, and insulting them.
2. Steadfastly refusing to respond to media revelations of government or state corruption and malfeasance.[10] The clearly intended message to media audiences and journalists alike has been that the media have no power, that they do not matter. And so: "If you [expose] something, and nothing happens once, twice, or even three times, you wonder, 'Why should I risk my job or health for this?'"[11]
3. Engaging in overt acts of intimidation, to include beatings, arrests, bombings, and the ransacking of editorial offices, acts that have been recorded at one time or another since 1989 in Albania, Bulgaria, Romania, and the Slovak Republic.
4. Accusing the media of everything from irresponsibility (often a well-deserved charge) to being unpatriotic by not toeing the official line or by not being sufficiently nationalistic.

Direct (and often successful) attempts at state or government influence and control over the media in the 1990s include

1. dominating the print media distribution;
2. monopolizing newsprint production;
3. monopolizing the major printing facilities;
4. interfering with the privatization of the press;
5. appointing as heads of public radio and television and as members of the councils that oversee national public radio and television, award licenses, and make operational rules only persons favoring government or state control of the broadcast media;
6. impeding, if not actually blocking, media coverage of government, the presidency, parliament, and the state; and
7. supporting new laws and regulations that favor government or state control of the media, or seeing that only slightly altered old laws and regulations are interpreted by the state-controlled judiciary to the same effect.

The problem with most works on the Eastern European media from 1990 to 2000 is that they have either been highly idealistic in nature—that is, concerned about how perfection can be achieved—or they have attempted to describe and critique the evolution of the media and even to predict their final form after the media have taken only the first few steps toward developing a professional journalistic culture and understanding of the roles they are to play in a democracy. In reviewing the media's privatization, as well as the history of their distribution, printing facilities, newsprint production, laws, and governing councils, this chapter will show that, however successful the attempts by states and governments to influence and control the media, their success was only short-lived; that these attempts have become ever less successful in the last eleven years as institutions have been altered by changes in personnel, politics, policies, and, to some degree, mentalities—and by the relationships between institutions.

Progress at curbing state or government interference in the media or staving off the return to state control and paternalism should go some way to allay fears that direct state and government control of the media in the region is a defining characteristic of the new post-Communist media, one that endangers their potential contribution to civil society and democracy.[12]

Media Privatization

In post-1989 Eastern Europe, the print media were privatized far more quickly than the broadcast media. For instance, in the span of a few days in December 1989, the daily *Romania Libera* was taken over by a cadre of its editors and journalists who formed the R Company. They were awarded the first commercial license in post-Communist Romania in February 1990.[13] The Czechoslovak press, too, and particularly the national dailies "were the first to respond to the societal changes marked by the Velvet Revolution," most passing into private hands, whether those of a political party, a commercial company, an association, or a group of individuals.[14] It was a pattern repeated in Albania, in Hungary, and in Poland, where the 1990 Law on the Liquidation of the Worker's Publishing Cooperative Press-Book Movement (RSW) established a liquidation committee to oversee the death of the Communist regime's print media monopoly.[15] In each country of the region, as I will show, privatization was spurred as much by political as by commercial motives.

This more rapid privatization of the print media came about for a number of reasons: (1) in some of the region's countries an underground press provided the initial and natural source of the new private press; (2) the collapse of any state and government control gave rise to quasi-libertarian conditions for the print media, in contrast to broadcasting, where frequencies if not licenses and the technical infrastructure remained under state or government control; (3) private print media outlets were far cheaper and easier to quickly establish than private broadcast media outlets; and (4) the multitude of former Communist newspapers afforded a system ready-made to be privatized, compared with the extremely limited number of television outlets available in 1989 in each Eastern European country. Moreover, especially in countries whose Communist regimes had been the most totalitarian (Albania, Bulgaria, and Romania): "The rapid privatization of the print media could be seen as a preemptive defense against expected retributive legislation punishing old-regime organizations."[16]

Regardless of the speed of demonopolization, the print media encountered obstacles to their development, as did virtually all private institutions throughout Eastern Europe. These obstacles ran the gamut from political manipulation and the absence of professional cadres, regulatory agencies, and laws, to the lack of investment capital and inadequate communications infrastructures; they were chiefly generated by government attempts to control the press through "financial pressures [such as] new taxes, the withholding of advertising and the impounding of delivery trucks," as well as "dangerously broad defamation laws."[17] Of the 106 Polish state dailies and weeklies that were approved for sale, only 69 were sold by mid-1995: there were simply no investors bidding for them.[18]

The obstacles thrown in the path of the newly privatized publications included but were not limited to high license fees, real and artificial newsprint shortages, and printing and distribution problems created by the state-controlled paper manufacturing, printing, and distribution enterprises. In some countries, Hungary, for example, state or government ownership of the media, far from disappearing, reasserted itself to some degree. Thus by 1994, the government established or controlled a number of important daily and weekly publications, and "assisted in the development of a conservative press whose ownership links to the state were more attenuated."[19] Apart from newspapers clearly owned by political parties, by the state or government, or by foreign companies, ownership of newspapers across Eastern Europe is more often than not difficult to pinpoint. Indeed, the Hungarian case, "where a web of immensely complicated corporate cross-holdings makes the very concept of ownership problematic and leaves managerial control mostly unchecked," is typical for the rest of the region.[20]

Broadcasting was slower to privatize for the reasons cited above, and because broadcast laws were slow to be rewritten. Specifically, private television stations with a national reach were the slowest to appear, not only because of relatively slow changes in the broadcast laws, but also because of the machinations of the new regulatory institutions set up by these laws.

In Czechoslovakia, despite a 1990 law on radio and television permitting the privatization of radio and television, private, commercial national television did not make its appearance until 1994 in the Czech Republic (e.g., Nova TV) and not until 1996 in the Slovak Republic (e.g., Marzika TV), although the first private radio station began operations in 1990 in Slovakia and the first private television station was established there just after the breakup of Czechoslovakia in 1993. In Hungary, private, commercial broadcasting also had to await the passage of a media law on radio and television.[21] Private, commercial television channels (e.g., MTM/SBS, Magyar Televiso, and Magyar RTL) were not launched until 1997. And not until 1998 was Hungary's National Radio and Television Board (NRTB) able to report that "the hegemony of the public service media [has come] to an end," with the success of those commercial television stations.[22] In Poland, although commercial radio licenses had been granted already in 1991–92, even before the enactment of the new radio and television law in 1993, a private national television channel, Polsat, did not make its debut until 1995, when several new cable and satellite channels were also introduced. In Albania, the country in the region slowest to officially privatize its broadcast media, twelve private local television stations and ten private local radio stations were already operating without licenses even before its new law authorizing private commercial broadcasting went into effect in 1998.[23] Yet, by then, it was claimed the Albanian state was "winning the battle for a monopoly over . . . radio and television."[24] In Bulgaria, private, commercial radio received temporary licenses in 1992, but demonopolization in television did not begin until 1994, with the launching of Nova Televiza in that year and of 7 DNI in 1995.[25] In Romania, the country fastest to privatize its broadcast media, private radio and television stations were introduced almost immediately after the December 1989 demise of Communism, even before the new radio and television law was enacted in 1992, although private, national television was not officially approved until 1995. Since then, a plethora of national, regional, and local television stations have sprung up (e.g., Pro-TV, Antena 1, Prima-TV, and others).

Cable television, a significant area of broadcast development in Eastern Europe, is almost exclusively in private hands. Between 1990 and 1994 alone, cable networks reached from 18 to 35 percent of Eastern European homes, and have grown by leaps and bounds since then.[26] Along with the print media, cable television was one of the initial targets of foreign investments, partly because it was poorly regulated, if at all. Consequently, American, Dutch, Australian, Danish, Sudanese, and German investors, among others, have invested in Czech, Hungarian, Polish, and Romanian cable broadcasting.[27]

Foreign investment in ownership and co-ownership of the media was extensive and rapidly undertaken in the Czech Republic, Hungary, and Poland in the first five post-Communist years, whereas it was nonexistent or very limited in Albania, Bulgaria, Romania, and the Slovak Republic until the second half of the first post-Communist decade. It remains a major aspect of media privatization in Eastern Europe. Print media outlets were the overwhelming initial target of multimedia corporations and private companies attempting to gain a market share. Newspapers were offered capital, technology, and know-how, all badly needed in the post-Communist era.[28] Foreign ownership or partnership was welcomed by media outlets throughout the region precisely because it offered the kind of financial support not available domestically and because it served to make the outlets' divorce from government control official.[29]

Gauging the level and promise of the market economy's development and taking advantage of the vacuum of media legislation in the initial transition from Communism, the Swiss Ringier AG Group and the German Passau Neue Presse invested heavily in the Czech media market, where they "met little political and/or popular protest."[30] By the end of this 1994 "invasion," few of the country's dailies remained in Czech hands.[31] Such foreign inroads into media ownership and investment were repeated in Hungary, where media giants such as Australian Rupert Murdoch's media conglomerate, British media magnate Robert Maxwell's media company, the German Bertelsmann media group, the Italian Carlo de Benedetti's media company, the Swedish Bonnier-Group, and the German Axel-Springer Verlag, among others, gobbled up substantial portions of the national press. They also invested in both the regional and the local press, with the result that, by 1994, an estimated 80 percent of overall capital investment in the Hungarian media came from the West.[32]

In Poland, the potential for foreign investments was at first severely restricted by the Liquidation Committee: only the French Hersant media group had any significant success in entering the Polish print media market. After the committee officially finished its work in 1993, the situation changed: the Passau Neue Presse media company along with the German Bertelsmann, the Swiss JMG Ost Press, the French Hersant, the Italian Finivest, the Norwegian ORKLA, and a number of U.S. media companies made important investments in the Polish press. In Albania, foreign investment was slight; the joint Italian-Albanian venture *Gazeta Shqiptar* is one of only two newspapers with a foreign partner. In Romania, significant foreign investment in the print media was slow to arrive, although newspapers such as *Romania Libera* greatly benefited from investment in their infrastructure by the now-defunct U.S.-based International Media Fund.[33] After 1996, the Swiss Ringier group acquired a number of newspapers (e.g., *Capital, TV-Mania, Libertatea, Gazeta Sporturilor, Unica,* and *Lumea Femeilor*).

Foreign investments in the broadcast media were made both before new broadcast laws were enacted (e.g., in the Czech Republic) and after (e.g., in Poland). By 1998 (see "Access to Government, State, and Parliamentary Information and Sources, Protection of Journalists' Sources" below), four of the countries examined here had enacted new broadcasting laws, legally limiting foreign capital interests in the broadcast outlets of Poland (33 percent) and of Hungary and Bulgaria (49 percent); Romania, the Czech and Slovak Republics have no limits on foreign investments.[34]

Whereas Western European companies dominate foreign investment in the Eastern European press, U.S. companies lead the parade of investors in the region's broadcast media.[35] At the head of the line is Central European Media Enterprises (CME), a Bahama-based U.S company with investments in Hungary, Poland, Romania, the Slovak Republic, and Slovenia, as well as in the Czech Republic, where "the majority of radio stations represent joint ventures with significant, albeit small, foreign participation," the most successful private national television station being the CME-backed Nova TV.[36] Italy's Berlusconi, America's Time-Warner Enterprises, Murdoch, Proctor and Gamble, Sardinia's Nicolas Grauso, France's Hersant, and Britain's New European Investment Fund, to name but a few, have also entered the Eastern European broadcast field. Foreign investments in cable television have been significant as well.[37]

Media privatization has been stymied by the failure of market economies to fully establish themselves anywhere in the region by the end of the 1990s.[38] With often substantial variations from one country to another, fundamental economic problems prevent them all from sustaining an economically viable media system; they can instead support only a limited number of individual media outlets. The unequal viability of even these few outlets across countries is reflected in average advertising expenditures per household for television time in 1996, an inequality that has changed little since then: $113 in Hungary, $47 in Poland, $30 in the Czech Republic, $24 in the Slovak Republic, $8 in Bulgaria, and $7 in Romania.[39]

Privatization has also been economically encumbered by government actions, principally through high taxes. The Albanian case is mirrored to one degree or another elsewhere in the region. The former Berisha government (1992–98) was accused of using taxation to deliberately "cripple the independent and opposition press," and the new Nano government that took power in 1998 showed no predilection for reducing these taxes.[40] Moreover, the deleterious effects of taxation have been exacerbated by the unevenness with which taxes are levied. In Bulgaria, the (privately owned) top four dailies "are taxed more heavily than publications owned by political parties."[41] In 1994, a value-added "killer" tax of 18 percent was assessed against all Bulgarian print media outlets.[42] High taxes also contribute to the shaky economic situation of the Slovak independent press.[43]

Privatization of the media has resulted in serious competition for state- or government-controlled "public service" broadcasting and an increasingly heated debate over what constitutes "public service," in a rush on the part of governments and political parties to influence and manipulate, if not control, private commercial broadcasting and print media content, and in banks entering the media business.[44] As one of its clearest benefits, privatization, insofar as it involves foreign investments, ownership, and partnerships, has effectively checked a return to state control through ownership of the media, short of a return to totalitarianism.[45] Indeed, where it exists, this foreign economic presence makes state control of the media virtually impossible in nations attempting to shape a democratic future, although, as circulation and competition grow and returns diminish, it remains to be seen how much longer it will continue to be a significant factor.[46]

Overall, monopolization of the media and globalization of media systems have not been significant factors in the first post-Communist decade. Whether their predicted benefits and drawbacks will manifest themselves in years to come depends on a host of social, cultural, and political factors.[47]

Print Media Distribution, Newsprint Production, Printing Facilities

The systems for distributing newspapers in Eastern Europe, all still state owned in the immediate aftermath of the collapse of Communism, posed a severe problem for the mushrooming print media. For one thing, the existing systems were inefficient and could not handle the rapidly growing number of titles. For another, some of the new post-1989 governments moved to impede the distribution of newspapers belonging to opposition parties, particularly during election campaigns.[48] By the end of the first post-Communist decade, however, most distribution systems across the region were either divorced from state control or augmented by private distribution systems; state-controlled systems still holding a monopoly on distribution no longer overtly interfered with the distribution of newspapers, whatever their political shade.

For instance, by January 1989 publishing in Hungary was declared a business activity and, therefore, divorced from state control. Initially, this state demonopolization did not have a salutary effect. The Hungarian Post charged newspaper publishers a high fee for its distribution service (38 percent of newsstand prices) and retained control over both the delivery and reader demographic information, for which it also charged a high fee.[49] As a result, newspapers were hard pressed to expand and maximize their potential income. On the positive side, it also spurred some publishers to set up their own distribution systems beginning in 1995.[50]

In Poland, the distribution system remains state-controlled, despite the liquidation of the RSW, with almost 100 percent of newspaper distribution being managed by RUCH (the national distribution network), whose inefficiency makes national distribution "particularly difficult."[51] Nevertheless, "there is no evidence that the government has used its control over distribution to suppress any publications."[52]

The move to establish private distribution systems picked up speed throughout Eastern Europe by the mid-1990s. In Bulgaria, a private distributors' union organized in 1995 attempted to negotiate the takeover of press distribution from the state.[53] By 1995, "the largest national and regional newspapers owned kiosks and trucks across the country. . . . Several newspaper companies even signed agreements to handle each other's distribution and subscriptions in order to save on commissions to other distributors."[54] Private distribution companies now also augment the state-owned distribution system in the Slovak Republic.[55] In Romania, the state-owned Rodiped remains the country's major distribution network, although many of the larger private publications have endeavored to build their own distribution system. In sharp contrast to the first six to seven post-Communist years, the Romanian press no longer grumbles much about the distribution system.[56]

In Albania, the region's unmistakable laggard in all areas of transition, the largely state-controlled distribution system does not reach all areas of the country, particularly not all mountain villages and towns.[57] Moreover, private distribution is subject to direct governmental interference. For instance, the daily *Koha Jone*'s delivery trucks were seized by police in January 1996, "preventing the distribution of the paper, as well as that of 11 other independent opposition titles."[58] This was followed in 1997, during the state of emergency declared by the government, with government-imposed censorship.[59]

Nevertheless, overall, there has been clear progress in extending the number of private distribution systems and limiting state control over distribution in the region. A far greater unresolved problem is the availability of newsprint, its costs, and its quality.

A lack of newsprint is endemic in the Slovak Republic, where costs are rising precipitously, endangering the independent press.[60] The Bulgarian and Romanian states still monopolize newsprint production and supply, with perhaps the most extreme manifestation of state control over newsprint distribution to be found in Bulgaria. So complete was this control that in 1990 the government allocated paper "to its preferred publications," agreed "that political party newspapers would be preferentially supplied with newsprint," and "reduced the quantity of paper for some of the most popular special interest titles by 22 per cent."[61] It was not until the mid-1990s that such policies were discontinued. Similarly, the Romanian press has been battling shortages of newsprint, deliberately engineered, or so some say, by President Ion Iliescu's government from 1990 to 1996, as well as steadily increasing prices.[62] From 1990 to 1996, a 15 percent tax on newsprint and a quota system for newspapers put extreme pressures on the publications that opposed President Iliescu, his government, and the Romanian Democratic Socialist Party (PDSR) majority in parliament.[63] In Poland, too, newsprint is expensive, as it is in Albania, where it is not only difficult to obtain but is characterized as resembling "Swiss cheese."[64] The importation of newsprint from Western sources is an expensive proposition that few print media outlets in Eastern Europe can afford, particularly when also faced with typically high import taxes.

As if high taxes, high prices, and short supplies were not enough of a burden, Eastern Europe's rapidly expanding print media outlets continue to be hampered by a shortage of printing facilities, the existing ones often being antiquated. This situation also contributes to inflationary trends in the publishing business. Not surprisingly, then, along with the quick privatization of newspapers came a concerted and expensive effort to build private production facilities. While the state-owned printing facilities continue to function in almost all Eastern European nations, by 1998 they were competing with a number of more technically advanced private facilities, particularly in Hungary, Poland, and Romania. The pace, extent, and success of efforts to establish private production varied significantly from country to country, however. Some examples:

In Poland, printing houses not handed over to the state treasury were sold into private hands.[65] "Printing is extremely expensive in Poland, and . . . prices skyrocketed after the economic reform program of 1990."[66] In the Slovak Republic, printing facilities are still deemed "inadequate."[67] In 1992, Prime Minister Vladimír Mečiar stopped the privatization of Danubiaprint, the plant that printed the nation's newspapers. "Control of the printing press [has] allowed government the ability to pressure journalists at will."[68]

In Albania, most newspapers are still printed by state-owned printing facilities operating with antiquated presses that date back to the 1930s.[69] In Bulgaria, the state-owned Rodina printing complex retained its monopoly, and set printing schedules and even the circulation of its client publications, as well as prices, until private printing facilities were established.[70]

Though uneven, progress was clearly made in 1990–2000 in demonopolizing the media's supporting institutions: distribution, newsprint production, and printing. Although this progress has only lessened the power of the state or the government over the media, it has all but eliminated the prospect of a return to full state control, short of renationalizing the now relatively numerous private facilities. Such a move remains highly unlikely despite the persistent belief among some politicians and state bureaucracies that state control of the media is desirable. The increasing emphasis of the media on entertainment may make that prospect unlikelier still. After all, if the media offer audiences "bread and circuses," they are less apt to pose a serious threat to politicians, the state, and government.

Access to Government, State, and Parliamentary Information, Protection of Journalists' Sources

It is a truism that journalists are only as good as their sources. And although detective work is at the core of good reporting, the expectation in a democracy is that journalists will have ready access to the workings of all institutions, whether government or state, that represent the people. Eastern

European journalists, however, have few if any legal tools either to gain access to government and state institutions or to protect their sources.

In Albania, the press law outlined after 1993 "ushered in an even more restrictive era for Albanian journalism," leading to "access to information being restricted."[71] In other nations in the region, neither new nor amended old media laws require that government officials give out information. Even in the Czech Republic, the regional front-runner in the democratization process, after the Czech senate rejected a freedom of information bill, approved by the Chamber of Deputies, which would have secured constitutional rights to information, the national Helsinki Committee felt compelled in 1998 to call for a reform of the still-operative 1966 press law to ensure "unhindered access to information."[72] Although a freedom of information act went into effect on January 1, 2000, providing for access to information controlled by local and national authorities, as well as other institutions affecting the rights of citizens, how rigorously it will be enforced remains to be seen.

Given the short post-Communist history of the region, one that includes the deliberate, politically motivated denial of access to a variety of events, from deliberations of certain bodies to press conferences, laws guaranteeing access to information and to the workings of government and state bodies are particularly important. For instance, piqued in December 1997 by what he considered low journalistic standards, Slovak Prime Minister Vladimír Mečiar sent a letter to his cabinet and other public officials prohibiting them from giving information to certain media outlets. Subsequently, "the cabinet press office announced that it would provide information only to the government media, not the independent media."[73] Mečiar also abolished the government's weekly press conferences.

A series of incidents in Romania also reflects the general mentality and actions of governmental and state bodies in the whole region.[74] Since December 1989, each chamber of Romania's bicameral parliament has taken turns attempting to restrict journalists' access to its public deliberations, this despite Article 65 of Romania's 1991 constitution, which explicitly states that "the meetings of both chambers are public." The election to power of the "democratic" opposition in November 1996 was supposed to have stopped such actions. It did not. In March 1997, the Romanian senate obliged journalists to be accompanied by "persons from the [Senate's] administration" and to "reflect the activities of the permanent commissions" only on the basis of information offered by the commissions' spokespersons. In other words, journalists were "under guard" and were essentially to function as disseminators of public relations releases.

One year later, on March 10, 1998, the Romanian senate finally reconsidered and modified the rules referring to press access to the working of this legislative body. The modifications specified that the "meetings of the [Senate's] commissions are public"—unless the individual commissions decide otherwise. On March 11, the education commission of the Chamber of Deputies, claiming national security, barred journalists from covering its debate on an emergency ordinance (no. 36) regarding the completion and modification of the education law. On April 22, 1998, the Ministry of Agriculture and Food Supplies demanded from journalists wishing to cover the ministry not only their general accreditation to cover the government, but a special accreditation, a curriculum vita, and a list of the journalists' articles dealing with the ministry. Nor is this ministry alone in its approach to the question of providing access for journalists.

When a new government headed by Prime Minister Vasile Radu came to power in 1998, all ministries and their organs demanded increasingly greater proof of press accreditation; various press offices disregarded the press credentials of journalists. Pending action by the Romanian parliament on a bill regarding public access to information, "transparency has become steam, doors are slamming shut one by one, and attempts to shut the journalists' mouths and to snatch the pen from their hands have increased."[75]

Hungary's Data Protection and Freedom of Information Law, passed in 1992 and strengthened "dramatically by the 1995 election of a parliamentary commissioner to oversee its implementation," forces government agencies to respond to requests for information within eight days.[76] Directly offsetting this, however, the Secrecy Law of 1995 grants the commissioner wide discretion in classifying information as state or official secrets. In Bulgaria, after recording more than 200 cases in which officials denied access to information, the Access to Information Program launched a "right to know" campaign, "complete with a how-to brochure on pursuing access claims."[77]

Despite these often well-intentioned efforts at reform, nothing resembling U.S. shield and sunshine laws exists in Eastern Europe. Significantly, even the current freedom of information laws are far from being as potent a weapon for journalists as the Freedom of Information Act is in the United States. "Where freedom-of-information legislation exists, it lacks implementing legislation or is contradictory and confusing. Understandably, then, it is neither understood nor enforced."[78] The fight to guarantee journalists access to information and to the workings of governmental agencies, and to provide them legal protection when they abide by any confidentiality agreements made with their sources, continues. Laws are only as effective as the mechanisms to enforce them; Eastern European judiciary systems are as yet neither independent nor fully competent to deal with the demands made on them by democratizing societies. Indeed, enforcement is an area where paternalism is a justifiably worrisome prospect.

The crucial issue of legal protections for journalists who refuse to reveal their sources has been left unresolved (e.g., in the Czech Republic)—or has been resolved by new laws denying such protection and requiring journalists to divulge their sources (e.g., in Albania and the Slovak Republic). In the Czech Republic, the 1995 media bill skirted the issue altogether, prompting journalists to label the bill "a bastard" that served "no one's interests and [that demonstrated] the inability of politicians to understand the concept of freedom of the press."[79]

When, in January 1995, an editor at *Gazeta Wyborcza* was fined and sentenced to a two-week prison sentence for refusing to name a source, the Polish Supreme Court ruled that the penal code took precedence over the press law that supposedly protected journalists' right to shield their sources.[80] The journalists' plight was finally alleviated in 1998, when a newly enacted criminal code granted absolute protection to journalists for keeping their sources confidential in all cases except those involving national security, terrorist acts, and murder. Moreover, under the new code "journalists who refused to divulge sources prior to the new code's enactment [could] avoid sanctions by invoking 'journalistic privilege.'"[81]

Media Law

The new or revised constitutions of all Eastern European nations except Albania provide for freedom of speech and of the press.[82] How well the constitutional principles of freedom of speech and of the press are respected and applied depends in large measure on how the laws relating to them are interpreted and enforced.

Media law in Eastern Europe can be broken down into press laws (principally directed at the print media), broadcast laws (regulating the new broadcasting industry and public broadcasting), and penal codes (defining offenses such as "defamation" and "insults" by media outlets and their journalists). As it stands now, media law in Eastern Europe almost exclusively addresses the sociopolitical and cultural concerns of lawmakers; there is a decided dearth of laws addressing the market side of media operations.

Press Laws

Attempts at establishing new press laws have almost uniformly failed, and the reformulation of old press laws has neither improved press freedom nor contributed to greater professionalism among journalists. In the first few post-Communist years, press laws were drafted by governments, parliaments, and even journalistic organizations, only to be rejected by most press outlets and their journalists. By the mid-1990s, there was no doubt that journalists in the region viewed press laws as unacceptably restrictive to their freedoms. The initial push to enact press laws was in line with a general European tradition, and reflected continuity in Eastern European mentalities from the pre-Communist to the Communist era.[83]

Before the Communist takeover in 1948, Czechoslovakia had no comprehensive press laws. Some laws addressing the press were incrementally introduced by the Habsburg Empire, with the Czech lands following Austrian law after 1918 and Slovakia operating under a system inherited from Hungarian law. Under the Communists, a comprehensive press law was enacted, whose latest version, the Press Law of 1966, was simply amended in March 1990 to eliminate any form of censorship. Ownership of and foreign participation in the Czech press are dealt with in the commercial code, which was revised in 1990. In similar developments, Hungary's Press Law of 1986 was modified in 1990 to deal mainly with privatization of the press, an issue addressed in Poland by enactment of the special Law of the Liquidation of the RSW, also in 1990.[84] Despite formal preparations dating back to 1992, however, Poland still did not have a press law as 2000 came to an end.

Denounced "as being too imprecise and too harsh for a country with poorly developed legal institutions," Albania's Press Law of 1993 calls for fines and confiscation of printed matter for those publications that, among other "crimes," publish materials the government considers secret or "sensitive."[85] A new law providing for broad press freedom, enacted by the Albanian parliament in September 1997, has been characterized as "extremely vague."[86] In light of the absence of a free press tradition in Albania, Skender Gjnushi, speaker of the Albanian parliament, declared in 1998 that a "complete legal framework of European standards" had to be established.[87] In February 1999, the Albanian parliament took a step in the right direction, scrapping Article 30 of the State Secrets Law, which subjected media institutions and journalists to punishments for publishing classified information.[88]

Not entirely without reason, governments and parliaments in the region viewed the so-called independent press in the early post-Communist years as dangerously out of control: politicized, partisan, sensationalistic, defamatory, pornographic, distorted, and generally lacking any "journalistic responsibility."[89] Press freedom as part and parcel of the process of democratization was viewed as at once necessary and dangerous. It is therefore not surprising that, for instance, Hungary's constitution and amendments to the 1986 press laws made in 1990 take "irreconcilable positions."[90] The perceived and actual lack of any journalistic ethics, as reflected in the "wild" use of press freedom, gave impetus to most attempts at regulating the press and its journalism.

In the initial post-1989 period, even some journalists had similar views. For instance, Bulgarian journalists in the early 1990s held freedom of speech and of the press to be "too fragile unless backed up by legal guarantees," only to reverse that position a few years later when they understood that guarantees could be secured through means other than press laws, as in the United States.[91] Sharing with their Bulgarian and regional colleagues a concern that the press considered freedom carte blanche to do as it pleased, Romanian journalists at first felt that only a press law could provide much-needed parameters for their profession.[92] Although several versions of a new press law were discussed over the first nine post-1989 years, all of them were ultimately rejected by the press and an overwhelming number of its journalists.

Breaking away from the general European trend, the majority of Eastern European journalists have adopted the view expressed by Count Michael Karolyi, first president of the Hungarian Republic, in 1918—the best possible press law is one that contains only two articles: one proclaiming that no one should control freedom of the press, and the other specifying the date on which the law becomes effective.[93] Karolyi's prescription for a press law makes eminent sense in view of the fact that all of the newly liberated Eastern European nations have constitutions guaranteeing freedom of the press and of expression. That press laws are not necessary, given the existence of other legislation addressing freedom of the press, is a view also shared by some politicians. "There is no need and [it is not] timely for a press law that will regulate the activities of the press and the profession of journalist," declared the Romanian prime minister in April 1997. "The legal rules already in existence in the Civil Code and the Penal Code are sufficient."[94]

The historical grounding for arguments that the press's conduct be subject to specific legal limits is embedded in the 1789 Declaration of the Rights of Man and of the Citizen: "Free communication of thoughts and opinion is among the most precious rights of man. Thus, all men may speak freely, write and publish, *provided they be responsible for any abuse of this freedom in cases determined by law"* (emphasis added).[95] The penalties for the abuses of freedom and the legal determination of their nature can be and indeed are outlined in defamation (libel or slander) articles in the existing penal codes in the region.

Penal Codes

Amended to reflect the non-Communist status of the societies they are to regulate, the penal codes of all seven states under examination are essentially versions of the old Communist codes. Depending on the extent of change in these societies, their media, and their journalism, and on the need to make the codes more effective in protecting individuals from media excesses and the media from the excesses of powerful individuals, governments, and states, these codes are revised and refined from time to time. Thus far, however, progress in improving the penal codes of Eastern Europe by eliminating articles that curtail freedom of the press and might have a "chilling effect" on wide-ranging journalism has been modest, from slight (e.g., in Hungary) to moderate (e.g., in Bulgaria).

Although the statute on "defamation" of the president of the republic was revoked in the Czech Republic in September 1997, the statute addressing defamation of the republic remains in effect.[96] Poland's penal code also includes punishment for those who "publicly insult, ridicule and deride the Polish nation, the Polish Republic, its political system, or its principal organs."[97] Similar if not identical provisions remain part of the penal codes of Romania, Bulgaria, and the Czech and Slovak Republics, meaning, in effect, that any criticism of persons governing or representing any of these five nations may constitute defamation of the country or nation and, as such, be punishable by fine, imprisonment, or both. Romania's penal code, giving "insults" and "defamation" equal legal weight, forbids "insults, libel or threats" against public officials while they are carrying out a function that involves the exercise of state authority, but, notably, does not spell out what constitutes an "insult." Albania's criminal code, enacted in 1995, presents similar impediments to free media and unfettered journalism.

The imprecise, ambiguous wording of most penal or criminal code articles dealing with "defamation," "libel," "ridicule," "derision," "threats," and "insults" allows authorities the widest latitude in interpreting and applying them. The dubious definitions of "defamation," and particularly of "insults" to individuals, have the potential "chilling effect" of curbing any criticism or bona fide reporting of wrongdoing on the part of elected or appointed public officials and civil servants. In Poland, to "advocate discord" on national, ethnic, racial, or religious grounds or to offend religious sentiment is punishable by fine or imprisonment. Thus in 1990–2000 those committing any of the various media offenses listed in the penal codes were punished with prison sentences, severe fines, or both, in Albania, Bulgaria, the Czech Republic, Poland, Romania, and the Slovak Republic.[98]

This intimidation of the press did not pass unnoticed, however, either in the region or abroad. When, for example, Bulgaria's defamation law, part of its criminal code, was used by prosecutors "to intimidate free expression in the press, particularly . . . expression . . . critical of the Prosecutor's Office," it came to the attention of international human rights groups and Western press freedom oversight organizations.[99] More than anything, the prison sentences prescribed by the codes as punishment for media offenses have brought angry responses from organizations such as the Helsinki Watch and Reporters Sans Frontières. In 1999, the Bulgarian Media Coalition, an association of journalists' unions and free expression groups, called for a review of the defamation laws and outlined recommendations for a draft Freedom of Information Act. Bowing to internal and external pressures, the Bulgarian parliament in July 1999 amended the criminal code to eliminate prison sentences for insult and defamation. Six months later, the Parliament's attempt to replace prison sentences with fines ranging from $2,500 to $15,000 was vetoed by Bulgaria's president, Petar Stoyanov.[100]

The defamation provisions of the present penal codes have the potential to "chill" reporting about controversial issues and on elected and appointed public officials. They can be and are used in the region to intimidate the news media and to punish enterprising reporters. It should be emphasized, however, that the cases being brought against the media and their journalists under these provisions are far from legion. As the short post-1989 history of media legislation shows, pressures both from the West and from within are forcing legislators, courts, public opinion, and the media alike to reassess the new laws, their interpretation, and their application.

Broadcast Laws

There are essentially two sets of broadcast laws in force in Eastern Europe: those regulating the broadcast industry in general and those regulating the so-called public service broadcast media. Each set has proved problematic for the evolution of broadcast media systems with maximum autonomy from states and governments. Both sets have been formulated by lawmakers "burdened by the old way of thinking," which former Polish President Lech Walesa has called "our greatest weakness and our biggest obstacle in this task."[101] Yet all countries in the region have seen both sets of laws changed, refined, or reinterpreted, once or several times since their initial post-1989 enactment, to permit increased freedoms, to open broadcast systems to greater pluralities of outlets, and (for public broadcasting) to effect greater separation from governments and states.

Broadcast laws in Eastern Europe continue to evolve, moving closer to compliance with European Union (EU) law. In the Czech Republic, the Broadcasting Law was amended seventeen times since its enactment in 1991–92. In January 1999, the Czech government approved changes to the broadcasting laws to bring them in line with EU standards. In Hungary, the 1995 Act on Radio and Television Services brought about a liberalization of Hungary's broadcasting system. Separate public trusts were established to own Duna Television, Hungarian Television, and Hungarian Radio. The latter two were also allowed by the new law to convert into limited companies, and new national commercial television and radio channels were given the green light to broadcast starting in 1997. In Poland, the Broadcast Law of 1992 was amended in 1995 and the regulatory framework continues to be reshaped.[102] In March 1999, President Aleksander Kwasniewski vetoed the amended 1995 law on radio and television, saying the law is "incompatible with the European Union Law."[103] In the Slovak Republic, the 1993 Act on Radio and Television Broadcasting was revised more than once to meet some EU requirements, starting in 1996.

In Albania, a partial broadcasting law was enacted in 1997, followed by a comprehensive law regulating both private and public broadcasting in 1998. The 1998 law was "prepared with great care and with substantial outside advice from the Council of Europe and others. On paper, it stands up well in comparison to many media laws in the region."[104] In Bulgaria, the Parliament adopted the Radio and Television Act in 1996, which it then revised in 1998. In March 1999, it ratified the European Convention on Transfrontier Television, joining Hungary, Poland, and the Slovak Republic (Romania, which has signed the convention, is also expected to ratify it). In Romania, many changes have been made over the years to achieve EU compliance. Starting in 1995, licenses were at last awarded to establish private, commercial television with a national reach, a development strenuously resisted under the Iliescu regime. In January 1999, President Emil Constantinescu signed into law a provision ensuring that Romanian television will broadcast European-produced television programs at the levels mandated by the European Union.

In the second half of the 1990s, the various councils and boards with responsibilities over sundry aspects of television and radio broadcasting have reinterpreted decisions made on the basis of post-1989 laws or have had their decisions overturned by courts of law. For instance, Hungary's Supreme Court ruled that the Hungarian National Radio and Television Board deviated from rules of evaluation and proceeded illegally when it accepted an invalid bid submitted by Magyar RTL and, therefore, had to rescind its contract with the television station. The Romanian National Audiovisual Council (RNAVC) amended an earlier decision to force all foreign-language broadcasts to provide Romanian captions or simultaneous translations, even for live broadcasts. Political pressures forced the RNAVC to "refine" its original rule to apply only to recorded television programs.[105]

In 1993, after surveying initial developments in Eastern European public broadcast laws, Owen Johnson concluded that

> all of the post-communist rulers of Eastern Europe have tried fervently to hold on to state control of radio and television broadcasting. Just like their communist predecessors, they have argued that as the people's elected representatives they must be able to deliver their message directly to the people, and not have to compete in the marketplace.[106]

The original and amended versions of these post-1989 laws either provide outright for links between the state or government and public broadcasting or are so vaguely worded as to allow such links to be readily developed. Thus the Polish broadcasting law clearly states in Article 22 that public radio and television "shall in a direct manner enable the state organs to present and explain the policy of the state"; the Romanian broadcasting law specifies in Article 9 that "national public companies . . . are obliged to broadcast, on a priority basis and free of charge, communiqués or messages of public interest coming from the Parliament, the Presidency or Government."[107]

Making full use of their powers under these broadcasting laws, the region's rulers maintained considerable state or government control, largely through political appointments to the various councils and boards responsible for public radio and television. Their efforts have met with some resistance, however. Indeed, from 1990 to 1999 the decisions of political appointees regarding personnel, programming, fees and finances, and even divestitures of public radio and television outlets have aroused continual controversy.

In response to this controversy, the pressure to change public broadcasting laws, to eliminate government interference in public radio and television, and to alter the makeup of the various councils and boards responsible for public radio and television has increased. Hungary's media watchdog, the National Radio and Television Board (NRTB), has repeatedly called on the Parliament to restructure the boards responsible for public radio and television, asking, in 1998, that "the political independence of public service programme providers, who ensure the authentic information of the citizens and mediate cultural values . . . be strengthened."[108] In Bulgaria, while reserving the right of the president, prime minister, and the National Assembly chairman to address the nation via public broadcasting, the government promised not to interfere in the operation of public radio and television.[109] In Albania, the opposition parties grouped together in the Union for Democracy and Albanian United Right demanded in January 1999 that

> pluralism in the public media outlets be guaranteed by law [and] that the Albanian Radio-Television guarantee equal conditions for the ruling parties and the opposition to express their opinions, respect the proportional allocation of air time on the basis of the percentage of votes won in the last parliamentary elections, and also provides the minimum necessary airtime for the small parliamentary and nonparliamentary parties.[110]

The politicization of Eastern European societies remains a clear and present impediment to substantial and expeditious changes in broadcast laws and the absence of independent judiciaries allows for continued manipulation of the broadcast laws by political interests. There is no denying that the initial versions of these laws and the work of the various broadcast councils and boards have allowed state and government paternalism to be reestablished to some degree. It is also true that increasing pressures from internal and external forces to bring laws and their interpretations, as well as the councils and boards, in line with the standards found in the West, specifically those of the European Union, have met with incremental success.[111] Such limited success is significant in recognizing that Western standards are the baseline. It is only the beginning of a long road to establish a legal framework that will foster pluralism and diversity in the broadcast systems and guard against state and government interference.[112]

Broadcasting Councils

With the enactment of their respective broadcasting laws, the Czech Republic (1991 and 1992), the Slovak Republic (1992 and 1993), Romania (1992), and Poland (1992) also became the first to establish bodies charged with overseeing their respective broadcasting fields: the Czech Council for Radio and Television Broadcasting (CCRTB), the Slovak Council for Radio and Television Broadcasting (SCRTB), the Romanian National Audiovisual Council (RNAVC), and the Polish National Radio and Television Council (PNRTC). Hungary and Albania followed suit, passing laws that established the Hungarian National Radio and Television Board (HNRTB) and the Albanian National Radio and Television Council (ANRTC) in 1995 and 1998, respectively. In Bulgaria, the Radio and Television Act came into force in 1996, creating a nine-member National Council on Radio and Television (NCRT) appointed by the Parliament and the president; the Parliament adopted a new Radio and Television Law in 1998.

One of the immediate and most serious controversies arose over who was to appoint the members of the national councils or boards: the Parliament alone (Albania, the Czech Republic, Hungary, and the Slovak Republic), the Parliament and the president (Bulgaria and Hungary), or the Parliament, the president, and the government (Romania).[113] The perception that these councils or boards allow the government and, through it, the political party or parties in power to control their work was thus, at least on its face, justified. Indeed, in the case of the Slovak Republic, the "crushing majority of [council] members were elected by the votes of the majority government coalition."[114]

In Poland, where the PNRTC members are appointed by the Parliament and the president, there have been wide-ranging accusations of politicization and favoritism toward governments and the party or parties making up the ruling regimes. Although PNRTC members are required by the broadcast law to renounce their membership in political parties in order to lessen political party conflicts on the council, they are nevertheless "chosen for their political allegiances and nominated by the Sejm, the Senate, and the President following political bargaining, raising serious questions about the independence of broadcasting oversight from political influence."[115] The council was also accused of treating private, commercial broadcasting unfairly. Indeed, under its sweeping powers the PNRTC "gave state broadcasting interests control, among other things, over the access of would-be commercial broadcasters to the airwaves and a built-in advantage against them should the state authorities wish to use it."[116]

Occasionally, however, political appointments backfire. In 1994 in the Czech Republic, over parliamentary objections, the CCRTB issued a license to a private news radio station (Radio Echo) to broadcast on a medium-wave frequency previously assigned to state-controlled Czech Radio. Three months later, the Czech parliament dismissed the entire board.[117]

Nor is overdependence on parliaments limited to broadcast councils and boards. As Milan Smid explains with regard to the Czech Broadcasting Company (CBC):

[The] heavy CBC dependence on the Parliament stems from the belief prevailing in many East European post-communist countries in those early days of political change, that the best and only representation of the public is the parliament because the [legitimacy] of democratically elected deputies is indisputable. However, this state of affairs raises doubts about the independence and impartiality of the CBC in the future, since the legislation not only does not protect them sufficiently, but also enables very easy transformation of the independent and professionally minded CBC to the quasi-parliamentary commission controlled by the instant party political interests.[118]

Accusations that the RNAVC, Romania's broadcast council, was highly politicized in favor of the Iliescu regime in the 1990–96 period, and that it retarded the privatization and growth of Romanian broadcasting, particularly of private, commercial national television, were legion.[119] By 1998, the primary accusations leveled at the RNAVC dealt with its inability to carry out its regulatory assignment, having failed to keep itself abreast of developments in the Romanian audiovisual sphere. Media transparency itself simply does not exist in Romania, partly because of the inadequacy of the law regulating broadcasting.[120]

Politically based controversies, both over their makeup and over their work, have plagued the region's broadcast boards and councils since their establishment, and there seems to be no end to them in sight. For example, in Hungary the HNRTB was accused of bias in awarding television licenses well into 1997. Not to be outdone, the Slovak Republic had similar accusations leveled against the SCRTB for imposing "inappropriate and politically unfair" sanctions: "The so-called licence council contributed to the prolonging of the media chaos in the pre-election period with its unprincipled assessment of licence conditions by the private media."[121] In 1998, the Association of Slovak Journalists refused to send representatives to the SCRTB, claiming that elected council members represented only the political interests of their parties.[122] In Bulgaria, there is concern over the continuing control of the national radio and television boards by the majority party in Parliament.[123]

With each change in governments and in the political makeup of the various parliaments, there is at least the potential for a change in the composition of the councils, assuming that vacancies in the regular turnover process are available during any particular party's or coalition's tenure in power. Thus the perception or reality of political manipulation by these councils or boards of rules, regulations, and edicts concerning a wide range of issues that affect broadcasting in the region will remain a political issue for the foreseeable future. The work of these councils or boards becomes even more controversial during election years, when most are tasked with laying out the ground rules for television and radio coverage of the political election campaigns and with policing adherence to these rules. The responsibilities of these boards and councils vary from country to country: CCRTB, the Czech council, has limited regulatory responsibilities for policy making, while PNRTC, the Polish council, has broad interpretive powers.[124]

The potential ability of any Eastern European broadcast council or board to control or micromanage private commercial television for partisan political purposes is great. Indeed, these boards and councils are arguably the most direct avenue, short of a wholesale change in laws to restrict the independent media, to a return to state control of the broadcast media. Yet their ability to serve as such an avenue is at least partially restricted by these nations' desire to join the European Union, which has certain requirements regarding the state of the audiovisual media, program production, and the importation or exportation of programs, among other matters. If they are to be EU members, Eastern Europe's broadcasting boards and councils must adhere to EU standards. Furthermore, the Council of Europe, the Organization for Security and Cooperation in Europe (OSCE), Reporters Sans Frontières, the International Center for Journalists, and the International Press Institute are just a few of the many international organizations that are monitoring developments in the transition to independent media in Eastern Europe. But the strongest opposition to a return to state control of broadcast media comes from within these countries, from some political parties, elements of civil society, journalists, and journalistic associations.

Public Broadcasting

With state and Communist Party control over broadcasting gone, Eastern European nations turned to the West for inspiration in developing independent public service radio and television. The public broadcasting systems developed by Germany, Britain, Italy, and France were looked upon as models: the laws and regulations governing them were, to one degree or another, adopted at the systemic level with the intention of turning the former state-controlled radio and television into public service broadcasting. The reality of the new "public broadcasting" falls short of its intended objective of providing the "fundamentally democratic trust" that constitutes the marriage of public with private life.[125] That is, it does not yet provide what modern democracies need: decentralized and localized public service media outlets that disseminate an unlimited range of opinions and tastes, and that allow citizens to fully benefit from and participate in programs and programming. With John Keane, many media scholars see such public service media as

a vital requirement of an open, tolerant and lively society in which great big dogmas and smelly little orthodoxies of all kinds are held in check, and in which, thanks to the existence of a genuine plurality of media of communication, various individuals and groups can openly express their solidarity with (or their opposition to) other citizens' likes and dislikes, proposals, tastes and ideals.[126]

Eastern European public service television falls short of this prescription. This is hardly a surprise because even in Western European countries, where such television may meet the general spirit of Keane's characterization, its audiences have been shrinking and have become as selective as those for commercial television. The deliberate distortion of the public service role of national television and radio stations in Eastern Europe is best exemplified by remarks made in 1996 by the chairman of Polish Television's supervisory board, Ryszard Miazek. Identifying the mission of Polish Television as serving society, and equating society with the state and "its democratic structures," Miazek declared that Polish Television "should not aspire [to express] independent opinions, because such opinions are formulated by parliament and other representatives of the state."[127] Miazek drew support for his remarks from the Polish broadcast law, which requires public television to provide direct access for state organs and the country's president.

A similar problem exists in the Czech Republic, where, even though the broadcast law prescribes that public authorities are not the owners of information, Czech Television "appears to be breaking its own statutes."[128] Jan Culik argues that public service Czech Television, by being neither professional, independent, critical, nor analytical, fails to "play a crucial, stabilizing role in the current period of political uncertainty and economic stagnation."[129] The Czech example is anomalous in that the staff is rejecting professionalism even as the council running Czech Television is attempting to bring greater professionalism to it. Across the border in Hungary, the government has been "unwilling" to nominate members to the board of governors for the Hungarian Television (MTV), thus freezing the board's activities. The acting chairman of MTV in 1998 was "forced to ask the government for financial help," a situation interpreted by the liberal opposition Alliance of Free Democrats (SZDSZ) as a signal that the chairman "must fall in line with government's wishes if he is to get any help."[130] The SZDSZ has accused the government of launching a comprehensive campaign to subjugate the public service media to its control.

Accusations of political patronage in staffing key positions in public television throughout Eastern Europe abound. In Romania, where Romanian Television had been accused of overt partisanship during Ion Iliescu's presidency (1990–96), the new government that took office in 1996 came under fire for appointing senior TVR officials sympathetic to government views, "ignoring regulations that did not permit such nominations to take place without parliamentary consent."[131] Not until 1999 was the democratic opposition in the Parliament able to replace the TVR leadership council.

State-owned Slovak Television continues to be accused of being highly politicized. Stephen Flanagan, special advisor on Eastern European Affairs to President Bill Clinton, left Bratislava after a May 1998 visit "convinced that public Slovak Television marches to a government drum."[132] Although the Slovak government approved legislation designed to boost the public character of Slovak Radio and Slovak Television in the fall of 1998, how this will affect the two institutions' public affairs and news programs remains to be seen. In Poland, the chairman of the Sejm's commission on the media and culture, Jan Maria Jackowski, declared in 1998 that the management of Polish Television was so politicized that it was "it impossible for it to carry out its public mission."[133]

After years of turmoil, state control, and accusations that it is serving the post-Communist powers that be, Albanian national television is now officially public service television, charged with informing, educating, and entertaining the public, "while serving the nation, all groups of society, also including national minorities."[134] As with Bulgarian Television and the new broadcast laws governing it, only time will tell if Albanian Television will actually function as genuine public service television. Most likely, it will continue to make incremental progress toward its ideal role. Thus Albanian Radio and Television coverage, which did not represent the diversity of Albanian society in 1996, had, according to "most international observers," made "a significant improvement" in that regard by 1998.[135]

Ethnic diversity is now a feature of most of the region's national broadcasting services. For instance, the local affiliates of Bulgarian Television (BNT) broadcast programs in Turkish in areas of Bulgaria where there is a large Turkish-speaking population, although BNT's promise to occasionally broadcast national programs in Turkish remained unfulfilled as 2000 drew to a close. The Czech Republic broadcasts television and radio programs in Romani; Hungary broadcasts two-hour daily radio programs in Romani, Slovak, Romanian, German, Croatian, and Serbian; the Slovak Republic broadcasts national television and radio programs in Ukrainian and Ruthenian; and Romania's national television and radio have programs in the languages of most of its ethnic groups.

Despite progress in the region, the major obstacle to an independent public service television model, however such a model may be defined, is the political elite, which continues its attempts to secure a monopoly, or at least significant levels of influence, over public television.

> The concentration of political and economic power in the hands of an oligarchy with an understanding, experience and tradition of democracy different from that of the West European elites leads in reality to the formation of a different relationship in the media world even when, outwardly, in the making of media laws one can note the adoption of West European standards.[136]

The short history of post-Communist public service television is filled with incidents of resistance and revolts against the overt politicization of public television on the part of public service broadcasting's personnel, unions, parliamentarians, political parties, and members of governing councils. Although this continuing tendency and the small successes on record hold hope for the future, political independence for public television is going to be difficult to achieve for three very basic reasons: (1) the political parties that control the various Eastern European parliaments and governments hold the purse strings to financing for public television; (2) the dominant political culture among the elites dictates that they attempt to control public television; and (3) public television personnel have not made sufficiently serious, sustained efforts to become truly professional, to raise the standards of their medium and journalism, to demand independence, and to educate their audiences about the need for such independence and for supporting media personnel in this regard.

Even should public service televisions gain their independence, it is doubtful that they will adopt the most idealistic prescription of their role and function, much of which depends on the practical definition of "democracy" and, specifically, of the type of communication necessary to sustain it (more will be said on this in chapter 5). Sparks and Reading outline two conditions for the success of public service broadcasting: (1) statutes or regulatory bodies that compel broadcasters to offer public service programs; and (2) funding that allows broadcasters to embark on a "non-optimum programme strategy."[137]

Normative and prescriptive definitions aside, defining what in practical terms constitutes "public service" is problematic. Indeed, Sparks and Reading's first condition lends support to arguments for continued government control by suggesting that such control, and the resulting choice of programs, might constitute "public service." Defining the audiences for public service television in the most inclusionary ways, ones that give voice to each and every interest, whether ethnic, religious, social, cultural, or other, as well as to individual interests of citizens, is simply unrealistic; there are not enough hours in the broadcast day to accommodate such diversity, even if it were possible to produce the programs needed to do so. Furthermore, policies regulating the content of the public service media to pursue programming ends "deemed to constitute public service," no matter how well meaning, could easily fall under the rubric of "positive" freedom, amounting to paternalism that is manipulative and restrictive in nature.[138]

But the more significant problem is that the same audiences for which the public service media are to be defined may either object, in whole or part, to the programming—or may simply not be willing to expose themselves to the myriad of individuals or groups professing support or opposition to particular issues. Yet, without this sharing of all differences and commonalties, can public broadcasting truly meet its idealized goals? If, as Keane suggests, the new public service broadcast media are to be "held accountable to their audiences through democratic procedures," with the majority of these audiences insisting the media reflect their sociopolitical and cultural preferences, what is to stop these media from becoming far less diverse and pluralistic than ideally envisioned?[139] Furthermore, how would one go about gathering the kind of financial support that would allow the public service media to pursue Sparks and Reading's "non-optimum programme strategy?"

Today's Eastern European public service broadcasting is supported by a combination of dues, tax moneys, and advertising revenues. Yet all three sources pose potential problems for the public service mission. Dues may shrink if news, public affairs, and entertainment programming becomes objectionable to a growing segment of the public, who object to financially supporting something they personally oppose. An increasingly displeased public, one that listens to public radio or watches public television infrequently, if at all, may press their political representatives to cut back or even eliminate tax support. Reliance on advertising will subject the public service broadcast media to the same pressures allegedly placed on the commercial media. Moreover, resorting to legal coercion to force payment of dues or tax moneys to support the public service media in the name of "diversity" and "pluralism" and "the public good" would only hark back to the authoritarian or totalitarian regimes the Eastern Europeans overturned in 1989.

This is not to be construed as an argument against the institution of the public service broadcast media. Quite to the contrary, they can be an important part of the array of media available to Eastern European audiences. My objection is to their idealization as the saviors from the political or commercial media, as the only guardians that can hold in check the "great big dogmas and smelly little orthodoxies of all kinds," by giving voice to various individuals and groups to express their views and interests.[140] The assumption that these individuals and groups do not get to express their views and interests in other types of media is just that, an assumption. For instance, the Rom, long persecuted before, during, and after Communism, now receive some coverage in the "mainstream" media in most countries of Eastern Europe; in some, they even own their own newspapers and produce their own broadcast programs. Thus, even though the public service broadcast media in the region are still controlled or strongly influenced by governments and the political party or parties in power, there has been significant progress toward greater independence and greater diversity in the public service media.

State Control of the Media Revisited

A number of observers have expressed concern over a possible drift toward, or even a possible return to, state control of the media in Eastern Europe. Their perceptions of what might favor such a possibility vary. For example, Patrick O'Neil relates it to the market and the state; Karol Jakubowicz, to the state, the growth of civil society, and the politicization of public life; and Slavko Splichal, to the virtual cabal of media owners and the political elite.[141]

There is no question that since 1990 there have been continual attempts at increasing the degree of state control over the media through (1) rules, laws, and regulations, and the official bodies charged with their definition, enactment, application, and enforcement; (2) state and government manipulation of the public service media; and (3) state ownership or control of the means of distribution, printing, newsprint manufacture, and broadcasting. Most attempts were complete or partial failures. Over the first post-Communist decade, the laws and policies pertaining to licensing, frequency allocations, and other state means of controlling or influencing the media were revisited by parliaments, new presidents, and governments either on their own initiative or because of pressures brought by journalists, their professional organizations, or international media institutions. The attempts at state paternalism by way of controlling newsprint allocations and print media distribution have had mixed results, thanks in part to the ability of publishers to purchase paper abroad and the establishment of some independent distribution systems. Controlling journalists' access to the working of governmental or state bodies has met with relatively greater success but also with continual challenges.

In short, there is no proof that a return or even a drift toward state control of the media has taken place, or that paternalism has become entrenched in the state-media relationship. The story of the first post-Communist decade is one of failed attempts to bring back paternalism and continuing battles to enlarge and secure the autonomy of the media from governments and states. Ironically, in those few instances where governing parties have achieved such state control, as in the case of Hungarian Television (MTV), the media outlet being dominated is a minor one; indeed, those controlling MTV "seem unperturbed by the fact that they are increasingly speaking to themselves alone when they hold forth from MTV's sparsely watched shows."[142]

The relationships between Eastern European states, governments and the media have slowly but surely benefited media autonomy in most instances. Examining the evolution of laws, rules, and regulations, on the one hand, and of the media, on the other, it seems clear that governments have at least officially given freedom of the press a solid foundation since 1989. Nevertheless, I agree with the conclusion that "formal rules, the mere existence of laws, even formal prohibitions on state intervention in the media will make little difference without the machinery of enforcement."[143] To safeguard the growing independence of the media, that machinery, namely, independent judiciaries and independent regulatory bodies—together with a democratic political culture—needs to be firmly in place.

4

The Media as an Institution

The remaking of the news media as an institution, of their corps of journalists, their professional ethos, and their journalism, was to be accomplished at the same time as the reshaping of other institutions, the reshaping of Eastern European political cultures, and the development of civil society, politics, and the market economy. More than that, these media, their journalists, and their journalism were expected to serve as catalysts, models, facilitators, and vehicles for all other societal changes. It was a reasonable expectation, particularly if one believes that the media can play an instrumental role in resocialization and modernization by teaching a new way of participating in politics and socioeconomic life and by encouraging new individual and national aspirations.[1] The news media were also expected to inform, provide diverse views on the issues of the day, set the agenda, and help shape public opinion on all matters related to democratization in a direction consonant with that process. Equally important was the expectation that they were going to carry out their tasks in a mode different from the highly politicized, partisan, propagandistic, mobilizational mode of the now-defunct Communist media, using a journalistic approach and language different from the "wooden" ones of the Communist era.[2]

In short, during the first post-Communist decade the Eastern European media were viewed as powerful forces, not a surprising perception: the region's political culture retains vestiges of the Marxist-Leninist belief in the absolute power of the media, and the "power of the press grows in a political culture characterized by this belief."[3] The perception was reinforced and heightened by the proven effectiveness of the indigenous (underground and alternative) and foreign media in contributing to the overthrow of Communism. The perceived power of the post-Communist media, most particularly among the political elites, was further multiplied by the rapidly growing number of media outlets and by the attention paid them, their journalists, and journalism by internal and external actors.[4] Regardless of this perception, however, the "hopes that television, along with the press, [would] play an important role in reestablishing a more open and honest political life" have only partially been fulfilled.[5]

Although few observers of Eastern Europe's post-Communist evolution challenge the notion that freedom of the press is now pandemic in the region, many question the autonomy of the media as an institution and their efficacy in informing and contributing to the reeducation and resocialization of the polity, their service to democratization, and how well they represent civil society and promote its development. The systemic alteration of the media as an institution was nearly completed by 2000. Still needed is a redefinition of the perceived and actual role of the media, their journalists, and journalism, their purpose and uses, characteristics, sources, organization, and ethics. Legacies, politics, culture, and the very nature of new societal institutions (including the media) are looked upon as central to defining the new nature, role, and effects of post-Communist journalists and journalism. What is seldom examined is the collective and individual professional culture of those who *are* the media—editors, news directors, journalists, owners, and publishers. Specifically, what is still missing is an analysis of their interests, abilities, and success in reshaping their professional culture and its product and how these can escape the legacies and the pressures of politics and extant political cultures, as well as pressures from other institutions.

How and in what ways has the culture of the media as an institution, and that of their leadership or elite and journalists, helped or hindered the remaking of the institution, and how is it affecting the journalism practiced? How has political culture affected the media's professional culture? Do the Eastern European media have the power that other institutions perceive they have?

Media Elite—Elite Media

Journalists, editors, news directors, and others who worked for the Communist media or for the underground media, where they existed, immediately took over the newly fashioned political party, commercial, and private media in 1989–90. The explosive growth in the number of outlets created a plethora of journalistic positions for which no new, trained, professional cadres and leaders were available.

Many of the media elite—the leaders of the thousands of journalists in the post-1989 era and the "stars" of Eastern European journalism, the analysts, commentators, and editorialists—were from the Communist or anti-Communist old guard. This was also the case in other institutions and even in those nations where new journalists replaced or outnumbered the old at a very rapid pace. For instance, even though, by the mid-1990s, 90 percent of Romanian journalists were new (post-1989) journalists, the overwhelming majority of media decision makers were people who had spent the bulk of their professional lives in the Communist media.[6] This "in with the new, in with the old" reality prevailed in the Polish media as in those of other countries in the region:

> Former publishers and editors of underground periodicals found themselves working alongside those who had weathered the storm working for official media. The old guard—insecure and fearful in the new situation, afraid that the general hatred of the old official media in their propagandistic role might now turn against them and prompt a witch hunt (which never came)—thought it best to play safe and to toe what they perceived to be the government's line. In other words, they performed true to old form.[7]

In addition, another type of journalistic leader emerged, principally in the "soft" dictatorships of the Czech Republic, Hungary, and Poland.[8] Having worked for the underground or alternative media, these new leaders focused on the propaganda or advocacy of anti-Communism, and not on a journalism meeting Western standards or roles. In his analysis of Poland's media elite, Jakubowicz accurately describes a situation common in the Czech Republic and Hungary, which also had an underground or alternative press during the Communist era:

> The new guard, people who had risked a great deal working for underground media or had been involved in other forms of underground activity, now understandably sought to support the new government they identified with in the extremely difficult situation it faced. Consequently, they were unwilling to expose its weaknesses and point out its mistakes. Thus both groups [the Communist and the anti-Communist media elites]—though for quite different reasons—were inclined to depart from

the ideal of objectivity and the watchdog role, conspiring, as it were, to practice a brand of journalism somewhat less independent and aggressive than expected.[9]

Neither the Communist media elite nor its underground counterpart was prepared to impose, lead, or serve as models for a Western-style, fact-based journalism. For instance, Polish journalists who worked for the anti-Communist media and served as managers and editors in the 1990s had "no experience in producing well-balanced perspectives and views."[10] Everywhere in post-Communist Europe, those who had worked for the Communist press, accustomed as they were to practicing "the 'old-style' journalism, based upon political criteria," were hard pressed to adopt "a 'newer' model based upon objective reporting."[11] In Poland, as elsewhere in the region, the old Communist "civic attitude" of taking sides in the struggle between Communism and democracy has the members of the new media elite doing their best to advance the cause of their own political and personal views. This is a substitute for providing objective information and "a cool and dispassionate (such an attitude was wholly out of the question) analysis of the situation."[12]

This special legacy of the region's Communist and anti-Communist media elite, combined with the long-standing legacy of partisan, politicized European journalism, helped to divide it into factions supportive of the political parties making up the new, post-Communist governments and factions supportive of the opposition parties, themselves widely varied groups. In both cases, the media elite became effectively a mouthpiece for the new political elites, at least in the initial half of the first post-Communist decade. In Hungary, for example, the new media elite disseminated what the governmental or oppositional political elite wanted to say and thus could "work only like a technical mediatory channel on which the political elite—being in power or in opposition—[spoke] to the audience."[13] In an even more extreme case, the Albanian media elite was "transformed into a loudspeaker [that] amplifies and spreads its opinion [and] that of the political elite."[14] From country to country throughout the region, the same theme was sounded, varying only in degree and in cultural expression. Such a finding closely agrees with those of mass communications scholars in the developing countries of Africa, Asia, and Latin America since the 1960s:

In many of the new countries the journalistic profession has little opportunity for independent development because the most rewarding careers with the mass media tend to be with essentially propaganda agencies for either the government itself or for the dominating political party or movement. Under these conditions writers and communicators may be able to play a constructive role in facilitating the nation-building process but they cannot assume the lead in training the citizenry to appreciate the virtues and the possibilities of non-partisan, and hence essentially constitutional, institutions.[15]

Granted, in Eastern Europe, save perhaps for the now-divorced Czech and Slovak states, there is no question of nation building in the strictest sense; still, after years of vassalage to Moscow, varying degrees of nation rebuilding are necessary throughout the region. Nevertheless, Eastern European journalism in the initial post-1989 years and journalism in the developing nations of the Third World in the 1960s shared another striking similarity—a heavy representation of intellectuals. The political, partisan approach to what was supposed to be a new, post-Communist, democracy-enhancing journalism was not helped by the addition of these intellectuals to the ranks of the media elite; even those generally inclined to support some form of democratization were simply not capable of being "journalists" and journalistic leaders in the modern, democratic-minded, Western sense. Serving the audience, fulfilling a public trust and interest, and helping to develop a social consciousness were generally not accepted as guiding ideals, although many journalists speciously argued that their journalistic polemics and their biased analysis, presented as news reporting, were intended to help the audience develop a democratic political culture.[16]

This reinjection of intellectuals into the media, in large measure a return to pre-Communist days, or a continuation in countries with anti-Communist media, was a process helped by "the phenomenon of the polarized political life."[17] More than that, because the media were profoundly involved in political battles, their communication took the form of a discourse in opinions, a genre comfortable for intellectuals.[18] Indeed, this was a continuation of the general European tradition of melding journalism with literature, with public relations, and with social, political, and cultural leadership. Seeing journalists as active participants in politics and public affairs wanting to influence audiences and politics according to their own beliefs is a wholly European view.[19] Notwithstanding the marriage between journalist-polemicist, on the one hand, and essayist, novelist, academic, poet, or artist, on the other, however, only a handful of bona fide Zola-type journalistic stars or leaders were created in post-Communist Eastern Europe.[20] Indeed, by the mid-1990s Zola-like journalism was increasingly reserved for the commentaries and analyses in major newspapers or in the strictly intellectual, low-circulation weeklies, such as Romania's *22*, which featured a plethora of analysis pieces and interviews.

The gradual withdrawal of intellectuals from public life and from the media by the end of the 1990s is both positive and negative: positive because it makes room for the possibility of journalistic professionalism and negative because it deprives the journalistic world and its audiences of another possibility, a deeper, intellectual examination of the issues. If we accept the notion that intellectuals constitute a class apart from the political, managerial, and mass leadership classes, being a "spiritual aristocracy," as Raymond Aron describes them, and thus a potential alternative voice, their more limited participation in the media restricts the scope of societal, cultural, and political dialogue.[21]

Ideally, the media elite should exert considerable influence on society as a whole and on the media as an institution.[22] It has failed on both counts in Eastern Europe's first post-Communist decade. The media elite had "an important impact on the dismantling of the system," especially in the nations with an organized anti-Communist movement and press, yet it "lost much of [its] influence on the public" after the 1989 revolutions.[23] In those countries where the media elite was essentially an ex-Communist elite, any immediate "success" it had in the first few post-Communist months quickly dissipated in the wake of its continuing application of pre-1989 mentalities and methods. Contrary to what Karl Deutsch might contend, there is no documented evidence that the media elite played a pivotal role in forming or shaping public opinion in any but a few isolated cases, depending on the issue, the country, and the individual members of that elite.[24] Even when the media elite assumed such a role, it often did so in the service of personal opportunism. A case in point is Nova TV's former general director Vladimir Zelezny, who used the very popular "Volejte rediteli" (Call the Director) program "to mesmerize the ordinary Czech viewer and to manipulate him into absolute submission. It is a self-promotion program, where Zelezny will say anything, often absolute manipulative rubbish."[25]

Still worse is a "leadership" of neglect, which allows control of a media enterprise to slip into the hands of an ad hoc group of individuals not responsible to anyone. This was the case at Czech Television's news and current affairs department in the late 1990s:

> The editor-in-chief did not run the Department. He spent his time liaising with the outside world, going to lunches and dinners with politicians. Like in many other Czech institutions, Czech TV's news and current affairs de-

partment was run by an informal group of five or six individuals, mutual friends, who met in the canteen, in the corridor or in the smoking room and decided there and then what was to be put on the air, what line to follow. This informal set up was structured in such a way that nobody was accountable for mistakes. The department worked a little like a secret paramilitary organization: a number of individuals informally assumed large decision-making powers in order to make themselves indispensable.[26]

As to the influence of the media elite on the media as an institution, it was and still is attenuated by

1. the lack of preparation, willingness, or both on the part of its members to lead journalism in a Western-style, professional direction;[27]
2. the partisanship that divides its members into supporters and opponents of the governments or parties in power, a situation only slowly and selectively changed as the 1990s came to a close;
3. the political ambitions of its members, which transform some into members of the political elite;[28]
4. the exigencies of dealing with the daily problems of newspapers, magazines, and radio or television stations;
5. the struggle with politicians, political parties, governments, states, and their various organs, sometimes carried on for partisan reason and sometimes not; and
6. the traditions and legacies of the pre-Communist and Communist eras.

In the 1990s, another more basic, self-serving reason for the media elite's lack of leadership in changing the institution and its product may have been present: they would not, indeed could not, support a journalistic role and practices that would likely make most of them obsolete. Of course, the media elite denied such a motivation, all evidence to the contrary.[29]

Now that the former Communist and former underground media elites are free of the Marxist-Leninist context in which they worked, for or against, they are much like Pavel, the middle-aged television cameraman in Ivan Klima's 1993 novel, who, busy with one small job after another, never fulfills the professional possibilities that the new freedom affords him.[30] There are some highly visible exceptions among Eastern Europe's media, journalists who, it is hoped, will serve as beacons guiding their colleagues to a level of professionalism that matches the best of their Western counterparts.[31]

Meanwhile, aside from the clearly inadequate leadership that the media elite has exhibited in shaping public opinion, in agenda setting independent of politics, political parties, and other special interests, and in changing journalism and the media as an institution, it has shown a predilection for an arbitrary management style, whether for personal or political reasons. When, for example, the news staff of Czech Television charged that the appointment of Jiri Hodak in December 2000 was politically biased and refused to work with him, Hodak responded by firing the rest of the management team, as well as some prominent journalists.[32]

Members of the media elite have also shown an inclination to join the political elite.[33] A unique example, by virtue of sheer numbers, is provided by the Czech Republic, where members of the underground or alternative media elite, such as Václav Havel, Jiri Dienstbier, Václav Klaus, and Rita Klimova, made the almost instant leap to high political office. For them, concludes a longtime observer of the Czech scene, "samizdat journalism had been only a political alternative until such time as they could enter the public arena."[34] In the Slovak Republic, too, "it is not accidental that many within the media have become members of the political elites themselves."[35] Adam Michnik, one of the Solidarity leaders and editor of *Gazeta Wyborcza,* served in the new Polish Sejm from 1989 to 1991. The owner and news director of Albania's daily *Koha Jone,* Nikolle Lesi, is a member of Parliament. There are many others in the region.

But election or appointment to political office was and is not the only way to become part of the post-Communist political elite. In all Eastern European nations, appointments to the leadership of so-called public broadcasting are still made on the basis of political loyalty to the parties in power or to powerful politicians. Jiri Hodak's appointment to the directorship of Czech Television was perceived as a political appointment made by the Czech Television council on behalf of Hodak's friend Václav Klaus, the speaker of the Czech parliament and a former prime minister, whose rivalry with President Václav Havel had dominated Czech politics since 1997.[36]

Elections or appointments to leadership positions in public broadcasting represent, for all intents and purposes, a change in status from the media elite to the political elite, or at least the straddling of the thin, not-so-tall fence separating them. In some cases, it may even be considered a sort of melding of the two. In an extreme definition of "public service broadcasting" and of journalistic roles, Ryszard Miazek, the former chairman of the Polish Television Supervisory Board, announced that, because the state and "its democratic structures" *were* society, public service television had to serve the state if it was to fulfill its mission in society.[37]

With the national election of 1996, Romanian Television, accused throughout the first post-Communist regime of being in the regime's pocket, appointed Alina Mungiu-Pippidi, one of the new government's staunchest supporters, to the top job in the news department. A scandal in January 1998 only reinforced the distinct impression that TVR was still not an independent news organization and was being manipulated by those in power.[38] Romanian Television's Rasvan Popescu was appointed to head the Public Information Department of the Romanian government controlled by the National Christian Democratic Peasant Party (PNTCD); *Romania Libera*'s Gilda Lazer and Eugen Serbanescu were appointed spokespersons for the Ministry of Foreign Affairs and for one of the Romania's post-1989 prime ministers, respectively; Ion Vaciu, a former deputy of the Romanian Television's Union, was appointed personal advisor to Adrian Nastase, a high official of the Romanian Social Democratic Party (PDSR), ousted in 1996.

Of course, this anointing of individuals from the media elite as members of the political elite could backfire on the political appointee. For example, Istvan Palfy, a political appointee who headed the Hungarian Television news, was fired in May 1995 for "what the government saw as excessive criticism of its actions in the news."[39] Nor were government reprisals limited to political appointees: that same year, seven Bulgarian journalists were summarily dismissed from Bulgarian national radio after protesting against censorship at their station.[40] And in a curious twist, in 1998 the young political appointee heading the Albanian State Television's news department quit, complaining that the government and opposition parties attempted to influence his work.[41]

Being either for or against the ruling party or coalition as a stepping-stone to joining the political elite is not unusual among members of the media anywhere in the world, especially not in transitioning or transforming societies.[42] In Eastern Europe, however, such behavior by members of the media elite does little to establish or enhance their credibility and legitimacy with audiences, or their ability to contribute to public opinion formation. In the most extreme case in the region, the Albanian media elite is "eclipsed by . . . the pro-government part of the media elite, by the political elite and the opposition one, by the artistic and scientific elite."[43] The limited credibility, legitimacy, and power of those who belong to the media elite may also be partly due to their perception, and the audiences', that they *are* an elite.[44]

Thus the rift between the media elite and its audiences is as great as it is between any other type of elite and the population in general. In the context of media professionalism, Adlai Stevenson's version of Lord Acton's famous dictum aptly describes the Eastern European media elite in the first few post-Communist years: "Power corrupts, but lack of power corrupts absolutely." Yet another problem impinging on professionalism and the media elite's leadership involves the musical chairs played with media management positions as a result of politics—particularly in public broadcasting—and the desire to improve one's financial condition and one's status as reflected by the media outlets employing one. The lack of stability does not allow members of the media elite to acquire professionalism, nor to serve as educators, models, and professional leaders for their journalists, old and new. Consequently, nowhere in Eastern Europe do they support changes; they only reject or endorse them after the fact.[45] If, indeed, the media "can serve democracy only when those who manage them feel a passionate responsibility to create it and maintain it," most of the news media in Eastern Europe did not serve democracy in the first decade of post-Communism because their elite, with some exceptions, simply failed to acquire that passion.[46] Even the few media managers who did feel a passionate commitment to democracy had no real understanding of a working democracy.[47] Most important, the media elite has not taken on the one element crucial to liberty, namely, responsibility. Nor have its members a clear sense of for what and to whom they might be responsible. Nevertheless, its power and influence increased in the latter part of the 1990s.

The media's official break with political parties in each of the region's countries in the first few post-1989 years and the increasing willingness of media outlets to be somewhat less partisan, if not less political, have served to amplify their power and status, at least in the eyes of the political and economic power elites. By the end of the 1990s, a segment of the region's media elite was engaged in a deepening struggle with the political elite over editorial autonomy.[48] Both sides based their struggle on some warranted concerns but also on a number of fallacious assumptions.[49] As Tomasz Goban-Klas aptly explains, both elites judge the media to be the main instrument of politics: "Their vision of the media is one-dimensional, overpoliticized and simplified, believing in a missionary role for journalist and an idealized press."[50]

Although editorial autonomy took a step forward, the reason for taking this step was still short of an appropriate understanding of the role, function, and professionalism of journalists and of journalism in a democratic society.[51] It is not clear to what extent members of the media elite can secure their independence, and thus "alienate themselves from their national elite and its goals," by seeking out "their natural mass audience."[52] It is equally unclear whether they mirror the intellectual and political elite with respect to the nature of democracy they envision, itself unclear.

An example from Romania illustrates how politicians and the public perceive the media and how members of the media elite perceive themselves, and how derelict their leadership has been in professionalizing journalism. In April 1998, Prime Minister Victor Ciorbea was forced out of office by political infighting in the Democratic Convention, the collection of parties that won control of Parliament and the government in the November 1996 elections. One Romanian analyst, Cornel Nistorescu, recognized that politicians spent more time on television and talking with journalists, particularly those considered members of the elite, than working "in the real sense of the word," and that they assigned blame for the prime minister's downfall to the media.[53] The public blamed the media for the political disorganization and chaos, and even politicians worried about the "terror" of the media.

> That the Romanian politician is hungry [to be on] television, which most often leaves him mangled and smeared, cannot be said to be the responsibility of the [media], but must be seen as his own irresponsibility. This explains why politicians have wanted [their own] newspapers, tried to influence them, and have stuck their tails even in television. . . . Ultimately, this invoked terror of the [media] is nothing but a sign of a freedom wrongly used, coupled with the weakness of politicians.[54]

Coming from a nation considered among the less reformed in the region, this Romanian example also applies to nations considered to be ahead in their transformation into substantive rather than just systemic democratic forms. In Poland, for example, there is also a "deep feeling of insecurity among the media elites and the ruling political forces. Each is afraid of the other."[55] In Hungary, "the mutual distrust which had existed between journalists and politicians [under Communism] was carried into the new system and exacerbated by events."[56] These "events," cutting across state boundaries in the region, had another, more positive effect, however, moving the media and their elite from a heavy if not exclusive dependence on politicians and political parties to a relatively more balanced power relationship.

Still to be achieved is a consensus among members of the media elite on a journalistic paradigm for Eastern Europe. The absence of consensus is partly attributable to the elite's continuing partisanship, politicization, and its very elitism, and to the self-protection embodied in not allowing for major change within the news media and their practices. It is also attributable to the lack of professionalism in politics: professional politicians would invariably have called for professional journalism.[57]

Last but not least, the absence of consensus persists because well-entrenched, extensive commercial media, divorced from political forces, do not yet exist, and because what commercial media there are do not rely strictly on the market for their existence (see chapters 2 and 3). Genuinely commercial media could counterbalance the political forces, while reinforcing a new, formative political culture. Moreover, "oriented toward the market logic," they would tend "to abide by professional practices."[58] Such media would also produce a media elite that could redefine or help redefine journalistic roles and practices or, at the very least, could provide competing ones. Should market-oriented media come to dominate in the twenty-first century, and indications are that they might, the media elite may have the opportunity to play a significant role in shaping and orienting public opinion from different and more varied perspectives than the purely political.[59]

Of course, there are no guarantees that commercial media will play only a salutary role in cultivating a responsible journalism with collective responsibilities and interests. To put it another way, commercial media cannot serve as pure vehicles for addressing the public interest or uniformly seeking public trust as long as they define their audiences as consumers rather than as citizens.[60] Nevertheless, because market-oriented media must maximize the size of their audiences if they are to maximize their profits, their journalism has to be, at the very least, less partisan and more uniform in professional standards, always subject of course to the danger of tabloidization.

Furthermore, the creation of media elite with their own powers, independent of the political parties, politicians, states, and governments, may set the stage for an evolution in their perception of media roles and functions, of journalistic professionalism and a professional ethos. In turn, this may allow for the establishment of elite media in each Eastern European nation. To date, no truly elite media outlets have surfaced in the region, even if there are some that have gained a modicum of independence, credibility, and status within their respective societies—for example, *Gazeta Wyborcza* and *Reczpospolita* in Poland, *Koha Jone* in Albania, *Adevarul* in Romania, *Nepszabadszag* in Hungary, and *Pravo* and *Mlada Dnes* in the Czech Republic. Still, these newspapers do not have the national standing and professional respect, and certainly not the international recognition, awarded, say, the London *Times, Il Corriere della Sera, Frankfurter Allgemeine, Neue Züricher Zeitung,* the *New York Times,* or *Asahi Shimbun,* to mention but a few of the world's elite newspapers.

What defines elite media is elite journalism, encouraged, guided, insisted upon by the media elite—journalism of the kind that "diplomats, educators, writers, theologians, economists, and scientists take seriously . . . that serves as a kind of model for the mainstream serious journalists and newspapers. It is that which is most quoted, alluded to, and respected."[61] Such journalism works to unite its audiences, not to segment them, by providing ample fact-based information along with its diversity of opinions and analysis. Most important, elite journalism in Eastern Europe would establish a standard for responsibly serving the informational needs of the public and of society.

Journalists and Political and Professional Cultures

When the possibility arose in late 1989 and 1990 to join the ranks of a profession that was strictly regulated until then by the Communist Party, state, and government, hundreds of individuals flocked to the rapidly multiplying media outlets. This was particularly true in Albania, Bulgaria, and Romania, which lacked the underground or alternative media that had existed in Czechoslovakia, Hungary, and Poland, although it was true in these countries as well. The great majority of the new journalists were men and women in their twenties and thirties. They were drawn together by powerful magnets, even if these did not serve to unify them or make them professional. Indeed, few if any of those entering journalism in the early 1990s had any journalism training or education, a situation only partly rectified by the end of the decade with the proliferation of questionably effective journalism programs at universities, trade schools, and professional associations.[62] They came from all walks of life and with a wide range of academic and nonacademic preparation.[63] The absence of a shared sense of purpose, role, ethics, ethos, and practices made the Eastern European journalist corps far more heterogeneous than its Western counterparts. In its widely varying journalistic conceptions, sociopolitical and economic backgrounds, and educational, personal, and other experiences, the new corps of journalists well represented the diversity of its societies, and its very absence of a professional culture served to "democratize" it.[64]

While the still persistent Eastern European journalistic "tradition" (a mixture of various conventions, some already changed by the Communist era and some being discarded since 1989) is melding with Western European and American media traditions in a world news culture penetrating ever more deeply into the region, the old ways, pre-Communist and Communist alike, are slow to change. Writing about Polish journalists in the nineteenth century, Goban-Klas paints a picture of individuals with a literary education entering journalism because they were not sufficiently talented to become novelists: "Polish news people were never dedicated professional information providers, but were usually educators, politicians, propagandists, and creative writers."[65] The same can be said of Albanian, Bulgarian, Hungarian, Romanian, Czech, and Slovak journalists of the nineteenth century.[66] In turn-of-the-century Hungary, information was disseminated "by gray, nameless reporters," while "great men and famous reporters" set about purposefully influencing public opinion.[67] In Romania, pre-Communist journalists availed themselves "of the prerogative of not knowing anything, to harangue about . . . unimportant things in the name of the country [and] to preach morality from the pulpit of immorality."[68]

Thus Eastern European journalists did not have to take a giant leap into the Communist era when they became a "living 'transmission belt' between party and society."[69] The role of journalists as self-styled "teachers, preachers, and spiritual leaders of society" was continued quite naturally in the Communist period through monocentric media, and is just as naturally practiced today, in the post-Communist period, albeit in a far more atomized political and journalistic milieu that provides a sense of déjà vu with respect to the pre-Communist years.[70] In spirit and practice, the post-Communist professional transformation is as difficult for Communist journalists as for anti-Communist journalists. Adam Michnik, the editor in chief of *Gazeta Wyborcza* and a Solidarity founder, explains the ongoing struggle in the mid-1990s to change the activist, anti-Communist journalism practiced during the Communist period:

It is difficult to change one's views; it is difficult for a dissident, a member of the underground to become the editor in chief of the most popular newspaper in a democratic state. The reality of democracy is so different from the world of dictatorship. . . . That world was inevitably a black and white one: Goodness struggled against evil, the truth struggled against lies, freedom staged the battle against enslavement. . . . In the world of democracy, the prevailing color is gray. This world is ruled by

arguments which are divided and not complete, by partial and contradictory interests.[71]

Eastern European journalists in the 1990s followed a well-set pattern observed by their counterparts in other nations undergoing transition or transformation, where "politics, literature, and journalism come together."[72] Indeed, as Herbert Passin notes, "to the extent that writers take as one part of
their vocation the work of public enlightenment, there is not too much difference between their conception of themselves as writers or journalists, or
even as politicians."[73] This is translated into journalists thinking of themselves as intellectuals, which is not of course to equate journalism with intellectual labor. Moreover, too many of them view and present themselves
as so many Romanian journalists in their early twenties do: as "analysts"
instead of reporters, when almost all of what they write springs from their
own partisan political interests or those of the party they feel they must represent, and not from unbiased consideration, factual knowledge, and clear
understanding of the matter at hand.

The tendency to think of themselves as analysts, critics, or commentators rather than as reporters or explainers led Czech journalists in the second half of the post-Communist decade, working in a country often touted
as the most advanced of the Eastern European nations, to consistently mix
their own unsubstantiated opinions with facts.[74] Moreover, because they
were often influenced by politics or a particular ideology, their reporting
was just as biased and incomplete.[75] Polish journalists in 1990–92 lacked
"the basic skills of objective news reporting and analysis or the ability to
unravel fully and completely for their audience the immensely complex
process unfolding on the political scene."[76] By 1997, they were still "fundamentally deficient in terms of their comprehensiveness, objectivity and
professionalism" and, to this day, when they "try to separate news and opinion, they . . . continue to perform an advocate function."[77] Ironically,
Polish journalists consider it their main function to inform, a view shared
by their colleagues in the region.[78] An identical situation was found
throughout the 1990s in Romania, where journalists were more devoted to
ideological or political than professional values, and mixed opinion and information in their reporting without much attention to objectivity. Consequently, newcomers and Communist-era journalists were equally inclined
to write propaganda.[79] In Albania, where "journalism is an intellectual passion, not a real profession," it has remained a tool for indoctrination, "to
fight the enemy of the party, the opposition."[80] Thus throughout the region,

defeating the "opponent," a continuation of the Communist mentality, was in the 1990s more important than reporting, informing audiences, supplying verifiable facts, using credible sources, and being complete and unbiased in the selection and presentation of news items.

Worse yet, journalists in the region believed, with their Hungarian colleagues, that freedom of the press meant "freedom to write anything without attention to truth and privacy."[81] Nestor Rates, the news director of Radio Free Europe's Romanian department, a frequent visitor to Romania, and a careful observer of the Romanian scene, states that as a journalist he is often "frightened" of how little Romanian journalists care about verifying information, the quality of their sources, and the "destiny" of the information after it is published. He considers the absence of standards of accuracy and professional responsibility "the gravest negative in journalism in the present phase."[82]

Partisanship and bias aside, the general lack of competence and professionalism noted throughout the region, with the exceptions shining brightly only because they are exceptions, is a result not only of Communist and pre-Communist legacies, but also of contemporary political, economic, cultural, and institutional problems. The persistent string of media outlet closures has put many journalists on the unemployment line; as the media field begins to stabilize, there are fewer new outlets offering journalists employment opportunities.[83] Fearing the loss of their jobs, journalists raise few objections to their working conditions and often follow their editors' orders unquestioningly.[84]

Low pay also forces many journalists to work at other jobs (journalists in Bulgaria, for example, were also "encouraged to sell advertising for a commission"),[85] making them divide the attention required to professionalize, a process already impeded by the absence of role models and meaningful guidance. In some cases, journalists work for two different media; the daily switch from print to broadcasting or vice versa further interferes with their professionalization, each medium having its own particular requisites for the presentation of news and information.[86] Thus there are few real opportunities to develop and hone reporting and writing skills. Moreover, journalists often draft political campaign messages for politicians and political parties at the same time they are reporting on the campaigns, and even take bribes for "news stories."[87]

Thus both economics and politics threaten the stability and professionalization of journalism on the institutional and individual level. As we have seen in chapter in 3, journalists' fears of being fired for being "politically incorrect" are all too often justified, and in the 1990s these fears combined with the still fresh memory of Communist rule, when political correctness was a constant factor of public life. For Czech and Slovak journalists, and no less for their colleagues in the region, "that experience has produced a journalistic 'schizophrenia,' with journalists wanting the right to be independent and professional but also to be active advocates of party positions."[88] This "schizophrenia" was clearly present in the early 1990s, when the head of Slovak Television emphasized "the need for impartiality in television broadcasts," while also noting that Slovak Television was "'an important informational medium of the Slovak parliament and Slovak government' to serve the democratization of Slovak society."[89] And in 1995, when the chairman of the Union of Hungarian Journalists (MUK), a group that supported the rightist government and whose members had called for "national," partisan journalism, is reported to have said, "We do not want free speech, because free speech is turning into spitefulness. . . . We want decency in the press."[90] (He did not explain what he meant by "decency.")

This journalistic dissociation should logically prevail only among those who were employed by the Communist media, and who were in the minority among working journalists by the end of the 1990s. Yet it is pervasive among the young, new additions to the profession, partly for the economic and political reasons mentioned above, and partly because the new journalists have received no professional guidance or only the guidance of those still suffering from the journalistic "schizophrenia" of the Communist era.

In his survey of the Eastern European region and the former Soviet republics, Dean Mills notes that journalists' views of how their roles and practices are to be understood and carried out are affected at least as much by their respective cultures and individual interpretations of journalism as they are by other institutions and the post-Communist political cultures. Journalists

> are far from unambivalent about their proper role in post-Communist Europe and about the proper kind of journalism. . . . The lack of clarity stems in part from a blending of roles caused by many current-day journalists' individual backgrounds as partisan activists, and in part by a mind set that still views journalism as partisan by nature.[91]

This contradictory view of the journalists' role and place in society, when considered together with the economic and political threats to job security, may also explain the journalists' difficulty in defining journalistic autonomy and their uneven attempts at defending a truly independent journalism in the first post-Communist decade. Hungarian journalists, like their colleagues elsewhere in the region, equate independence with support for their own positions, confusing personal with professional independence.[92] Governments use awards and prizes to praise and reward journalists who support them, and they demonize journalists who do not, as in the Czech Republic, where none other than Prime Minister Václav Klaus called them the "biggest enemies of mankind"; and in Romania, where democratic-minded president Emil Constantinescu (1996–2000) called them "waiters and barbers," suggesting they could easily be bought off.[93] Like other Eastern European journalists, Czech journalists "are still struggling to define what constitutes a free press."[94] Without a clear, universal definition, one accepted and defended by all journalists and by their respective societies' political cultures, their journalistic dissociation and their lack of professionalism will persist.

The contradictory and incompatible elements in Eastern Europe's journalistic practices and ethos have given rise to other problems. Thus the region's journalists, as individuals or in organizations, seem unwilling or unable to

1. Close ranks in professional solidarity. Journalists' organizations are often split along political lines. For instance, in 1992 pro-government journalists formed the Union of Hungarian Journalists (MUK), which wrangled with the anti-government National Association of Hungarian Journalists (MUOSZ).[95] In Bulgaria, too, "journalists did not see themselves as a community" in the first five post-Communist years.[96]

2. Take a leadership role in professionalizing journalism. The Polish case epitomizes the situation in the rest of Eastern Europe: "Journalists' associations are not standing up to the task of remodeling the profession."[97]

3. Adopt or enforce professional codes. In Romania, a professional code was articulated as early as 1991, and a new one formulated in 1998.[98] But it was to no avail. Given the inability of any one organization to enforce its code, none of the codes are meaningful in regulating journalistic behavior or standards. In Poland, as elsewhere in Eastern Europe, "the most serious obstacle to the independence of the . . . media is the lack of a professional code among journalists."[99]

4. Tolerate their differences or resolve them amicably. Bulgarian journalists who worked for the party press saw each other not as colleagues but as opponents; those working for the private media outlets

viewed their counterparts at state-owned media outlets as "incapable of practicing independent journalism; and those who worked for the state media resented the commercialization of private media journalism."[100] Polish journalists "quarrel among themselves, sue one another, despise each other."[101] The same holds for the rest of Eastern Europe, where many of these lawsuits, called "firecrackers" in Romania, are filed by quarrelsome journalists simply to draw attention to themselves.[102]

5. Exercise professional caution in their reporting. Repeated over the region is the Czech experience, where "less than fully professional reporting leaves journalists and publications open to legal action, and a string of libel suits is constantly before the courts."[103] Although many of these suits are politically inspired tantrums by elected and appointed officials and politicians, others are clearly not, and arise from the absence of journalistic professionalism.

Based on observation of and testimony from Eastern European journalists, it is safe to conclude that the lack of a clear sense of the professional values underlying the journalistic enterprise has led the region's journalists to

1. have no respect for verifiable information or for their audiences' ability to digest such information;
2. believe they are the discoverers of the truth rather than only providers of accurate, verifiable, balanced, complete facts and information to help audiences arrive at the truth;
3. believe they are sociopolitical and cultural leaders when they are only facilitators of leadership, public involvement and discourse, and education;
4. refuse to cooperate with their colleagues. In Western Europe and the United States, it was found that, because such cooperation serves to elevate professional expectations, the influence of professional standards grows stronger.[104] Cooperation among journalists is as yet rare in Eastern Europe.

Thus Eastern European journalists have not developed a professional culture strong enough to counterbalance the political forces that dominate their societies. And despite claims to the contrary, their professional culture is not yet tied to market forces. Still, by the very end of the 1990s the beginnings of professionalization had resulted in "a stronger commitment to impartiality."[105] Journalists all over Eastern Europe had begun to distance themselves from political parties, from state and government influences. Their tendency to view themselves as either "for" or "against" those in power seems to be slowly weakening.

Young journalists exposed to Western European or American journalism, whether directly or indirectly, are keen to adapt it to their own practices.[106] Media outlets that are foreign owned or co-owned have also brought a Westernization to the indigenous journalism, most noticeably in television. But it would be wrong to mistake the polished, very Western façade of television news for Western or American professionalism (more on this in "Journalism" below).

The resistance to adopting more Western journalistic standards and practices comes from most members of the media elite. But it is the exceptions, such as Adam Michnik of Poland and the few Young Turks throughout the region, who are gaining experience, credibility, and even positions of responsibility, that bodes well for the future of Eastern European journalism. It is a future that may see journalistic professionalism, ethics, ethos, and practices defined, adopted, and maintained endogenously by the media institution and its journalists—in other words, genuine media and journalistic independence. The few exceptions in the region have already proven it can be done. In Poland, as elsewhere in the region, professionalization of journalists "reduces bias, in many cases introduced not so much by publishers and editors, *but by the reporters and commentators themselves*" (emphasis added).[107] Professionalization may also lessen the owners' and publishers' biased influence on journalism. On the other hand, for journalism to fulfill its professional mission, journalists need to "behave in an extremely selective manner toward themselves and toward third parties"; thus, or so some argue, "the full professionalization of journalism would . . . in the long run, undermine the reputation and functional ability of journalism."[108] Perhaps. In any case, Eastern European journalists are a long way from having to be concerned about the consequences of being fully professional.

The Roles of Journalism and the Media

Changes in the pattern of journalistic practices accepted in a particular society depend on changes in the culture, distribution of power, market con-

ditions, media ideology, and the corps of journalists in that society.[109] The
region's cultures are changing, but very slowly; political and economic
power remains predominantly in the hands of members of the former *nomenklatura,* although more in some Eastern European societies than in others.
Market conditions have changed considerably: there is now a bona fide market in most countries of the region, albeit incomplete in most. The media's
ideology has also evolved: from being heavily dependent on, to being parallel with, to being relatively independent of political parties, although with
varying degrees of overt political partisanship. And finally, neither most journalists nor media elites throughout the region have developed any concerted
interest in changing the principles or practices of their profession.

At first glance, it appears that the Eastern European media and their journalism were carried away by the flood that ensued when the nearly perfect
Communist dam built to restrict freedoms was demolished. Their new role
lacked definition and was tinged by pre-Communist and Communist legacies, ties to political parties, and individual political biases among the media elite and the rank-and-file journalists.[110]

More than any other factors, the polarization of the media into supporters and opponents of the new governments, and the perception that other societal institutions were not up to par in dealing with the problems engendered by the transition and transformation phases, severely impacted the
media's role. It led the media as an institution to define their role in the transition and transformation phases in ways that were significantly at odds with
the role of the media in Western democracies vis-à-vis supplying information and explanations about events, people, and issues and the well-
grounded analysis and commentaries necessary to carry out a public debate
over the issues of the day. Yet, ironically, playing this role contributed to the
transition and transformation (see chapter 5); furthermore, there is some validity to the claim by the region's "opposition" journalists that they "keep
an eye on government."[111] The Eastern European news media became vehicles for political battles between political parties and politicians, themselves trying to find definition and to win or retain power, which suggests
that the roles of the media and journalism were defined by forces outside
the institution and the profession. However, judging from media ownership
in the immediate post-Communist period, as well as from the corps of journalists and their experience, training, and professional culture, or lack of
same, a case can also be made that media partisanship and politicization
were actually functions of the media's endogenous definition of their roles
and journalistic practices.

That the underground and foreign media and their journalism had a significant effect on overthrowing Communism, the ebullient welcome given the liberated indigenous media, and the voracious appetite of their audiences in the first months of post-Communism engendered a certain haughtiness, arrogance, and overblown self-estimation on the part of media elite and rank and file alike. These attitudes quickly translated into the notion that they were the "movers and shakers" in the new post-Communist societies, that they stood above society, observing and directing it, filling the voids created by the absence of strong institutions and leaders capable of guiding the process of democratization. Thus most Polish journalists, while recognizing they had a function to inform, criticize, and "monitor," also felt throughout the 1990s they had to expose "dark matters" and to "intervene," with intervention taking precedence over exposure.[112]

The "civic attitude" inherited from the [Communist era now leads] editors and journalists to do their utmost to promote the cause of their own political camp and its version of reality, rather than to inform objectively and provide a cool and dispassionate analysis of the situation (such an attitude was wholly out of the question). As a result, the Polish press market has become dominated by politically affiliated journalism masquerading as objective. That was particularly obvious during election campaigns.[113]

This mentality, universal throughout Eastern European journalism, speaks to the regional similarities in the post-1989 political, social, cultural, and professional situations, although it is more overtly and clearly articulated in Romania than elsewhere. In 1995, Alina Mungiu, a leading analyst and commentator and the Romanian Television's news director from 1997 to 1999, characterized the Romanian news media's role as follows:

The mass media [were] more in 1990 and less so subsequently but persistently in our days, a substitute for all the absent structures in Romanian society: a substitute of power, and of opposition [to it], a substitute for a political class which has only recently and incompletely been educated, a substitute for justice [system] often weak and inefficient, and for some hesitant investigative organs.[114]

From an outsider's perspective, only a superficial case can be made for the media's playing a "substitute" role in any Eastern European country.

First of all, the news media became highly heterogeneous, as did their audiences. Instead of transforming into mass media, save perhaps for their national television stations, the post-Communist Eastern European news media became very specialized, focusing on relatively small groups of readers, listeners, and viewers.[115] Each media outlet espoused the views of a particular political party, politician, or ideology to a self-selecting audience, at least initially seeking reinforcement, reassurance for their views, and ready-made answers to pressing problems. Parties and politicians owning the media outlets, state and government control over national public television, and then, the parallelism between political parties and the media ensured that the media would start the post-Communist era in the specialized stage. In any case, an argument can be made that if a "substitute" role is to be effectively carried out, the media must be mass media before anything else: they must reach large numbers of people, instead of addressing relatively small, isolated segments of the audience with "news reports," analysis, and commentaries from a distinct political perspective. Yet only since 1995 have individual media outlets taken the first, tentative steps toward becoming mass news media, experimenting with less partisan news content aimed at attracting audiences who had known nothing but partisanship. The major impetus for these steps appears to have been predominantly economic, rather than a socially conscious reformulation of media roles and journalistic professionalism, although, in all fairness to certain journalists, such steps may also represent the beginnings of professionalization.

Second, the news media can play an effective "substitute" role only when they have high credibility (and in 1990–2000, save perhaps for the media in the Czech Republic, they did not) and only when they and their audiences have "different news values" (and there are no data to substantiate such a claim).[116] Indeed, there is no evidence to suggest that their audiences had any news values at all, even though they keep searching for something, perhaps reliability and credibility, judging from the high turnover in newspapers coming onto and going off of the market. Such a persistently elevated turnover during the 1990s suggests that audiences were searching for a different type of print journalism than the one being practiced.

Additionally, the suggested "substitute" role implies that the media, their elite journalists, and journalism are serving as reformers in the transformation period. Yet there is no evidence that this is so, nor should we expect it to be.[117] As Walter Lippmann rightly argued in 1922, "the press is no substitute for institutions."[118] Furthermore, the "substitute" view of the media's role suggests that the media are "more powerful, more independent, and more determined to pursue their own interests through a professional culture of their own making" than is clearly the case; nor is there any indication of their taking on "political functions formerly performed by party and party-controlled media, such as political socialization and providing information to the public about politics and government."[119]

That the Eastern European media did not, indeed very likely could not, perform that role in the 1990s is neither entirely their fault nor the fault of other institutions influencing or even controlling them. For the media to take on this more powerful, influential role, which goes beyond reinforcing to shaping and leading public opinion, two things would have to happen. First, the intrinsic importance of public opinion in the region's societies would have to be heightened for politicians, elected and appointed officials, and political cultures in general.[120] If and when that happened, "the roles of the traditional political intermediaries—the parties, the mass media experts, and the governing elite—[would] decline," with information, a variety of opinions necessary for a public debate, and media outlets that can supply such fare becoming more important.[121] Second, the nature of citizenship in the region's societies would have to be redefined in both theory and practice (see chapter 5).

In the context of a government versus opposition mentality, there is another suggested media role, that of a counterpower. Yet, as Jean-François Revel is quick to point out,

> the press has no business claiming to be a counterpower [automatically] and in every circumstance. Besides, the very notion is absurd, for if things really happened in this way, and if the government in power invariably deserved to be opposed, it would be sufficient reason to despair of democracy, for it would mean that a democratically elected government is always mistaken, and therefore that the people electing it are afflicted with a congenital, incurable idiocy.[122]

Furthermore, the vision of the news media as a substitute or "counterpower" is far removed from the notion of an adversarial role for the media, at least as (ideally) defined in the United States. The adversarial role adopted in Eastern Europe is generally politically partisan rather than independent, although there were signs some degree of political independence had selectively crept into journalistic practices as the 1990s came to a close. As I will show in chapters 5 and 6, a political adversarial role for the media is not wholly negative in the context of the liberalization of the unconsolidated democracies of the region. Indeed, an adversarial role that is political without being partisan to a party or a politician can arise the moment the news media elite as well as the rank and file change their attitude toward public and political authority from one of "opponent" versus "supporter" to one of impartial skepticism. On the other hand, it has been argued that the media cannot be truly adversarial because they rely on what Gaye Tuchman calls "the news net" and on official acknowledgments of what the journalists have discovered:

> Challenging the legitimacy of offices holding centralized information dismantles the news net. If all of officialdom is corrupt, all its facts and occurrences must be viewed as alleged facts and alleged occurrences. Accordingly, to fill the news columns and airtime . . . news organizations would have to find an alternative and economical method of locating occurrences and constituent facts acceptable as news.[123]

In Eastern Europe there are two parallel realities in regard to this "news net." One reality is that there is no "news net" per se. Access to information, more in some of the region's countries and less in others, is curtailed by bureaucratic and political mentalities that are legacies of the past (see chapter 3), although, particularly in reporting on politics, journalists focus on the political leadership, what they do and say and their disputes.[124] The other reality is that journalists do, of course, depend on sources within the same institutions they often attack. Political infighting, personal squabbling, and jockeying for position, and, in isolated cases, genuine revulsion over the excessive politicization of policy making, corruption, nepotism, and the like make for good sources, who are not going to disappear regardless of how much the media attack the institution that employs these individuals. There is even the practice, considered wholly unprofessional in American journalism, of having sources "authorize" articles written about them, that is, vet articles prior to publication.[125] A more Western or even American adversarial role for the media would be much easier to adopt in Eastern Europe if access to information laws, open meeting laws, and something akin to the U.S. Freedom of Information Act were in place and enforced there (see chapter 3), and of course if Eastern European journalists had the needed reporting skills and investigative skills, as well as the inclination to consistently use them.

But the biggest problem remains the interpretation of what "adversarial" means. Most Eastern European journalists or news media take an adversarial stance vis-à-vis a politician, political party, or government if and when they are in political agreement with, or even represent, another political party or politician. Hence the vehement attacks on the media on the part of politicians and officials during the first eleven post-Communist years (see chapter 3). A rancorous adversarial relationship also develops when politicians, parties, and government officials do not cooperate with the media they consider to be "on the other side."[126] In theory, this undermines the media's legitimacy and thus the very institution they perceive as essential to their political survival.[127] By way of contrast, in the United States the media and public officials deliberately "strike a careful balance between surface conflict and . . . consensus" on underlying values.[128]

For the second half of the 1990s, one can argue that the slow professionalization of the media and its adoption of a less partisan (though still highly politicized) approach to news reporting have done away with the one consensus on values that might have been present in the first few post-Communist years. Indeed, it is this absence both of a consensus on journalistic values, roles, and standards and of fact-based, complete, accurate, verifiable, sourced reporting in a meaningful context that has blocked the establishment of a true Fourth Estate, essential to the checks and balances needed in a democracy. The criticism that whatever Fourth Estate exists is the progeny of commercial media seeking only to enhance the political and occupational status of their journalists and to legitimize opposition to state control may be no more justified in Eastern Europe than it is in the West.[129] For one thing, opposition to state control of the media in Eastern Europe is a direct outgrowth of more than forty years of Communist state and party control; there is no need for a Fourth Estate to legitimize such opposition. For another, the political status of journalists is very high, even if their occupational status may have fallen in the transformation period.[130]

Whether there will be a true Fourth Estate in Eastern Europe thus largely depends on the adoption of a principled adversarial stance favoring fact-based over polemical journalism and presenting audiences with varied commentaries and analysis. Such a stance would take on the political elite, societal institutions, and policies on behalf of society and its citizens.

Some progress is discernible. Thanks to the changes occurring in the second half of the 1990s, the region's post-Communist media are no the longer the lapdogs of political parties or politicians, although, because of their dependence on the power structure for access and their limited legitimization, they are not yet guard dogs either. Nevertheless, their input into, and at least indirect veto power over, the media laws being passed, on the one hand, and the uneven, incomplete, and not always effective control over access exercised by the powers that be, on the other, have heightened their guard dog-like attributes.[131] At the risk of belaboring the canine metaphor, for reasons already discussed, the Eastern European media might be better characterized as attack dogs on their way to becoming guard dogs. Thus, in the post-Mečiar Slovak Republic, the media "are actively participating in the public discourse without being pro- or anti-opposition."[132] In Poland, *Gazeta Wyborcza*'s credibility rests on its political independence. The newspaper works for a "democratic Poland" and has no intention of working for Solidarity union bosses "or for any other political party."[133] But the media in Poland and elsewhere in the region still have a way to go in performing their guard dog function.[134] In the Czech Republic, TV Nova, which is not beholden to any political party, tackles governmental corruption, legal injustice, and financial wrongdoing, "but usually does not rise above a simplistic style that avoids deeper investigations of the country's problems."[135]

One notable, extreme exception is Albania, where the partisanship of the media outlets and journalists makes most of them willing participants in the manipulation or control exercised by their respective party bosses.[136] Until recently, Romania was yet another exception. The Romanian media began to change during the long-awaited "real" democratization period that began with the defeat of President Ion Iliescu and the election of Emil Constantinescu in 1996. The "press of opposition," as so many media outlets labeled themselves before November 1996, changed almost overnight into the "press of transition." By mid-1998, the Romanian media gave the impression they were slowly (though perhaps unwittingly) beginning to define an independent role for themselves, a pattern developing in the other Eastern European nations to a greater or lesser extent.

Media roles are defined by their importance not only to public opinion formation but also to agenda setting. The situation in Bulgaria is typical for the rest of the region:

> Instead of showing us what is going on around us, journalism is trying to tell us what to think. . . . In general, the possession of competence is not considered a necessary condition which will then allow [us] to make commentaries. . . . Instead of serving the reader, journalism places itself above the reader.[137]

A more salutary view, at least ideally, looks at agenda setting from a bottom-up rather than a top-down perspective, one that requires audiences to play a more active role and the media to focus more on gathering and disseminating information and less on "interpreting" it—providing balanced instead of biased analysis.[138] Some of the problems intrinsic to this view will be examined in chapter 5; suffice it to say here that the bottom-up view recognizes that public opinion formation and agenda setting are also affected by personal experience, interpersonal communication, and real-world indicators of the importance of an issue or event, that is, variables that measure "more or less objectively the degree of severity or risk of social problems."[139] In a democracy, the media's agenda is to combine, and interrelate, with the public's agenda (what the public wants, what it perceives and thinks) and with the policy agenda (what is being proposed and carried out by those in power, or what is being proposed by those who wish to be in power) to form society's agenda.

Indeed, social change and social stability can be productively studied by examining agenda setting in a society.[140] Since 1989, the Eastern European media's agenda-setting goals have been predominantly political and have combined far more with the policy agenda than with the public's agenda. Importantly, the media's symbiotic relationship with the political and economic elite began to change by the mid-1990s, with audiences becoming more and more selective of the news and information they read, viewed, or listened to, and with media outlets exploring more effective ways to be "marketable."

The top-down approach to agenda setting in the post-Communist era may well represent a continuation from the Communist era. During the Communist years, the power of the media was an article of faith in the extant political culture of the Communist apparat. It remained so after 1989; indeed, it was strengthened by the proven contributions of the underground, alternative, and foreign media to overthrowing Communism.

The three primary media functions identified by Harold Lasswell—surveillance of their immediate and distant environment, correlation of all elements of a society with society as a whole, and the transmission of society's cultural heritage—become crucial in times of sociopolitical turmoil, particularly of the extreme kind experienced by Eastern Europe since 1989–90.[141] It stands to reason that, under such circumstances, the media should play an even more central role in the ability of society to gather, explain, analyze, and act on all relevant information.[142] But during the transformation of Eastern European nations, the media need to play still other roles: they need to serve as resocializers, as champions of a democratic political culture, and, to that end, as teachers and mobilizers (in the larger sense of the word), and not simply as guard dogs and disseminators of information. Although they do play some of these roles, they do not always play them directly and purposefully in the service of democratization.[143]

Some analysts view news as culture, a culture that creates and conveys a hegemonic ideology.[144] Such a view suggests that the mission of the media is to defend or oppose the status quo.[145] That was not the case in the first eleven post-Communist years in Eastern Europe, where there was no status quo to defend or oppose. In another version of this top-down view of news, reality belongs to those who have the power to interpret it and to communicate their interpretations.[146] In either version, the top-down view has no room for a professionalism intrinsic to journalism and developed by the media institution. A different view, however, one that encourages such professionalism, is slowly and selectively taking root in the region among media leaders and rank and file alike. One such leader is *Gazeta Wyborcza*'s Michnik, whose ten commandments of good journalism have borne fruit by bringing respect and credibility to his newspaper.[147] Michnik is not alone. In 1998, Ivan Kytka, newly appointed head of the Czech Television news and current affairs department, insisted on factual, accurate, independent reporting and an end to the department's sycophancy toward government.[148] Only when Eastern Europeans, as citizens, members of the elites, and journalists, clearly define the roles they wish the media and journalism to play in their societies will the media come of age and serve the larger interests of those societies.

Journalism

Some would argue that journalism is a craft, an art, a trade, but not a profession. Yet the issue of "professionalism" is at the core of most contemporary criticisms of American journalism, a point of debate in Western Europe, and the focus of how Eastern European journalism is evolving.[149]

A survey of journalists on both sides of the Atlantic yielded conclusions that encapsulate the main distinctions in definitions of "professionalism" between U.S. and European journalists, distinctions that are becoming blurred as U.S. journalism increasingly takes on a European flavor. Nevertheless,

Although [U.S. journalists] like political influence, they do not pursue this goal by championing their subjective values and beliefs—as do their German and Italian colleagues—but by digging out relevant information through their own research. Most journalists in the United States will uphold norms of objectivity, fairness and neutrality.[150]

"Objectivity "as a journalistic concept is now being questioned on both sides of the Atlantic, however.[151] The charge that news has became a corporate commodity—neutral, factual, routinized, even formulaic—reverberates throughout the United States, most particularly in the universities. Ultimately, it is argued, the "constraints of organizational routines and pressures" and the quest for "objectivity," the very core of professionalism, have combined to produce news stories that are "negative, detached, technical, and official."[152] According to this argument,

1. including both sides of the story in a news article heightens the appearance of conflict;[153]
2. dependence on official or "expert" sources emphasizes the official perspective;[154]
3. verifiable information and "facts" in great measure also depend on those official sources;[155]
4. fairness is not an issue when the news is the result of a tug-of-war between different powers;[156] and
5. leaving out personal or editorial opinion does away with the role of journalists as cultural storytellers.[157]

Furthermore, it is argued that journalistic detachment can be a "crutch for avoiding responsibility."[158] U.S. journalism, more so perhaps than its Western European counterpart, focuses on the isolated event, the particular episode that is new, bad, dramatic, available, and easily understood, without addressing the larger context and continuity.[159] Notwithstanding their heightened sense and practice of professionalism, U.S. journalists have been driven by economic necessities to blend professional ideals with entertainment-oriented approaches to attract ever larger audiences and thus to sensationalize.[160]

Eastern European journalism of the 1989–2000 period also suffered to some degree from the sensationalistic and entertainment-oriented approach associated with the economic exigencies of the media business. However, when it focused on the larger context of a story and its continuity, such focus was more often than not related to a political or ideological goal, although it unwittingly incorporated most if not all of the "corrective" measures suggested by critics of U.S. journalism's concepts of professionalism and objectivity. More significantly, it has suffered from the absence of even rudimentary aspects of professionalism.

In Poland, the quality of journalism was generally low, with "frequent factual mistakes, such as misquoting sources or omitting important data. Usually only one-sided stories [were] published—either for or against"; reportage was "fundamentally deficient in terms of its comprehensiveness, objectivity, and professionalism."[161] A new journalistic style emerged, which Goban-Klas calls "rap" journalism: "a style of writing and interviewing that begins with a definite political standpoint and an aggressive stance."[162] Not to be outdone, the Czech press at the tail end of the first post-1989 decade was at least as biased.[163] In Romania, journalists manipulated the news through their selection and presentation of news and information, and by not covering certain issues, events, people, and institutions. Journalism, particularly political journalism, became a sort of "Don Juanism" in the service of politics and political parties, themselves engaged in seducing voters to attain and retain power.[164]

In Hungary, in the early 1990s journalists felt that "giving the news in itself" was "not enough." They felt they had "to act . . . to speak out . . . to unveil the bad guys. And independently of a journalist's political leanings, the result [was] to damage impartiality."[165] Hungary's news media and journalists continue to resist adopting Western European or U.S. journalistic standards and reporting approaches. Either they rely on official sources, are unreliable, or, as Goban-Klas found in Poland, "they criticize everyone and everything."[166] The Czech and Slovak media, while thoroughly reporting official actions and statements, have been remiss in reporting the findings of their own research and news gathering.[167] The Romanian media appear to be in a permanent "electoral campaign" mode, resulting in a plethora of partisan opinion pieces and a dearth of articles that simply inform.[168] Journalism in all of the region's countries is likely to resemble the Slovak case for years to come, lacking balance and objectivity and remaining partisan.[169]

In addition to committing the journalistic "sins" already discussed. Eastern European journalists have responded to waves of corruption, crime, and crisis with tabloidlike, yellow journalism and, like their Polish colleagues in the early post-Communist years, with "pandering to low instincts and prurient tastes."[170] Altogether, the region's journalism remains a dubious blend of advocacy reporting, reporting of rumor in the guise of "news," and objective, fact-based reporting.

In its most positive characterization, Eastern European journalism has adopted a Zola-like stance of social responsibility, with journalists serving as "analysts" of events, people, ideas, and so on, from a normative or ideological perspective, their own or one assigned to them. The sociopolitical, cultural, and, mostly, political or ideological goals of the media, their elite, and their journalists, and their interpretation of "social responsibility" have been deciding factors in what is and what is not "news," what facts are chosen for presentation, and the "spin" put on them. And herein lies the basic problem for journalism in Eastern Europe, and one increasingly shared by U.S. journalism. As Harvard Professor Thomas Patterson warns, when journalism adopts an analytic rather than descriptive style, particularly one with a foreordained goal, "the story line gets assembled first," and then the facts are gathered. "That kind of journalism is a swamp in a way that the older [descriptive] style wasn't."[171]

The Zola-like stance combines "a didactic journalistic norm, leadership and guardianship/stewardship roles vis-à-vis the audience, a special form of the social responsibility paradigm, [and] a critical/dialectical role in society, assigning to the audience mostly the roles of 'pupils,' citizens, partisans and followers," with the result that, across Eastern Europe, debates on salient international and national issues are "generally emotion—rather than fact-based."[172] What is worse, the region's journalism resorts to "outright disinformation . . . manipulation and the triumphalist and anesthetic effect."[173] Eastern European television in the mid-1990s was actively inimical to the region's evolution, "encouraging political passivity and cynicism."[174] The shortcomings of Czech Television's newscasts in 1998, shared by public television newscasts in other Eastern European nations as the decade came to a close, included

1. overdependence on the national news agency;
2. reporting that was "passive, unimaginative and without independent critical thought";
3. "too many news items in the news bulletins," making each "excessively short and superficial";
4. "news reports and interviews [that were] often badly structured" and that lacked "proper professional research backup . . . to explain issues clearly and cogently"; and
5. emulation of Communist-era approaches to newscasts: "Czech TV often feels that it first has to show on main evening news that Parliament and the Government [are] in session. Only after these initial, perfunctory reports is space made for what should be the main items of the day."[175]

Such shortcomings go well beyond the documented notion that news "is produced by people who operate, often unwittingly, within a cultural system, a reservoir of stored cultural meaning."[176]

Furthermore, the absence of a status quo is testimony to the radical transition if not transformation of the region's political structures. It thus makes little sense to argue that "radical change of the media's role and function is unlikely because the existing political [structures have] not been sufficiently transformed."[177] As regards the role of the free market, it seems reasonable to subscribe to the thesis that "if market forces can both expand and diminish the democratic possibilities of the media, the same can be said for the professional norms and practices of journalists."[178] The claim that media outlets owned or co-owned by Westerners have brought a Westernized (more professional) journalism to their audiences is not supportable.[179] Despite the evident change in the "packaging" of the news reports, there simply is no evidence that the operative political and professional cultures of Western journalism hold sway. Commercial journalism, purportedly practiced by the Eastern European media outlets owned or co-owned by Westerners, has not markedly improved the professionalism of journalists in those outlets, let alone others in the region, not because commercial journalism is driven by market forces rather than by traditional journalistic practices, as is argued in a number of works in the past twenty-five years, but because traditional Eastern European journalistic practices hold sway in the commercial and noncommercial media alike.[180]

Professionalizing and developing a professional culture have proven to increase the independence of journalists, and to lead to the adoption of universal professional values and standards in journalism.[181] The view that professionalization, with its impartial, objective journalism, can only be brought about by the establishment of powerful commercial media conglomerates, which demand such impartiality "to serve a diverse audience, and the desire not to offend any significant section through the adoption of a partisan stance," is at once too one-sided, too cynical, and too likely to be politically motivated.[182]

Eastern European journalism lacks the very essence of good journalism: reliable information from which audiences can reach valid conclusions, whether helped or not by the overabundance of opinions and political stances that to date are the jumping-off point for gathering, constructing, and disseminating what passes for news in the region. Good journalism is about gathering and disseminating complete, unbiased, balanced, well-sourced, verified, and accurate information to an audience. It is about explaining this information in a context that is both reality-based and socially responsible, without the spin and bias associated with a political or ideological goal and other personal interests that amount to propaganda or advocacy communication.[183] The ideal of providing such information and of being fair and impartial in one's reporting is not yet recognized by most Eastern European journalists or by the media elite. At the core of good journalism is professionalism, as defined by journalistic objectivity, by no means a perfect criterion, yet an altogether serviceable one. Indeed, rejecting the validity of journalistic objectivity "is too often a refuge for mental laziness . . . mere trickery," or outright dishonesty and political demagoguery.[184] Professionalism requires a common education and training program, a degree of standardization in news gathering and the presentation of information, without being formulaic, and ways to review the quality of what is produced.[185] Professionalism also requires a constant search for ways to improve the practice of journalism.

Notwithstanding the region's legacies and limitations, by the end of the 1990s it became clear that some good journalism, particularly in economic and investigative reporting, was being practiced there by a handful of journalists working for a select few media outlets. A less partisan journalism has also proved possible and is being tentatively and selectively practiced, as dramatically shown by the private media's coverage of the 1996 local, parliamentary, and presidential elections throughout the region.[186]

Thus an endogenous definition of journalistic roles and practices is possible in the Eastern European media, whether market-oriented or not, one led by those members of the media elite and rank and file with a passion for professionalization. Furthermore, a quick review of national newspapers reveals a dramatic increase in the range of topics covered as the twentieth century came to a close, with regular sections on topics such as society, politics, agriculture, industry, the economy, business, culture, science and technology, health and medical news, foreign news, and even the media, and an attendant increase in the number and quality of voices through which information and views are disseminated.

Eastern Europe's journalism has been and very likely will continue to be slow to evolve. Nevertheless, in Hungary as elsewhere in the region, "the formation of an objective, less ideological press shows promise, but only in the long run."[187]

5

The Media, Civil Society,
Political Democracy, and the Market

Wherever they were successfully established in Eastern Europe, the underground or alternative media played a crucial role before 1989 in facilitating a non-Communist public sphere.[1] These media were part of a larger, indigenous non-Communist communication system that included book publishing, magazines, newspapers, newsletters, radio, and the exchange of audio and video cassettes. The public sphere they represented was, admittedly, a limited one because only a few citizens (except in the Solidarity movement in Poland) gathered "as public bodies" to "discuss the issues of the day, specifically those of political concern."[2] These issues predominantly if not exclusively centered on dissent, opposition to or removal of the Communist authority. The underground or alternative media exemplified, helped create, and supported a limited degree of collective social life and involvement in public affairs outside the Communist system, the extent of this involvement varying from one country to another. These media provided information, views and opinions, and entertainment not readily available from the state- or party-controlled media, serving as alternative or oppositional outlets for public communication; their roles extended from combating Communism to establishing a non-Communist public world, the "second society" described by Elemer Hankiss.[3] Altogether, in the years leading up to 1989, the underground and alternative media helped liberalize the Communist system, that is, to expand the possibilities for political opposition and competition for some modicum of nongovernmental, non-Communist, sociopolitical power.

While independent of the state and the Communist party, these media were not autonomous, but were instead attached to, or elements of, movements specifically created as sociopolitical and cultural counterparts to

124

Communism and the institutions that represented, defined, and protected it. They were not expressions of civil society per se, given their somewhat restricted roles and the equally limited definitions of "civil society" as an almost exclusively anti-Communist movement.[4] Unwittingly perhaps, Jakubowicz illustrates this point when he argues that the underground media and samizdat were a "mainstay" of civil society. He defines this civil society in oppositional terms, and characterizes it as amounting to an incipient independent public sphere. Describing the underground media as vehicles of information and communication, he adds that "they performed an . . . organizational function [beyond] the development of distribution networks . . . because they could guide the work of underground organizations and mobilize the general public to oppose the authorities and their policies."[5]

These media sought to create "a 'civilized' society that would prepare people to act apart from communist rules by giving them alternative ideas and publicizing the failings of the system."[6] Yet, in many ways, the "civilized" non-Communist public sphere and its media were as limited as those they were meant to counter. Like their Communist counterparts, they were far from being democratically oriented.[7] Rather, with the alternative and underground media mirroring and facilitating it, the non-Communist public sphere appears to have taken on a more modest role as a limited avenue of polemics, information, and communication for a small (Czechoslovakia) or larger (Hungary and Poland) community of disparate elements with anti-Communist goals or with other sociocultural needs that could not be met by the Communist system.

Where no alternate media existed (Albania, Bulgaria, and Romania), and where there were no organized non-Communist associations and social movements, there is little justification to argue that a non-Communist public sphere even existed. What did exist were private or intimate spheres.[8]

Embedded in these pre-1989, alternative and underground media was an element of direct or participatory media democracy, an element that appears to be present, perhaps exclusively, during revolutions and opposition to authoritarianism or totalitarianism. In Eastern Europe, it comprised "professionals," that is, journalists who worked for the Communist-controlled media, but whose sympathies were with the anti-Communist groups, and citizen volunteers, predominantly but not exclusively intellectuals, motivated by anti-Communism or by the opportunity to exercise a self-granted intellectual freedom and thus to enlarge their private sphere of activity. This element of direct or participatory media democracy was confined to a relatively few people with limited political and sociocultural goals.

Eastern European revolutions, concluded some scholars, "emerged on the border between the economy and the state and were motivated neither by profit nor by power maximization but rather by moral efforts to re-create a public sphere based on democratic ideals."[9] Yet it was precisely the lack of political power and influence and the chance for public involvement free of the Communist straitjacket that motivated individuals to organize in non-Communist or anti-Communist voluntary associations and media and to disseminate messages consonant with them. *Pace* Michnik, not all of these non-Communist or anti-Communist individuals, associations, organizations, and media outlets shared the same democratic ideals, if indeed they shared any (see chapters 1 and 2).[10] This is clearly demonstrated by the post-1989 breakup of the anti-Communist coalitions, by the wide diversity of post-Communist political parties, and by the equally wide diversity of new media outlets. While the old anti-Communist or non-Communist opposition certainly included individuals and groups sharing democratic ideals, it also included a mélange of those whose ideals were different and whose politics and ideology found a home in new, less than liberal democratic post-Communist political parties. Or they found a home in relaunched traditional parties, some of which constituted the "resurgence of neoromantic, populist, anti-modern forces in the region."[11] What united the non-Communist "civil society" and "public sphere" was a collective definition of what they were against. This negative unity led to revolutions that were essentially ones of "rejection" in 1989.[12] The revolutionaries showed themselves seldom capable of agreeing on or even articulating what they stood for in a post-1989 world.[13]

Not surprisingly, there is disagreement as to how democracy and civil society (see chapter 1) are to be defined and what their status was in the first post-Communist decade in Eastern Europe. Furthermore, there is disagreement over whether civil society is necessary for the transformation to democracy. Some observers see the Eastern European experience as negating any universal conclusions about the need for civil society in democratization.[14] Others see it as proof of such a need, whereas still others argue that "the phenomenon we called 'civil society' was not one meant to transform systems."[15] The third position finds some support in that civil societies created after the establishment of the state "were and are in trouble," with their "citizens [having] to borrow power from those whom they want to keep in check."[16] To make this "borrowing" possible, liberalization has to be accompanied by the establishment of crucial elements: a "democratic order," a democratic political culture, and competition, citizen participation, and civil and political liberties.[17] Finally, there are some who argue that even the presence of a high degree of social activity and of a developed civil society may not, in itself, lead to democracy.[18] The reason it may not—of particular relevance to Eastern Europe—is that "the 'we' claiming sovereignty in democratic rule" comprises "different organized interests," whose "interrelation . . . may be such as to undermine and even destroy democracy."[19]

Eastern European democracies fit one or more of several democratic models that share common attitudes, tinged by a lingering Communist mentality. C. B. Macpherson discerns three democratic models: (1) the protective, (2) the developmental, and (3) the equilibrium models.[20] The first two models parallel to some degree the "frozen" or restricted and the unconsolidated forms of democracy, such as are found in Latin America and in Africa.[21] The third model better describes the balance and evolution of the two dimensions of democratization identified by Robert Dahl: liberalization and participation.[22] Where liberalization is in ascendance, we have a political democracy; where participation is, we have a more advanced, autonomous democracy, as described by David Held.[23] A clearer transition model, based on Dankwart Rustow's work and with the requisite "background condition" of national unity, has society moving through three phases:

1. the preparatory phase, in which there is a breakdown of the nondemocratic regime;
2. the decision phase, in which a democratic order is first established; and
3. the consolidation phase, in which democracy is further developed and becomes ingrained in the political culture.[24]

During the third phase, the values, attitudes, behaviors, and mentalities of a society transform themselves into those consonant with a functioning democracy. This last, democracy consolidation phase is defined by Juan Linz as

one in which none of the major political actors, parties, or organized interests, forces, or institutions consider that there is any alternative to democratic processes to gain power, and that no political institution or group has a claim to veto the action of democratically elected decision makers. This does not mean that there are no minorities ready to challenge and question the legitimacy of the democratic process by nondemocratic means. It means, however, that the major actors do not turn to them and they remain politically isolated. To put it simply, democracy must be seen as the "only game in town."[25]

In the Eastern Europe of the 1990s, regardless of how each country's evolution might be characterized, democracy fits an unconsolidated, developmental model, one in the decision phase, to use Rustow's schema. In some countries, democracy was seemingly "frozen" or restricted, a condition in which economic changes have serious political consequences, such as the delegitimation of political parties and political actors and even of democracy itself, and lead to social dislocation. Even though Dahl's eight conditions for polyarchy—covering the main provisions of political democracy (competition, a modicum of citizen participation, and civil and political liberties)—had been met, it is clear that not all conditions favorable to the evolution of a stable polyarchy were present in the 1990s.[26] Thus by 2000, (1) a modern, dynamic, organizationally pluralist society did not exist in any of the nations under discussion here; (2) a political culture and a system of beliefs favorable to the idea of democracy and the institutions of polyarchy were not firmly entrenched among either common citizens or politicians; and (3) the nature and effects of foreign influence or control were not always clear.

Because the social values consonant with a democracy are not ingrained in the political culture of Eastern Europe, citizenship is defined in a limited way, one that seemingly detracts from robust participation in voluntary social, civic, and political groups. What is certainly missing is direct citizen participation in "the diagnosing of collective, problem-situations and the proposing of policies to meet them."[27] This yet-to-be secured democracy-supporting political culture is additionally hampered in its evolution by the profound socioeconomic changes or crises experienced by these societies. Stated another way, socioeconomic dislocations, material poverty, and the daily struggle for economic survival make the teaching, learning, application, and practice of democracy-oriented attitudes, behaviors, and values difficult, if not impossible. Admittedly, this is far truer in some Eastern European countries than in others. In short, most citizens in the region participate by giving or withholding their consent to those whom they have elected to govern: "a decisive but negative role—'decisive' because their decision is necessary before [political] action(s) can be performed; 'negative' because they merely respond to initiatives put to them by someone else."[28]

Which type of democratic government should be operative in Eastern

Europe and elsewhere—government by consent or government by the active and continuous participation of citizens? Both are strands of liberal democratic theory, yet each contributes to a different definition and role of civil society, of the public sphere, and of the media and their function and nature.

This chapter intends neither to define what democracy or civil society should be in Eastern Europe nor to characterize the strengths and weaknesses of either. Its intent is rather to examine whether the media and their journalists and journalism, as described in previous chapters, served and represented the region's unconsolidated, political democracy with its limited civil society and public sphere throughout the 1990s, whether they can facilitate or catalyze the establishment or evolution of civil society, and, indeed, whether they *are* civil society in Eastern Europe's transition and transformation phases.

Theoretical Expectations for Eastern Europe's Post-1989 Media

As we have seen in chapters 3 and 4, Eastern Europe's post-1989 media systems comprised the former Communist media outlets, put on a non-Communist footing; the underground or alternative media outlets transformed into the "mainstream" media, and the new media outlets, both indigenously and foreign-owned or -co-owned. These media, at least in theory, were to be the most conspicuous of civil society's institutions and the principal institutions of the public sphere.[29] As such, they were to play an effective, proactive role in democratization by helping to socialize and educate the public in and for new roles and social values in an open society. The conflict over their specific role in democratization centered on the conflict between Lippmann's view of the media as "manufacturers of consent" and Dewey's view of the media as empowerers of the public, chiefly by disseminating the exchange of opinions between citizens.[30]

In the eyes of most media scholars, the Eastern European media were to be outgrowths of civil society and not of the state or the new political forces, or of the newly established market.[31] They were to be this despite the transition pattern already noted: systemic liberalization and the establishment of a political democracy and a quasi-market economy, and even though privatization proceeded faster in some countries than in others. All media, or at the very least some of them, were to constitute civil society's "own communication system" in order to make civil society "less vulnerable than it is now."[32] In the most utopian and esoteric "differentiation" formulation, as already pointed out in chapter 1, the media were to separate themselves not only from governments, political parties, and markets, but also from "classes, regions, and religious groups."[33] Furthermore, in what is termed the "radical theory," the media were to come under "popular" control by democratizing themselves.[34]

In summary, the media of Eastern Europe were to be transformed after 1989, moving from state control, in whole or part, as in the former Czecho-slovakia, Hungary, and Poland, to full autonomy, indeed, becoming more ideal and advanced than any found even in long-established Western democracies. Or, at the very least, they were to embark on a road leading there. The same was expected to occur in Albania, Bulgaria, and Romania, countries lacking even the most rudimentary form of what was loosely labeled "civil society," the beginnings of a public sphere, and underground or alternative media.

Without a doubt, the idealistic expectations of how the media were to change and the nature of their new roles and journalism were in no way met in the first post-1989 decade. Nor could they have been. First of all, these expectations were largely based on the mistaken assumption that the liberalization phase begun in 1989 or shortly before had ended shortly after and that most of the region's societies had entered the "consolidation" phase of democratization. The problem lay not with the idealistic striving to improve society, institutions, sociopolitical, and economic conditions, or professions, but with unrealistic expectations and assumptions. Milovan Djilas aptly called society "unperfect": any attempt to perfect it invariably leads to the loss of societal and individual freedoms. Indeed, those intent on analyzing post-Communism and its evolution, as well as the media's role in democratization, would do well to consider what Djilas has to say about ideals and "social reality":

> Men must hold both ideas and ideals, but they should not regard these as being wholly realizable. We need to comprehend the nature of utopianism. Utopianism, once it achieves power, becomes dogmatic, and it quite readily can create human suffering in the name and in the cause of its own scientism and idealism. To speak of society as imperfect may seem to imply that it can be perfect which in truth it cannot. The task for contemporary man is to accept the reality that society is unperfect, but also to understand that humanist, humanitarian dreams and visions are necessary in order to reform society, in order to improve and advance it.[35]

What is still not available is a realistic, practical, universally agreed on explanation of how the transformation to democracy-serving media is to happen, and what their contribution should and can be to the transformation of societies having

1. no professional journalistic standards nor the means and interest to enforce them, and no shared professional culture;
2. no or scant economic means to help the media's evolution;
3. no democracy-oriented political culture prescribing a consonant use and role for the media and their journalism; and, finally,
4. only the rudimentary prerequisites of political democracy.

In part, the absence of a universally acceptable explanation is a function of the sudden beginnings of the region's transition and transformation and the uniqueness of its Communist past. It is also a function of disagreements among scholars, politicians, and members of the media regarding the theoretical and practical definitions of "democracy," "civil society," and the "public sphere." The three main theoretical and practical approaches of the first post-1989 decade were (1) the "materialist theory," which held that privatization or commercialization of the media was the sole means of democratizing Eastern European nations and empowering their civil societies; (2) the "idealist theory," which held that private and (independent) public service media needed to be empowered to establish and sustain civil society; and (3) the "standard theory," which held that the media needed to be privatized and the public service media to be controlled by the political elite.[36] Although these theories closely fit the thinking of societies emerging from Communist domination, they were roundly criticized by a small but influential group of scholars for not meeting idealistic, let alone utopian, expectations.

Whether the media are expressions or institutions of civil society depends largely on whether one views civil society and the public sphere as existing in the new Eastern Europe. It also depends on the media's nature, composition, and actual role in the transformation. First and foremost, it depends on the nature of democracy, its level of evolution or maturation in the region's nations. Civil society has grown at a faster pace in some countries than in others. In the Czech Republic, Hungary, and Poland, civil society is relatively well developed, although, according to some observers, it still lacks muscle; in Albania, Bulgaria, Romania, and the Slovak Republic, civil society is still viewed as underdeveloped and relatively weak.

Yet, even where civil society is still weak, but especially where it is stronger, it has made a significant contribution to democratization. To mention just three examples: civil society played a significant role in the outcome of the 1996 Romanian election, in ending Mečiar's authoritarian regime in the Slovak Republic in 1998, and in the evolution of Poland's democratic consolidation.[37]

The Media and Political Democracy

Eastern Europe's post-1989 media changed in much the same ways that their societies at large did. The initial, rapid expansion and wild proliferation of media outlets, ensuring varying degrees of diversity and predominantly political pluralism, occurred somewhat chaotically and independently of both states and yet-to-be developed national markets. Such changes were most pronounced in Albania, Bulgaria, and Romania and slightly less so in Czechoslovakia, Hungary, and Poland, where opposition movements, alternative media, and small, limited market economies already existed, facilitating media demonopolization and expansion, and where (Poland being the exception) the initial absence of regulation permitted the almost uncontrolled entry of foreign investment and ownership into their respective media systems.[38]

Most observers of Eastern European developments concede that the media have separated themselves from actual state control. Justifiably, they also point out that the media are still subject, to a greater or lesser extent, to the direct influence of politicians and political parties, commercial and cultural forces, their respective states and governments (through state- or government-controlled newsprint production and allocation, distribution, licensing), and other elements of society (organized religion, unions, ethnic groups, associations of intellectuals).[39] Based on these observations, it was concluded that the sociopolitical and cultural prerequisites for media autonomization do not exist; hence, as things stand, diverse, pluralist media providing access to and representing all individuals and interests in society (organized or not) cannot develop. The attempt to impose a single, idealistic model of media freedom on Eastern Europe in transition and transformation was therefore bound to fail, as were attempts to find a corresponding Western model of media freedom against which to measure the region's progress.[40] Indeed, judged to be "sometimes irrelevant" on both sides of what used to be the Iron Curtain, the media "in some instances act as forces against democratization."[41]

The central dispute over the new Eastern European media reality is whether the media can or should facilitate social change and participation in the sociopolitical life of nations in transition and transformation from Communism to democracy, when the political cultures of these nations have shown themselves unsuited to democracy. According to Daniel Lerner, the Third World media "teach people participation" by presenting them with choices among new ideas, situations, and opinions; only "with the spread of curiosity and imagination among a previously quietistic population," he argues, "come the human skills needed for social growth and economic development."[42] But Eastern Europe is not the Third World: literacy is high, Eastern European history is tied to that of Western Europe, desires and ambitions are "European," Enlightenment ideas have penetrated the educated classes, and the nations of the region have centuries-old press traditions— all the more reason to suppose that the media are capable of aiding social change, mobilizing citizen participation, and serving as conduits to new ideas. Moreover, at least in theory, they should be capable of reeducating and resocializing the citizens of their fledgling post-Communist societies. But they cannot do this alone, nor in a vacuum. There are no studies suggesting that even media systems with unlimited, ideal autonomy, with extreme pluralism and diversity, could accomplish these tasks by themselves.[43] Nor are there any studies suggesting that these tasks can or should be accomplished through the media.

Despite the constant emphasis on the importance of the media to every society, there is still no clear, useful theory of the media's role in sociopolitical change. If we accept that they are important, three possibilities come immediately to mind: (1) society and the media influence each other; (2) the media influence society; or (3) the media are neither influenced by society nor directly influence society but serve as vehicles through which leaders and other institutions influence society.[44] Examining only the first two possibilities, Jakubowicz argues that, even where the media can be shown to influence society, whether directly or indirectly, they are not independent agents, which leaves the first possibility, interdependence, as the only operative one. Taking his analysis one step further, he concludes that society "or some segment of it, for example, the power structure" determines the principal role of the media in social change.[45] Thus an *active* society, in whole or part, influences *active* media, which in turn influence society.

It is difficult if not impossible to discern this pattern in Eastern Europe; there is no evidence to date to suggest a set role for the media, one successfully determined by society, as a whole or any segment of it. In the initial transitional phase of the 1990s, although there is tentative, limited evidence of society influencing the media—audiences consistently rejected certain types of media outlets and in this sense influential—there is no evidence of the media directly, purposefully influencing society (see discussion of agenda setting in chapter 6), even if there are abundant examples of attempts to use the media to do so on the part of institutions and individuals from a political, ideological, or religious point of view.[46] Although such a tendency may seem to validate Lippmann's view of the media as "manufacturers of consent," I contend that the Eastern European media serve rather as a battleground in the continuous struggle over *who* should manufacture this consent—political leaders and parties, government and state institutions, institutions of civil society, or the newly minted citizens themselves.

Whether political parties, governments, markets, audiences, or even the media themselves have attempted to define a role for the media is not the salient question here. Rather, have the media successfully played the role or roles assigned them, whether by others or by themselves? There is no clear evidence that they have. Moreover, the media can be "active," whether society is or not, as long as society remains open. The very battles over the Eastern European media, the controversies surrounding media content, and the journalism being practiced suggest as much. On the other hand, because whatever influence the media appear to have on society is not direct, neither is it predicated on their level of "activeness."

Thus we are left with a slight refinement of our third possibility, that the media, though somewhat influenced by society, do not directly influence society, but serve as vehicles for political, socioeconomic, and cultural institutions, organizations, associations, and leaders seeking to influence society. Indeed, in political societies that lack broad participation, such as those of the transition and transformation period encompassing the first post-1989 decade, this may be the natural role served by the Eastern European media system, as I will show in the next section of this chapter.

The thesis that the media and their journalism are irrelevant and even counterproductive to sociopolitical change and to democratization in post-Communist Eastern Europe, unless they play the Western-style journalistic role prescribed by Dewey, Habermas, and others, is thus open to debate. Furthermore, the special reality of the Eastern European transition and transformation may require a different interpretation, not only of the role played by media autonomy, pluralism, and diversity in contributing to citizen participation, but also of journalistic professionalism itself.

Media Autonomy, Pluralism, and Diversity

Prescriptions of ideal or utopian media autonomy have at their core the notion of an idealized participatory rather than representative democracy in which participatory fervor is kept at a constant high pitch. For such a democracy, only the purest kind of pluralistic and diverse media will do, which is to say, only media through which all interests, concerns, and ideas are given currency, no matter how outlandish or how miniscule their support and potential consequences. Such media are seen as providing "the support needed to create a new social structure."[47] It turns out that, in the first phases of democratization, what creates new social structures is the ability to overtly, legally "oppose" or "support" and the freedom to choose. The very changes in the status of the media and their journalism—that they are no longer simply Communist or anti-Communist; that their role is now undefined, in contrast to the pre-1989 era; that they are extremely partisan and politicized in support of widely varying political orientations or ambitions; and even that they lack professionalism—contribute to their pluralism and diversity

While numbers alone do not tell the whole story of media diversity and pluralism, the dramatic multiplication of media outlets representing different allegiances and concerns suggests that a great variety of outlooks and interests are now being addressed. Most dramatic was the expansion of broadcast media outlets, which before Communism's demise were represented by state-owned television and radio stations. By the end of the 1990s, however, private radio and television stations dominated the airwaves in the region, with 30 private radio and 30 private television stations in Albania; 30 private radio stations, 18 private national and local television stations, and 200 private cable stations in Bulgaria; 60 private radio stations and 2 (of the 4) national television stations in private hands in the Czech Republic; 72 private television stations, 162 private radio stations, and 900 private cable networks in Romania; and 27 private radio and 78 private television and cable stations in the Slovak Republic.[48]

A sampling of the press's evolution since 1989 shows a dramatic growth in the number of publications available to the region's readers. There were 1,200 periodicals in Czechoslovakia in 1989 and an estimated 2,000 by the mid-1990s, with "the content of current publications [ranging] politically from distinctive left to distinctive right, and their typology from sensational tabloids and nude magazines to quality newspapers."[49] In Romania, there were only 495 publications before the overthrow of Ceausescu's Communist regime.[50] By the end of the 1990s, however, Romanian readers could choose from among some 1,800 publications, concentrating on everything from sports to religion, from humor to labor issues, from economics to pornography, from ethnic concerns to political orientations. In Bulgaria, the number of publications grew from 540 in 1990 to 907 in 1992, across the full range of political and ideological philosophies present in the country.[51]

The media that developed in Eastern Europe from 1990 to 2000 are an extreme representation of the Western European model of pluralistic, diverse media with a full array of politically, religiously, ethnically, and culturally oriented, as well as market-oriented, outlets. Media pluralism is clearly serving the liberalization phase of Eastern Europe's unconsolidated democracies. Two aspects of the Western European media still missing, however, are a bona fide public service function and journalistic professionalism, itself a controversial yet crucial topic. As the 1990s came to a close, the media became subordinate or answerable to a large number of varied interests, predominantly (though not exclusively or unalterably) political and commercial. Their ownership and the degree of their subordination and that of their journalists and journalism to these interests vary from medium to medium, country to country, and have seen small but important changes in the 1989–2000 period. In any case, ownership of the media is an insufficient gauge of their autonomy or subordination, and Eastern Europe appears to prove once again that it is the "overall cultural mix . . . that will tend to fix the position of the media on [the subordination-autonomy] continuum."[52] The problem is, in a transformation such as the region is undergoing, we cannot pinpoint where the media stand on the continuum because the "cultural mix" is constantly changing and the legal, conceptual, structural, and even normative constraints on the media are equally as unsettled, undefined, and unsecured.

Therefore, assessing media autonomy as a test of democratization and of media contributions to it is, at best, highly speculative and, in the end, fruitless. In the 1970s, George Gerbner suggested that independence per se, as an ideal, normative state, is less important to democracy than "by whom, how, for what purposes and with what consequences are the inevitable controls exercised."[53] Of course, he was addressing the situation in established democracies, where his proposition may indeed be sound. Gauging the source, nature, and effects of the controls exercised over the media and news content may be all but impossible in Eastern Europe. Who controls or influences the Eastern European media has changed many times during the

1989–2000 period, and so has the way this control or influence is exercised, the purposes for which it is exercised, and its consequences. A much more useful and realistic interpretation of autonomy and the important questions related to democratization, particularly in the liberalization phase of the democratization process, is articulated by Monroe Price, the editor of the *Post-Soviet Media Law and Policy Newsletter* and longtime observer of developments in the post-Communist world: "Independence can be measured as the capacity of an opposition to provide useful critique of the government in power."[54] The independence to provide such a critique in Eastern Europe exists. Whether it would be either effective or useful is another matter, one divorced from the issue of media independence per se.

Significantly, while there is still government *influence* on the media and journalism, there is an absence of overarching government *control,* save perhaps, ironically, in the public media sector. Such control fluctuates from country to country and from year to year and has by no means become entrenched, however, making "control" too categorical and far too conclusive a word to use here. The Slovak example perhaps speaks most strongly to this point: the Mečiar regime routinely harassed opposition media via the broadcast licensing process, taxation, and so on; such harassment ended abruptly with the ouster of the regime in 1998. Other such examples abound. The new public broadcasting laws in the region continue to be fine-tuned in favor of eliminating government control (see chapter 3); the constant debates, battles, and assorted professional controversies over public broadcasting staffs signal the potential for minimizing if not eliminating government control and influence, if and where they still exist (see chapter 4, "Media Elite—Elite Media"). If that happens, a public broadcasting system representing a variety of interests, groups, and views is not out of the question. But whether this public medium, with its wide representation of varied interests, groups, and views, will attract a sufficiently broad audience to fulfill its mission remains to be seen.[55]

Not being controlled by the state or driven by the market may not, in itself, make the Eastern European media more effective components of civil society, democratization, or democracy. The media's autonomy and courage depend in large measure on "the state of morale and vigor of other bodies, from schools, trade unions, and churches to legislatures, governments, and courts of justice."[56] Indeed, separating the Eastern European media from the very institutions that are facilitating, even if only unwittingly and indirectly, the consolidation of democracy is likely to be counterproductive. Ultimately, the absence of a well-developed civil society, or even of agreement on what it should be and what or who should represent it, makes any assumptions about media roles and effectiveness meaningless, as it does the relationship between media effectiveness and the extant political and professional cultures.

How the media can be completely autonomous from societal institutions is never explained in the available literature on the subject. At the micro level of the individual, each journalist, editor, or broadcaster also belongs to another institution, whether political, social, or civic, and thus represents a living link between the media and other institutions, eliminating any possibility of an idealized, pure autonomy. And, finally, media effectiveness, diversity, and pluralism, their role and contribution to democratization, and the degree to which they represent "all society" depend on the individuals who make up their leadership and rank and file and, ultimately, on the individuals who make up their audiences and how they choose to use the media.[57]

The Eastern European media's systemic evolution, their self-prescribed or imposed roles, their journalism, and their level of professionalism mirrored and served democratization as it evolved in the 1990s. That is, the media mirrored and served liberalization by their demonopolization from Communist Party and state control and by their extreme politicization (thus pluralization) after the fall of Communism. They also served the cause of intellectual and economic pluralism. Finally, they served the cause of sociocultural diversity, as expressed by ethnic minorities, labor unions, organizations of retired persons, and other groupings.

In short, the Eastern European media represent a diversified communication system. Their independence appears to be less a function of ownership or any other type of relationship with other institutions than of self-asserted professionalism, although, apart from a few select cases, professionalization has not occurred. On the whole, the main enemies of the free Eastern European media, as Michnik rightly judges the situation in Poland, include "the domination of ideological conviction over informative reliability" and a form of journalistic "blindness, which leaves one able to make only trite observations."[58] Other observers of Eastern European post-1989 evolution join Michnik in believing that the political and professional cultures have as much to say about media autonomy as laws, institutions, and ownership. A more Western-like concern about the media and journalistic autonomy may become more relevant if and when giant corporations begin to take over large numbers of news outlets and, in so doing, reduce the pluralism and diversity of Eastern Europe's media.

The Media and Citizen Participation

The Eastern European media, most particularly television, are said to play an "emasculating" role, thanks to their perceived lack of autonomy, pluralism, and diversity: they are considered tools "for political control not through direct censorship, as in the communist era, but through the cultivation of a feeling of apathy and powerlessness."[59] This claim, devoid of the solid research findings in support of similar claims in the United States,[60] is often presented in tandem with the opposite, albeit qualified, claim. Thus Hungarian television is judged to have "played an important role in thwarting and to a lesser extent aiding public participation in political events."[61] Such a judgment would seem to support the general assumption that "the greater the independence and pluralism of the media from the outset of the democratization process, the [higher] will be the level of civic trust and civic involvement"—hence, or so it might seem, the smaller the (perceived) independence and pluralism of the media, the lower the level of civic trust and civic involvement.[62]

The content of media fare and the context within which it is formulated, disseminated, and digested by media audiences may have a great deal to do with perceived media effects. We have no solid Eastern European data to determine such effects. What are available are mostly qualitative studies, descriptive and theoretical works based on observations and interviews. Pippa Norris shows there is a negative correlation between the amount of television watched and civic participation in the United States, although she also shows a positive correlation between watching news and news-related programs or reading newspapers, on the one hand, and civic participation, on the other.[63] Her second finding appears to hold for Eastern Europe as well. Overall media consumption is certainly high when one considers the large number of newspapers and radio, television, and cable stations accessed by the population (on proliferation of media outlets, see "Media Autonomy, Pluralism, and Diversity" above). Yet, while civic engagement is reportedly not very high in Eastern Europe, the number of nongovernmental organizations, groups, and institutions has drastically increased since 1989 (see "The Media and Political versus Civil Society" below). Furthermore, voter turnouts are still much higher in Eastern Europe than in the United States and also higher than in many Western European nations, even though they have been declining overall since 1989.

Clearly, factors other than the media are affecting popular participation in sociopolitical life in Eastern Europe. Indeed, the main reasons for limited citizen participation would seem to be the daily struggle for economic survival, limited discretionary time and money, the availability of a greater number of distractions, and the Communist-instilled culture of nonparticipation in public life.[64] Most important, the rapid erosion of trust in the new institutions and in the new political and economic leadership in the post-1989 period appears to have led to "a deliberate abandonment of the public sphere," although, again, that claim has yet to be confirmed by solid research data.[65] Nevertheless, that the public appears to mistrust the media does not make them a unique or primary cause for the public's withdrawal or nonengagement in public life.[66] Significantly, surveys show that, during the 1990s, the region's media were distrusted less overall than governments, parliaments, presidents, civil servants, the courts, the political parties, the police, the Church, patriotic societies, farm organizations, trade unions, private enterprise, and foreign experts.[67] This finding also suggests that, regardless of which other institutions influence or even control the media, the media's ability to influence society is separate from the credibility of these other institutions. Indeed, because the media have little effect on improving the credibility of these groups or institutions vis-à-vis society or media audiences, they are relatively ineffective vehicles for them.

Because voter turnout and overall participation in political party activities declined in the 1990s, Eastern European political parties "cannot be said to represent all society."[68] The existence of a political rather than a fully developed civil society (discussed in greater detail in "The Media and Political versus Civil Society" below) in no way disproves this conclusion. Nor, on the other hand, is civil society necessarily in retreat because citizens, discouraged by the unceasing political power struggles and by the lack of progress in solving the problems specific to their respective nations, have chosen not to be involved in public life.[69] "Polish society was more passive during the communist period and during the first phase of the transition than it is in the second phase. Low participation in formal 'macro' politics does not mean passivity. On the contrary, there are many signs of new forms of social activity."[70] And when mandatory "public involvement" ended in the former Czechoslovakia in 1989, new opportunities for public participation arose and new reasons for such participation emerged.[71] The welter of changes in institutional structures during the transition and transformation phases of democratization has thrown the citizens of post-Communist societies "back on caring for elementary needs individually, as a family, or in small networks,"which in turn has shaped their attitudes toward and use of the media.[72] This is not to suggest that Eastern Europeans have exchanged civic values for consumer values, as argued by Splichal, Jörg Becker, Charles De Bruyker, and others.[73] For, truth be told, how many held civic values, much less put them into practice, before 1989?

Furthermore, we need to reconsider the generalization that the struggles engaged in by political parties and politicians are irrelevant to people's everyday lives. As elements in a civil society, political parties, whether in power or not, are all representative in nature. Individuals will choose to get involved in civic life at certain times, or not to get involved at all, for very specific reasons. The "splendid thing" about civil society, writes Ernest Gellner, is that "even the absentminded or those preoccupied with their private concerns or for any other reason ill suited to the exercise of eternal and intimidating vigilance can look forward to enjoying their liberty. Civil Society bestows liberty even on the non-vigilant."[74]

Thus even when participation is low, there is no "phantom public," to use Lippmann's phrase. In the tug-of-war between John Stuart Mill's view that participation is the very essence of democracy and the view that democracy "in a narrow sense of the term can function without broad-based participation," the latter appears to be winning in Eastern Europe, where it is the only version of democracy that is realistically possible in the short term.[75]

Whether the nations of the region can move beyond a democracy with a relatively low level of citizen participation remains to be seen. If that is to happen, however, the nature of that participation is critical. It must, before all else, be based on informed public opinion. Absent clear knowledge and understanding of the facts, a government "by the people" becomes impossible. Politicians with their fingers in the wind of public opinion, as is increasingly the case in the region, are ill guided when public opinion is uninformed or misinformed. The nature of journalism, as the principal source of public information, is thus of utmost importance.

Specialized versus Mass Media and the Public Sphere

There is an irony in the Eastern European media's pluralism and diversity. By fragmenting the media, the new pluralism and diversity have rendered them marginal as educators, socializers, and mobilizers in the process of democratic transformation, for they have also fragmented the media's audiences, limiting, sometimes severely, their exposure to that very pluralism and diversity.[76] In so doing, they have compromised the media's ability to address the essential needs of resocialization and reeducation.

There is no denying that democracy requires informed citizens and that "their capacity to produce intelligent agreements by democratic means can be nurtured only when they enjoy equal and open access to diverse sources of opinion."[77] Eastern European audiences enjoy open access to diverse sources of opinion. Yet what is most important is that they have gravitated and continue to gravitate to like-minded media outlets, and have exhibited neither the inclination nor the financial ability, after 1989–92, to avail themselves of the whole spectrum of opinion available.

By representing a myriad of special interests and political parties, and catering to audiences with whom they shared beliefs and attitudes, most Eastern European newspapers almost instantly entered the specialized stage of evolution, bypassing the elitist and popular stages (see "Media Autonomy, Pluralism, and Diversity" above and chapter 4).[78] In Bulgaria, for example, "the number of medicine/hygiene newspapers increased from 2 to 18, sports newspapers increased from 4 to 286, and political/economic newspapers increased from 1 to 141."[79]

This trend toward fragmentation and diversification developed first in the press and then in the broadcast media, as local, regional, and national radio and television stations multiplied and diversified. The media's "specialization" was predominantly along partisan political lines; given that their "specialties" did not allow them to be mass media, the so-called national press cannot be said to be national in any but the nominal sense. Media audiences, as was the case in transforming societies elsewhere,[80] proved to be made up of individuals seeking to validate their predispositions. As Roumiana Deltcheva explains:

> The contemporary Bulgarian does not seek practical knowledge from the press; rather, he or she is looking for psychological satisfaction, a pseudocatharsis to be experienced from immersion in the scandal and the emotions of excitement, anger, empathy, at times even worship, thus triggered.[81]

Thus the nature both of the media and of their audiences appears to limit "the educational potentialities of the mass media and therefore casts in doubt the possibility that in the new states the process of consensus building can be rapidly realized by the conscious employment of the media."[82] At a time when the media need to perform a normative and integrating sociopolitical role, that is, to serve as models for democracy, to disseminate messages on its behalf, and to teach its ground rules as well as democratic behaviors, attitudes, and values,[83] their very "specialization" does not allow them to do so. Indeed, this may be the source of their greatest failure in the post-1989 transformation, as in the case of Poland, where "the demassification of transmission and reception . . . has created a diversity of democratic vistas and a multiplicity of voices that confront that country with a postmodern incoherence [and] a reassertion of its historical anarchic traditions."[84]

Consequently, what we have in Eastern Europe is not mass media eroding the critical functions of individual readers, listeners, or viewers, or resisting change in the political culture, but rather media that are fragmented and, as such, effectively incapable of educating or reeducating, socializing or resocializing the citizens of post-Communist political cultures in any unified, concerted way. This fragmentation severely reduces the ability of the media to be "the great multiplier" of those attitudes, behaviors, and values important to democratization.[85]

The negative effects embodied in fragmented media may be mitigated if citizens expose themselves to a wide variety of media outlets, as indeed they did in the first few years of post-Communist life. By the second half of the first post-Communist decade, however, individuals had settled for their "favorite" newspaper or radio and television news shows. Even when their sociopolitical and cultural outlook was more heterogeneous, their shrinking discretionary funds made it impossible to purchase more than one newspaper or magazine at a time, if they could afford even that. Thus, unlike in societies with a sparsity of media choices, Eastern Europe's pluralistic, diverse media play a far less potent role in democratization. Although they appear to be forces for dispersion and individuation, rather than integration, they have the potential to provide "lessons" helpful to democratization. For example, views and information provided by opposition media outlets counterbalance those provided by the nationalistic, xenophobic, racist media outlets, assuming of course audiences choose to expose themselves to such opposing views and information. What is also needed, however, and what has not been supplied by the media, are lessons emphasizing the meaning and importance of free, pluralist media in a non-Communist world and the reasons for them. At most, what is emphasized is that in democracies all journalists can write or say whatever they wish, without having to delineate their responsibilities to society at large and to each member of their audience.

Eastern European commercial television, as its reach and audiences increase, is slowly moving toward being more of a mass medium,[86] joining public radio and television, which have maintained their status as mass media despite decreases in audience size, and which are also relatively more partisan and less diverse in their coverage of topics and issues than their commercial counterparts. It remains to be seen whether these "new" media can more directly contribute to the process of reeducating and resocializing Eastern Europeans, and to increasing citizen participation. Mass media that endeavor to be more fact-based and balanced, if not also neutral, are better able to unify audiences in need of resocialization and reeducation, common lessons and common models. Indeed, experience shows that the mass media can promote nation building and other developmental agendas.[87]

Of all forms of media, only the mass media are touted as important and powerful elements of a public sphere, even when the public sphere is differently defined.[88] If we accept Habermas's notion that civil society is a precondition for a public sphere, and, further, if we grant that civil society exists in each Eastern European nation, then we can argue that each has at least the potential for a public sphere (see "The Media and Political versus Civil Society" below).[89] On the other hand, the virtual absence of mass media and of societies with a liberal political culture and attendant patterns of socialization, "united around the fundamental values of the existing social order," would seem to signal a corresponding absence of a public sphere, at least as defined by Habermas.[90] That is, an organized, open, rational-critical public discourse is not likely to be facilitated by media and audiences that are fragmented, even if what is being disseminated might otherwise promote such a discourse. This would be true even if Dewey's conception of a public sphere were adopted.

The assertion that only politicians' voices are heard throughout the Eastern European media was no longer true by 2000.[91] The political system and environment established in the first post-Communist decade, precisely because they were overpoliticized, have drawn other voices into the political fray, those of teachers, retirees, students, churchmen, workers, and small business owners, among others.[92] Yet, despite these new voices, and even if the Eastern European media were to become true mass media, prospects for a genuine public sphere remain bleak because, as Dahlgren points out, "a society where democratic tendencies are weak and [whose] structural features . . . are highly inegalitarian is not going to give rise to healthy institutional structures for the public sphere."[93]

One might therefore suppose that the political power, social hierarchy, and social structures hindering democratic development are well entrenched.[94] But they are not, indeed cannot be, during a period of societal transformation. One might also suppose that the institutional structures are themselves incapable of evolving into a more democratic form, let alone facilitating democratization. Yet there is sufficient evidence that the Eastern European media and their journalists have already begun to change in precisely that direction, indulging less in partisanship and becoming more professional, albeit thus far in only isolated cases, and that these changes have been brought about, not by those who own, control, or influence the media outlets, but by their journalists, editors, and news directors. Furthermore, there has been a significant increase in the presence of local and ethnic media, a facet of the Eastern European media scene that has not been sufficiently studied, especially not the very real contributions of such media to public discourse or the public sphere.[95]

Western nations engaged in aiding Eastern Europe's transformation assumed that what was needed to help establish democracy were media unbeholden to any major political institution, practicing professional journalism, mobilizing, educating, and informing the citizenry, and promoting comprehensive, diverse, and pluralist sociopolitical and cultural dialogue on behalf of and by "the people." Even if they were to exist in Eastern Europe (whose example demonstrates that they do not spontaneously arise in societies undergoing transformation), such media would not necessarily serve as "an agent of democracy."[96] Indeed, media that serve as agents of democracy are offshoots of already well-entrenched, evolving democracies. Nevertheless, this does not negate the substantial contributions to democratization made by media and journalism representing the very opposite of the conventional Western ideal.

The Media and Political versus Civil Society

There is general agreement that what quickly emerged from overlapping processes of event-driven and enacted changes in the region after 1989 was a "political society," civil society's "other" form, and the market.[97] The rapid and wild proliferation of political parties, media, voluntary and civil associations and groups, on the one hand, and businesses, on the other, were changes that paralleled those directed, encouraged, supported, and enacted by states or governments, that is, changes in laws, regulations, and policies. With variations from country to country across the region, such enacted changes affected and were affected by the event-driven changes.

The prevailing view among media scholars is that the new Eastern European media and their journalism do not represent, are not expressions of, and do not enhance the growth of civil society.[98] According to this view, the region's media and their journalists are responsive not to the public or to civil society, but to political parties, politicians, and the new capitalists or the market. Consequently, the public sphere is seen as being dominated by politicians or political activists, by businesses controlled by former members of the Communist *nomenklatura,* by the newly formed "mafias" impudently operating in several countries, and by foreign-owned or -controlled media enterprises.[99]

Despite their faults and shortcomings, their politicized and tabloidlike journalism, their initially close, even symbiotic relationships with politicians and political parties, and their overall lack of professionalism, the post-Communist media express and represent the existing political society. Moreover, they express and represent the post-Communist political culture, and, as such, they contribute indirectly and unwittingly to the remolding and resocializing of political society. For this and other reasons, I believe that civil societies are indeed emerging in post-Communist Eastern Europe, however fragile and unconsolidated they currently may be.

As the 1990s unfolded, and to this day, the range of those who directly or indirectly influence the media and who are covered by them has steadily widened, to include, among many others, unions, religious organizations, and educational institutions, as well as associations of ethnic minorities, intellectuals, professionals, businessmen and financiers, media audiences, and the journalists themselves. Without suggesting that their political impact or media influence has kept pace with their rapid growth in number, nongovernmental associations and organizations are now a significant factor on the sociopolitical, cultural, economic, and media scene. It is virtually impossible for the Hungarian media, for example, regardless of their relationships with the government, political parties, or commercial forces to ignore the nongovernmental organizations and associations, which numbered more than 30,000 by 1992 in this country of 10 million people.[100] Even in the Slovak Republic, there are more than 5,000 national nongovernmental associations, groups, and organizations, with thousands more at the local level.[101] Not only has media coverage of these elements of civil society increased in the region, but so has the coverage of the issues important to them: human rights, women's issues, ecology, political corruption, labor disputes, the plight of retirees on fixed pensions, changes in the educational system, corruption, health issues, children's issues, ethnic issues, and on and on. Additionally, the new nongovernmental entities have discovered, to varying degrees, the importance of getting their messages out via announcements and press releases, at times published or broadcast verbatim by some media outlets.[102]

Exemplifying the event-driven establishment of liberalization, political competition, and, with them, diversification and pluralization, even the party press provided journalistic coverage of segments of the growing civil society in the first few post-1989 years. Whether intentionally or not, this press reflected and served the collective and individual reactions and opinions of its audiences, however biased they may have been, as well as elements of civil society, of political, personal, or other interest to a particular party or politician owning, controlling, sponsoring, or influencing one or more of its outlets. Given that many of the post-Communist political parties derived from the pre-1989 civil and social movements that fought to liberalize or overthrow the Communist regimes (e.g., Czechoslovakia's Občanské, Poland's Solidarity, and Hungary's FIDESZ), they already contained elements of what is traditionally labeled "civil society"—that is, they were voluntary, private associations or informal groups of individuals with varied political, social, civic, and cultural interests. In this way, the emergence of competitive party politics in the region parallels that in Western Europe, where political parties appeared "as representatives of pre-existing organized interests in civil society."[103]

In those nations without such movements to bring about the liberalization required to end Communist rule, some of the political parties that immediately emerged after the abrupt collapse of the Communist regimes became hybrids of political and civil or social movements for restructuring society, at least at first. For instance, in Romania, the Group for Social Dialogue, a collection of civic-minded, civil libertarian intellectuals contributed ideas to the political dialogue and individuals to the leadership of some political parties. Similarly, the Civic Alliance, also an association of socially conscious, civic-minded intellectuals, formed the Civic Alliance Party. They each had a media platform, a newspaper, the most noteworthy being the intellectual weekly *22,* established by the Group for Social Dialogue. In Bulgaria, too, the Federation of Clubs for the Support of Glasnost and Democracy, led by Petko Semeonov, Dimitur Ludshev, and Zheliu Zhelev, who became the first post-Communist president, the Committee for Religious Rights, Freedom of Conscience, and Spiritual Values, Ekoglasnost, and the Independent Association for the Defense of Human Rights were all social or civil movements and at the same time political entities.[104]

In the 1990–2000 transformation period, the political parties in each Eastern European nation, numbering from dozens to hundreds, were the most potent elements among the private institutions of civil society. For the time being, they directly and indirectly represent, align themselves, or have sympathies with a vast array of political, ideological, and social views, as well as civic and cultural interests. Their constituents include ethnic groups, labor unions, churches, environmental organizations, organizations of former political prisoners and former landowners, professional organizations, university associations, writers' unions, and actors' guilds, as well as civil rights and human rights groups, among many others. Parties exercising considerable influence are well covered by the media,[105] although some parties have been marginalized for lack of members and, in a broader sense, constituents and receive little or no coverage. That, too, is an intrinsic part of an open, democratic society, where choice is freely exercised in accepting or rejecting certain political, cultural, or socioeconomic visions, programs, parties, and ideologies.

It is undeniable that political parties, belonging to a widening system of private institutions, have more than their fair share of power and influence in post-1989 Eastern Europe. There are reasons for their dominance in the transformation period: they are crucial to the establishment of a political democracy and, even more so, to the process of democratization and the creation of consolidated civil societies rather than merely elements of them.[106] By the end of the 1990s, they managed to bring a modicum of stability to the party system and to the political process. In most, if not all countries of the region, they have also limited the uncertainty surrounding the political scene because "actors know the rules and have some sense of how to pursue their interests."[107]

Accordingly, it is not surprising that civil societies as they now exist in Eastern Europe are predominantly political, nor that the media, focused as they are on them, are politicized. Indeed, this new, post-1989 political life and the plurality of political parties could only have "emerged" with the help of the media.[108] Furthermore, civil society as political society is also an extension of the extant political culture, that is, the habits, customs, ethics, and operative definitions of citizenship. First the party-dominated press and then, in a less obvious and more diluted way, the parties and the press in parallel contributed to, represented, and served the political nature of society. The press continues to do so in the fledgling post-Communist civil societies, where the political, the civic, and the sociocultural constantly overlap.[109] Yet it has also contributed to the introduction and enhancement of new, varied interests among its audiences, and, in so doing, promoted the growth of the civil part of political society. Thus the position that politicized, partisan media, "whether private or state owned, are clearly not the best method to serve the creation of civil society," merits serious reconsideration in Eastern Europe.[110]

For instance, retirement pay for the elderly, welfare and unemployment benefits, taxation, university tuition, building codes in cities, land redistribution, health codes, abortion, education, and the environment are as much political issues as they are social, civic, and cultural ones. Whether in the name of a political party or in a politician's self-interest, to act on one or more of these issues is also to represent the interests of constituents and of nongovernmental associations, groups, and organizations. That these issues and the fight over them are presented and debated in the Eastern European media from political or personal perspectives and in less than professional ways signals neither a disregard for civic issues nor a lack of responsibility vis-à-vis the public. More important, the presentation of these issues serves to promote the formation and expression of opinions, leading to the organization of new nongovernmental groups and associations, and eventually, to the creation of civil society from the bottom up. Thus the argument that pluralistic, highly competitive party systems inevitably lead to "the demobilization of civil society either directly or indirectly by reducing its influence to the narrowest possible channels," namely, to politicized or commercial media outlets with limited interests, also merits reconsideration.[111]

As the 1990s unfolded, coverage of the political and social scenes, of various politicians and political parties, and of social and civic movements significantly improved. For instance, continued deficiencies in their professionalism notwithstanding, the media generally covered elections in the second half of the decade in a wider, more balanced, and thorough way than they had in the first, with opinion polls also becoming a relatively regular focus of coverage.[112] Such quantifying of opinions on a wide range of issues contributes to the formation of public opinion and the building of civil societies.[113] If, indeed, civil society "can express itself in a great variety of forms, from individual initiatives through social movements, clubs, associations and other organizations,"[114] one could argue that the highly politicized, pluralistic, personal, opinionated, and judgmental journalism with neither shared standards nor a professional, democratic-minded culture that prevails in Eastern Europe not only represents civil society but *is* civil society.

The general expectation that civil society is essential to the evolution of the media—that it is needed to "'deregulate' the dependence of the media on the state and/or the market, and to maximize freedom of communication"—is also off the mark.[115] Post-Communist Eastern Europe suggests otherwise. "Deregulating" Eastern European media dependence on the state was successfully begun in the 1990s—spontaneously, as a natural rejection of Communist or authoritarian regulation by the state, and deliberately, as an expression of the ideational, practical, and professional evolutions of journalists—at a time when civil society existed only in the most limited sense. The drive for media autonomy was spearheaded by media personnel as well as by some politicians, political parties, human rights and civic rights organizations (see chapters 2, 3, and 4). Even in the case of "public broadcasting," progress toward greater autonomy has been registered, and the fight continues (see chapter 3).[116] Also noteworthy is the building momentum of the drive for the enactment of media access and freedom of information laws, a drive almost exclusively led by journalists and journalistic associations (see chapter 3). Finally, the presumption that all elements of civil society stand for and encourage media freedom is faulty. They can also discourage or even attempt to suppress media freedom, as is in the case of Hungary.[117]

The Media and the Market

The literature on the post-Communist media in Eastern Europe is replete with lamentations about the commercialization of the media. There is no need here either to repeat or to dispute all the arguments about the real and imagined potential negatives of the commercial media in the democratizing nations of the region: they have been well presented and argued by Splichal, among many others.[118] Suffice it to say that Eastern Europe's market-oriented media, with their sensationalism, trivialization, and tabloidization in the push to increase profits by enlarging audiences, have the potential to diminish the informational value of what they convey. Are they a greater danger to the informational needs of the public than the political media, with their polemical, biased, often inaccurate, spin doctors? Can ideal public service media, in their rush to cover and please everyone, to be all inclusive, and to give every group and view its day in the court of public opinion, meaningfully distinguish the saliency of the news stories they present? Most critiques of the commercial media are based on normative, idealistic, even utopian visions of the media and democracy, some still Marxist or neo-Marxist, and some derived from the Western media experience since World War II. According to these visions, being seriously compromised, if not actually corrupted, by the profit motive, the commercial media

1. do not "stimulate the differentiation and increasing complexity essential for civil society";[119]
2. are not dedicated to the public interest, nor do they honor their special role and responsibilities in a democratic society; and thus
3. do not serve the informational needs of civil society.

Let us briefly consider the Eastern European media and the free market during the 1989–2000 transition and transformation from Communism toward democracy. As the 1990s came to a close, Eastern European societies were still struggling to establish market economies. Privatization in all sectors of their economies has not been completed and in some countries, notably Albania, Bulgaria, Romania, and the Slovak Republic, the process is considerably less advanced than in the Czech Republic, Hungary, and Poland. Even so, the evolution of their markets has created elements of civil society, that is, new associations, groups, and organizations, as well as new individual interests, views, and needs. In this situation, though they may have taken on the appearance of their counterparts in the West, the region's commercial media, with some exceptions, (1) are mindful of the political, sociocultural, and ethnic characteristics of their audiences (versus the purely demographic characteristics to which true commercial media pay attention); and (2) are governed by their official and unofficial connections with or their strong sympathies for political parties, politicians, and religious or ethnic institutions, among others. In short, they are "political institutions par excellence, not just commercial enterprises."[120] Yet they are also sociocultural institutions par excellence, specifically, ethnic and religious in some cases and highly personal communications platforms in others. This second observation applies even to commercial television, which is far closer to becoming a mass medium than the other commercial media, one in which the rules of a market economy should dominate, at least in theory. Thus in the first eleven post-Communist years, profit has often taken a backseat to other motives for the region's commercial media. Other motives are simply more important in highly politicized societies that lack a "civil religion" and a democratic political culture. Indeed, because the region's economic systems are not fully market driven, economic motives are intertwined with political, social, cultural, and ethnic considerations; satisfying other motives becomes necessary for economic survival. And because the other motives are diverse, as are their wellsprings and their constituencies, there is both pluralism and diversity in media offerings; even where the topics are the same (politics, social problems, the economy), they are treated from different perspectives.

The argument that "by forcing political communication to channel itself via the commercial media, the advocates of market liberalism transform public communication into the politics of consumerism" may be valid on its face but says little to separate commercial from other media.[121] It is clear that the "specialized" media outlets, particularly in the first few post-Communist years, were almost purely political and remained so until citizens no longer wished to "consume" their offerings. Thus the "politics of consumerism" is clearly present in Eastern Europe, whether one considers the party press or the commercial one.

The commercial media, far from having a negative effect on the evolution of the region's media system itself and democratization, have made demonopolization of the media and their infrastructure (distribution, newsprint acquisition, etc.) possible. In so doing, they have also increased freedom of the press. There is little if any indication that in the 1990–2000 period, "moves towards the extension of the market" could "easily [have been] combined with increased government intervention and censorship."[122] Quite to the contrary, while governments attempted to achieve these ends, most of their attempts failed, were short-lived (see chapter 3), or were countered by the commercial media. Furthermore, accusations that privatization and commercialization of the media have been used to reform civil society "from above" apply with as much justification to policies establishing the public service media. Indeed, because the assumptions underlying them are less realistic, it is questionable whether the public service media will better inform the public and better serve civil society and democratization.

In a region where the lack of press freedom was associated with the monopoly of a single political party, it is hardly surprising to find that "privatization of the media is often considered the most important prerequisite for press freedom."[123] In my interviews with journalists in Albania, Bulgaria, the Czech Republic, Hungary, Poland, and Romania during 1990–99, it quickly became evident that press freedom was defined firstly as a choice of media employers. In some cases, journalists said it was good to have employers to whom they felt a political, ideological, cultural, or ethnic kinship. Indeed, with the near demise of the political press and the absence of effective public service media, it is the commercial media that offer the pluralism and diversity needed for freedom of the press. The right to practice journalism unfettered by any standards, even if constrained by the employers, themselves diverse in their sociopolitical beliefs, cultural inclinations, motives, and views of their role in society, makes for remarkably extensive press freedom.[124] In short, Eastern Europe's commercial media are "free and thoroughly disputatious (although not always ideally objective—unless the standard is the London tabloids)."[125]

Related to the previous point (and a reiteration of a point made in "The Media and Political versus Civil Society" above), where civil society is not fully formed or powerful, the commercial media add to and represent media pluralism and diversity. Moreover, they help establish and promote other nongovernmental institutions, associations, and organizations. Where civil societies, however underdeveloped, exist, the commercial media serve as communication platforms for, and as means of expanding, them. They encompass a greater degree of diversity than other media, with the possible exception of an extensive (and extensively used) political press, particularly in the absence of ideal, effective public service media.[126]

Thus, as things stand, only the commercial media appear to have the potential to be mass media (the need for which during transformation is discussed in "Specialized versus Mass Media and the Public Sphere" above). Also significant in Eastern Europe, the commercial media appear to be the only media having the financial wherewithal for the technological retooling and the training, both technical and journalistic, needed to become true mass media. Given the current state of the region's economies, neither states nor political parties have the financial resources to fund the retooling and retraining of the public service media, nor can taxes be easily increased or the tax base enlarged to sustain state-run or "public"-run public service media.

The assumption that profit-based media are, by their very nature, barred from providing credible, varied, bona fide news coverage also needs to be reexamined. Commercial news media that lose their credibility, no matter how entertaining and sensationalistic they may be, also lose their profits and go out of business, if they continue to do so. On the other hand, because Oscar Wilde's observation that "the public have an insatiable curiosity to know everything, except what is worth knowing" appears to hold for Eastern Europe (as elsewhere in the world), the commercial media, no less than the political or public service media, are unlikely to meet the ideal of informing the people and involving them in active democratic life.[127] In fact, such an ideal represents a misunderstanding of how democracy really works, suggesting as it does that, unless people are in some way cajoled, directed, or even forced, they will simply not be interested in "what is worth knowing."

What needs to be kept in mind here is that Eastern European societies are not fully democratic and that what is occurring in their transformation is meant to establish the *preconditions* for a democracy in the political, social, cultural, and economic spheres. The media, together with other institutions, must be judged in that context. There is no proof that media, simply because they are not political and not market driven, are any better journalistically. No one has yet made the case that, say, BBC journalism is better than that of the London *Times.* Or that PBS journalism is better than that of the *New York Times.*[128]

As soon as professionalism is defined in relative terms, as it is in Eastern Europe, and increasingly also in the United States, the boundary between objective and advocacy journalism, between news and entertainment, is eroded. Even so, the assumption that the commercial media deny the citizens the "information they need to exercise rational political choice" has been shaken if not shattered by studies on both sides of the Atlantic.[129]

In contrast to purely political or state-controlled media, commercial media have to foster what James Q. Wilson calls "a reasonable concern for the opinions of others."[130] The old habits under Communism (see chapter 1) are now being slowly set aside in the commercial media, which do not reward laziness, rudeness, and mediocrity that went hand in hand with the devaluation of work in the Communist era. This is not to deny the persistence of those habits, but only to say they are changing for the better. Unfortunately (as pointed out in chapter 4), the predominant type of journalism practiced in the region also serves as a negative model for qualities necessary for civil society and democracy: tolerance, respect, truthfulness, and civility. Thus Polish journalists "use vulgar language," "blur the line between reporting and opinion," misquote sources, and omit "important data."[131] Some Bulgarian journalists use stereotypes in their reporting of Romany issues.[132]

In an era when efforts have been made to reduce or end the media's financial dependence on government and political parties, there have been no real efforts to reduce or end their dependence on the market, although not every commercial media outlet in the region depends exclusively on the market. The call for such separation from the market, based strongly on the notion that civil society is reduced to "economic society" where a liberal market economy is established, does a disservice to the region's transformation in and has its own narrow limitations.[133] Although there is a form of "market authoritarianism" brought about by corruption and the lack of economic regulation, we should keep in mind that the market economy promotes modernization and the accumulation of wealth. The commercial media benefit and contribute to this process in a number of different ways: intrinsically as businesses themselves, and also as facilitators of business or the market economy. Without wealth being generated by the market and distributed throughout society, admittedly in an extremely unequal fashion during the transformation, people would be preoccupied with their daily economic survival, would have less time or money to spend on the media, and would be less inclined to increase their participation in civic life. Seymour Lipset's thesis that "the more well-to-do a nation, the greater the chances that it will sustain democracy," appears to apply to the nations of Eastern Europe; it is a thesis subscribed to by others as well.[134] In turn, if and when this modernization and wealth lessen the socioeconomic inequalities now present in the region, they will temper the tensions produced by political conflict.[135] It is incontrovertible that, during the first post-Communist decade, the gap has grown between the few who quickly accumulated wealth and the many who have barely held their heads above economic waters or who are actually destitute. The building of a stable middle class has yet to occur.

Still, despite the region's socioeconomic inequalities, its news media moved away from their specialized role, increasing their contribution to and participation in civil society. In a situation akin to the one found in Hong Kong, the Eastern European commercial press "acts as a partial corrective to the gravity of political force."[136] Indeed, the commercial media, even if unprofessional, are an intrinsic part of the transition and transformation. There is no denying that the commercial media exist to maximize the profits and to reflect the politics, as well as the social, political, and cultural worldviews, of their owners. But the ability and the willingness of journalists, editors, and producers to mitigate the profit orientation is too often disregarded; it is too easily assumed that free enterprise is incompatible with the collective social and civic needs of audiences and that the market and civil society are strictly differentiated. The new Eastern European consumers are defined not merely "in terms of privatized individual desires" but also in terms of "social and collective needs."[137]

Whether the Eastern Europe media serve audiences or vice versa cannot easily be determined.[138] But the killing off of the party press, the general low trust in the media, the continued high turnover in media outlets, and the beginnings of journalistic professionalism all bear witness to the drive, however unwitting, to establish media *for* audiences. Furthermore, the move to commercial media necessitates a diversification of news coverage and views to respond to audiences so as to enlarge them and thereby the media's economic base. Perhaps the issue cannot be resolved in a black or white way.

After all, an open society should be able to accommodate overlapping purposes: media serving audiences and audiences serving media.

Market forces include elements of civil society, the same elements out of which, ideally, the media are to arise. Consumers represent one or more of those elements. Admittedly, the power of nongovernmental, nonstate, and nonpolitical groups in Eastern Europe is not yet as robust as it is in the United States, where environmentalist, children's advocacy, and women's groups, to name only the most notable, stage effective demonstrations and boycotts over print or broadcast items they find objectionable. That may come in time.

The truth of the matter is that neither the marketplace nor the political parties nor the media can or should guarantee "equality of freedom," itself a contradiction in terms, especially in the context of an open, free, pluralistic, democratic society. Indeed, as Kenneth Starck points out, "by its very nature [freedom] provokes inequality by encouraging diversity of action."[139] Freedom accentuates individual differences in talent, ambition, industry, and intelligence, dispensing awards according to these and other qualities and to individual contributions to society. That is, freedom works to destroy the egalitarian myth, which can be realized only by destroying freedom. Equality of the type advanced by idealistic, utopian, or specifically left-wing ideologies comes only at the cost of restricting the individual freedom of some in the name of others, and of simulating an equality that does not naturally exist.[140] The argument can also be made that individuals are the most important element of civil society and if their freedom is restricted, so are the freedom and the essence of civil society. This is by no means an argument in favor of a society that resembles a jungle, but rather an argument against a society that resembles a cage in order to avoid becoming a jungle.

Neither a market economy nor market-oriented media alone can assure the establishment of an open, democratic society. Without them, however, such a society cannot exist. The degree to which both the market economy and the commercial media are to be regulated also signifies the extent to which a society is open and democratic.[141] In particular, the antimonopoly regulations most useful in keeping large corporations from gobbling up news outlets need much attention and enforcement in Eastern Europe. Presently, they are weak, untested, threatened by loose interpretations in the courts, or, in some countries, nonexistent.

On the other hand, the commercial media should have to live with as few regulations as reasonably possible, always mindful of their obligation to supply citizens with verifiable, accurate, and complete information, presented in the fullest context, and with the greatest variety of views practicable. There is clear need for a professionalism well defined and enforced by the journalists themselves. This is not to suggest that media professionals are necessarily effective self-regulators, however, but only that other regulators are likely to be worse.

Which brings us back to just how much the government should regulate the media in the first place. When do regulations, imposed in the name of utopian ideals, become illiberal—or simply oppressive? Overregulation leaves only simulated freedom and creates a situation in which the cure becomes worse than the illness itself.

Freedom "is not something which can be realized in a definitive or perfect sense. It is an ongoing project without an ultimate solution."[142] Scholars calling for public regulations that "entangle" the media in the name of freedom of communication would do well to keep that in mind.

Finally, the notion that "not . . . to restrict the operation of the free market in the media is clearly [to be] in favor of *corporate speech* rather than *free speech*" does not readily apply to Eastern Europe's first post-Communist decade.[143] First, "corporate speech," though it does not, in itself, represent societal free speech, is nonetheless part of it. Second, during this decade, the Eastern European commercial media could not be said to represent "corporate speech" as understood in the West, being driven by wide-ranging, highly dissimilar, and constantly shifting interests and views, many well outside a strictly market orientation.

As "impure," politicized, and partisan in political, social, cultural, and ethnic terms as they are, and even while they struggle to establish themselves economically, the region's commercial media have helped establish the preconditions for democratization through their pluralism, diversity, and freedom. To retain these essential media qualities, Eastern Europe needs highly specific and enforceable antimonopoly laws.

6

Conclusion: The Media, Journalism, and Democratization

In the historical blink of an eye represented by the first post-Communist decade, the media of Eastern Europe did not live up to their expected role as appropriate, effective facilitators of democratization. Yet, despite their less-than-professional journalism, their systemic, personnel, and legal problems, and their failure to conceptualize a well-defined and commonly accepted role, they registered progress on all fronts, from informing and facilitating political change to molding public opinion and setting agendas. This chapter summarizes the successes, failures, and contributions of the post-1989 Eastern European media and their journalism vis-à-vis democratization, offering some thoughts on their future evolution and roles.

The News Media, Journalism, and Democracy in Eastern Europe

The countries of Eastern Europe have successfully moved from Marxist-Leninist authoritarianism and Stalinist totalitarianism to liberalization and political democracy. They remain unconsolidated democracies, however, struggling to establish themselves while initiating and being affected by profound economic changes. Indeed, even though their citizens have begun to organize and mobilize themselves in nongovernmental organizations, groups, and associations, the region's countries are far closer to being representative than participatory democracies. What has evolved in Eastern Europe are societies where opportunities and freedoms are now available to all citizens to participate in public life, at whatever level, with whomever, for whatever reasons or goals, and in whatever manner they choose—or not to participate at all. Most choose to vote, others to get involved with civic groups, professional organizations, and civil associations, and still others to exercise their right not to get involved.

Whereas Dewey held to an idealistic, even utopian vision of deliberative, participatory, or communitarian democracy, Schumpeter more realistically assessed the "material" with which democracy could be built. He implicitly questioned the ability of citizens to establish and sustain deliberative democracy. The ordinary American citizen, Schumpeter observed, has a "reduced sense of responsibility" and lacks an "effective volition"; he went on to say that

> ignorance and lack of judgement in matters of domestic and foreign pol-
> icy . . . are if anything more shocking in the case of educated people and
> of people who are successfully active in nonpolitical walks of life than
> [they are] with uneducated people in humble stations. Information is
> plentiful and readily available. But this does not seem to make any dif-
> ference.[1]

Although writing about the United States in the 1940s, Schumpeter might just as well have been describing Eastern Europe in transformation. Here, too, information is plentiful and readily available, albeit more often than not it is biased, unverifiable, incomplete, and editorialized. Granted that the more "deliberative," analytical, and "intellectual" weeklies "that once enjoyed a significant popularity have lost readership" across the region, and that television, with headline news and public affairs programs that often seem more like talk shows, is grabbing the bulk of Eastern European audiences, information is nevertheless available for citizens to use or not.[2] But here it does seem to make a difference. Indeed, Eastern Europeans seek to be informed, and, using that information, they deliberate privately among themselves, with family members, neighbors, coworkers, and sometimes with fellow members of various nongovernmental groups, organizations, and associations. They also publicly deliberate through their participation in polls, their letters to editors, statements to journalists that find their way into the media, and indirectly and vicariously through the lobbying and statements made by various nongovernmental entities to which they belong or with which they sympathize.

Eastern Europe's representative political societies do in fact contribute to the liberalization phase, and in some countries to the beginnings of the consolidation phase, of democratization. Just as in Latin America, where politicians must deliver on their promises to make reforms, establish new rights, and improve government if they want to get elected or reelected, so a similar process is slowly evolving in Eastern Europe.[3] The media serve not only as the means by which votes are pursued but also as critics and alternative sources of information and commentary, forcing politicians to be more responsive and at least somewhat more responsible to voters.

On the other hand, even though Eastern Europe's politicized, partisan media reveal the workings of the state apparatus and its employees, they do so in an interpretive way that varies widely from one media outlet to another. They put forth differing and changing criteria by which the state's work is to be judged. More important, they leave the impression that the state cannot be controlled; indeed, that nothing is controllable and that chaos reigns. Post-Communist Eastern Europe in transformation thus serves as a compelling subject for a Lippmann versus Dewey debate over the role of the media in democratic societies.

Lippmann's view of the nature and role of the media and journalism was in stark contrast to Dewey's.[4] For Lippmann, fact-based journalism was to provide citizens with snapshots of daily events and issues as a prelude to their forming opinions and debating the issues. A champion of representative democracy, he envisioned a debate based on "logic and the rules of evidence," that is, one based on verifiable facts and not just on personal opinions and the journalistic relativity associated with accommodating the demands or desires of journalists, editors, news directors, and media owners.[5] He had no way of knowing that Eastern Europe's media in the 1990s would precisely exemplify what he had warned against in a different context, that "the unrestricted right to speak" would "unloose [a host of] propagandists, procurers, and panderers upon the public."[6]

For Dewey, champion of participatory democracy, the media embodied the town meeting.[7] They were to facilitate conversation, discussion, and an exchange of opinions—and nothing more. In his refinement of Dewey's view, Christopher Lasch stresses the crucial role played by information: "Unless information is generated by sustained public debate, most of it will be irrelevant at best, misleading and manipulative at worst."[8] By defining information as a derivative of opinions and views, however, Lasch (and, with him, Dewey) dismisses the value of verifiable facts as the basis of journalism. Thus in this view, while freedom of the press may mean widespread access to "information," it also means the right to publish any and all unverifiable facts. That is, it relegates "truth" and "information," like beauty, to the "eye of the beholder," forgetting that "only opinion can be pluralist, not information itself."[9] Indeed, Eastern European journalists, whose "information" is nothing less than pluralist, would do well to heed Revel's sage observation: "The more a piece of information is pluralist, the less it is information."[10]

Thus, on the surface at least, Eastern Europe's media and journalism in the 1990s would seem to embody Dewey's view. But that they have proven inadequate in directly and purposefully aiding democratization should come as no surprise. It could not be otherwise. First, the ideal, rational democratic community Dewey envisioned as the environment for his type of journalism simply does not exist in the region. Second, the journalism of Eastern Europe is based almost entirely on opinion, analysis, and the interpretation of selective facts, precluding a public discourse whose logic and legitimacy are derived from verifiable and complete information. In fact, in their free and spirited exchange of opinions, the region's journalists, far from creating "truth," have helped shape an ill-informed, misinformed, and often confused citizenry, whose seeming indifference and whose reluctance to participate in sociopolitical life have been exacerbated through their reliance on a journalism of opinion and analysis rather than fact.

Based as it has been, with few exceptions, on rumor, innuendo, opinion, partisanship, political and personal combat, the region's journalism has given rise to widespread distrust among its audiences. Its all-too-often incomplete presentation of selected, unverified, and unsourced facts, its opinionated and slanted reporting, and its often vituperative and intolerant exchange of views are hardly a prescription for promoting the new "public virtues needed for Democracy": civility, mutual trust and understanding, and tolerance.[11] Although granting civil and political rights is a first, essential step toward civil and political citizenship, without the ethical and rational values and behaviors needed to sustain it, democracy cannot take root, much less flourish. As models of a new professional and societal ethic and as disseminators of messages that would help establish it, Eastern Europe's media have failed and thus must be judged to have made no contribution to a new ethical basis for a civil society.

Nevertheless, despite all the negatives attached to the region's overpoliticized and partisan media (see chapter 2) and their lack of professionalism (see chapter 4), there is ample reason to argue that these very deficiencies allowed them to register successes alongside their failures.

Media Successes, Failures, and Contributions

An institution or profession can be judged to have failed when the role it
has performed and the results it has achieved do not match expectations—
provided those expectations are neither misplaced nor unrealistically high.
Such was clearly not the case with regard to Eastern Europe's media, in their
first post-Communist decade.

The misplaced expectation that the region's media would directly, purposefully, and effectively contribute to its transformation stems in part from
the mistaken assumption that the media could remake themselves overnight,
even as they helped remake their post-Communist societies. They could not
do so because they were expressions of the very political and professional
cultures they were called upon to change. The institutional changes undertaken in 1989 altered these cultures only slightly and only in the sense that
they moved them away from the Communist models. The unrealistically
high expectations that the media would, through an ideal pluralism, diversity, and autonomy, help create a fully democratic society were derived in
large part from utopian visions, in some cases informed by leftist ideology
or one of its permutations, a post-Communist version of the "Third Way"
(see "The Future of the Media and Journalism in Democratization" below).
The expected "democratization" simply could not take place during the establishment of preconditions for democracy. It required broad citizen participation and a truly democratic civil society, neither of which was (nor is
yet) present in the countries of the region.

There is ample reason to conclude that, because they are chiefly engaged
in personal and political battles and their journalism is largely based on
opinion rather than fact, Eastern Europe's media more directly and effectively transmit a form of political information "than inculcate democratic
values."[12] They contribute to opinion formation but do not significantly
shape public opinion, despite their intent to do so. Whatever informational,
educational, opinion-forming, and agenda-setting role their journalists
fulfill, they fulfill it, for the most part, unwittingly or even accidentally.

This is why the region's media have not yet become a true "third force"
exerting "a significant influence" on societal attitudes and behaviors.[13] For
Eastern European journalists and journalism to become such a force, they
must adopt the sort of professionalism that recently evolved in Sweden,
where the relationship between the political leanings of Swedish newspapers and that of their journalists is now "very weak."[14]

What is most problematic about the region's news media is not the nature of their pluralism, diversity, autonomy, ownership, or infrastructure, but their lack of professionalism. As described in previous chapters, not only do the region's media generally misinform and fail to educate their audiences, except as an accidental by-product of their polemics and unbalanced analysis, but their journalists contribute to suspicions about democracy, rather than to an atmosphere of compromise, pragmatism, and flexibility vis-à-vis their political opponents, often increasing rather than decreasing intolerance toward opposing parties, beliefs, and preferences. Indeed, they do little to encourage moderation in political positions and partisan identifications, encouraging instead mistrust of the political environment and cooperation, and contributing little if anything to political efficacy and participation.[15] The media have also failed to "promote and maintain standards of ethical conduct in civil and public life."[16] For these reasons, and because of the way their newsrooms are managed and their journalists are beholden to owners, publishers, news directors, and editors, or to their own personal interests, mentalities, desires, and ambitions, Eastern Europe's media generally fail to serve as models of democratic beliefs, attitudes, and values.

Analyzed in the context of the liberalization phase of the transformation of the region's societies from Communism to democracy, the media have registered successes and made telling contributions. As we saw in chapter 5, they have helped create the preconditions for democratization, however indirectly and unwittingly. They have contributed to the evolution of civil society's institutions, economic transformation, and even the beginnings of a new political culture. They have also partially and again, it would seem, unwittingly fulfilled seven of the eight prescriptions for the media in a democratic society proposed by Michael Gurevitch and Jay Blumler (see "The Media and Democracy" in chapter 1).[17] The sole exception, and a principal part of their ethos in need of change, is their failure to respect their audiences.

As negative as the lack of a commonly accepted, well-defined role and of a professional ethos may be, these deficiencies enabled the region's media to make considerable contributions to a transformation process with some very special needs. The example of the former Czechoslovakia, later Czech Republic, speaks to these special needs. After 1989, explains Jiri Pehe,

> many communist-style habits quickly returned to the political area. . . .
> With the opposition so weak, why should the government consult with anyone? And why should it communicate with other political forces, or even the people? With a political culture based on a lack of dialogue, the notion of "we know it all" prevailed.[18]

In such a situation, the partisan, politicized "opposition" media played a crucial "counterpower-like" role; indeed, they were the only ones to force the government to communicate, to force a dialogue, however one-sided that might be. The same situation and outcome prevailed in the other countries of the region. Thus Eastern Europe's specific kind of highly politicized "oppositional" media (described in chapter 4), while not a "counterpower" per se, made a valuable contribution to the re-formation of political culture, a necessary precondition for democratization. Their most obvious success was that, by their nature, they provided political pluralism and diversity, characteristics that strictly profit-based media alone do not provide, at least not according to those who view such media as becoming increasingly entertainment oriented and bland.[19]

Thus, for their unprofessional, sensationalistic, partisan, politicized news reporting, the region's media were undervalued. As the West's experience with how journalism affects beliefs, attitudes, and values shows, even under optimal circumstances,

1. only indirect effects take place;[20]
2. these effects stem from reevaluations of the journalistic products in "consultation" with family, coworkers, neighbors, and so on;[21]
3. news constructs messages beyond its content;[22] and, ultimately,
4. the knowledge audiences share and their evolving political beliefs are largely determined by how actively they reinterpret the images, fragments, and signals they find in the media.[23]

Moreover, as was found in transforming societies outside Eastern Europe, "the non-political content within which political communication is imbedded may . . . make its own independent contribution to political socialization and modernization."[24] Indeed, Eastern Europe's media experience during the Communist era is a good example of how political and nonpolitical content can send unintended messages. That is, reading between the lines of what the Communist media disseminated became a valuable talent, one still put to good use in the post-Communist era and a contribution to unintended resocialization and reeducation. Unfortunately, the level and extent of media contributions to resocialization and reeducation in the region are neither known nor measurable with any degree of certainty or accuracy. If we accept Silvo Lenart's proposition that media effects should be examined in terms of the climate they create, rather than their direct impact, an argument can be made that the Eastern European media have positively contributed to the transformation, despite their negative side effects.[25] They have contributed to the creation of a public climate of competition between a wide range of competitors for political and economic power or for cultural predominance. This climate was largely missing prior to 1989, at least on the overt, legal, or official level. To reiterate, the negative side effect was that, with their journalism, they have also contributed to a climate of distrust, chaos, and insecurity. But this negative climate may itself be cause for their audiences, and indeed for the media themselves, to rethink extant values, behaviors, and attitudes, a process that has been slowly unfolding in the region.

The Eastern European media have been successful in informing their audiences, not by design, but chiefly by virtue of their overpoliticization and partisanship, and in the absence of fact-based journalism. Even as their overpoliticization and partisanship alienated some in their audiences, the media also brought to the fore new issues, new parties, new leaders, and potential leaders, new ideas and possibilities, and contributed to the creation of varied new nongovernmental groups, which is to say, civil society. In fact, many Eastern Europeans first learned of these new ideas, possibilities, leaders, institutions, organizations, and the like from and through the media. Furthermore, thanks to the media's role as a platform for political combat, an increasingly wider variety of issues relevant to the region's citizens were disseminated through news programs and through newly introduced political advertising by politicians and political parties vying for votes. In Eastern Europe, the political combat continues to revolve around both politicians and issues, unlike in the United States, where political contests are by and large reported like horse races, in a style that smacks strongly of sports reporting, and where issue-oriented reporting has become increasingly marginalized, if not eliminated.

As a platform for the newly established economic competition, and even for social and cultural competition, addressing issues such as who should get what share of public moneys, which ethnic or cultural group should get which rights, and what definition of "morals" should prevail, the region's media have again served to inform even when they were manipulated by and mobilized for various partisan political, economic, social, or cultural causes.

The very cacophony of the media's presentation of choices in the realms of politics, commerce, employment, education, culture, society, and psychology has evoked an immediate sense of change, of new opportunities. It has also indirectly helped recruitment for these new opportunities and has enriched the ferment of ideas out of which new political, economic, and cultural attitudes, behaviors, and structures will emerge. In Albania, Bulgaria, and Romania, the media both symbolize and present choices for non-Communist ideas and goals and for group and individual ambitions and interests that were, unlike in Czechoslovakia, Hungary, and Poland, almost completely missing from public life before 1989.

Although the changes undertaken in 1989–2000 may ultimately result in a new professional media ethos, and although the evolving new political culture may ultimately serve to strengthen such an ethos, no data exist to support the conclusion that either of these eventualities has yet come to pass.

What has clearly occurred, however, is that changes in the media as an institution, their diverse partisanship, and their politically biased reportage have allowed them to mirror the changes in their opening, liberalizing, quasi-capitalist societies. Their presentation of sociopolitical and cultural choices, an essential precondition of democratization, has, in turn, contributed to the slow resocialization and reeducation of these societies.

Indirectly and unwillingly, Eastern Europe's media have helped set agendas. As amply illustrated, the media's agenda was at first identical to the policy agenda and later in the post-1989 decade at least similar to it. That the public's agenda was and still is represented by the media from their own political point of view appears in no significant way to have affected their role as agenda setters. After exhaustively reviewing the available data, researchers concluded that the Western media, though they have a minimal effect on actual outcomes, nevertheless set the voters' political agendas.[26] The conclusion continues to be reinforced by studies of the media on both sides of the Atlantic.[27]

In their 1987 study of the effects of television on popular opinion in the United States, Shanto Iyengar and Donald Kinder demonstrated that the media set agendas via "priming," which they defined as "calling attention to some matters while ignoring others," and thus influencing "the standards by which governments, presidents, policies, and candidates for public office are judged."[28] In Eastern Europe, "priming" varies vastly from one news outlet to the next.[29] In a later study, Iyengar outlined a second way the media helped set agendas, "framing," which he described as the contextual cues embedded within a news story.[30] It is an understatement to say that the Eastern European media overdo "framing" in their reportage.[31] Nevertheless, their very diversity and obvious biases serve less to influence public opinion and attitudes than to reinforce them, if and when members of their audiences sympathize with the slant or the cues the media offer them. In attempting to convince their audiences how to think, the region's media have also endeavored to tell them what to think about.[32] Considering the varied and partisan interpretations of information, and the overabundance of views and polemics they present, there is some truth in the argument that the media are offering their audiences choices and asking them to take sides. It is not an insignificant step in the democratization process, given that the Eastern Europeans had little or no opportunity to choose before 1989.

The Eastern European media's most significant contribution in the initial phases of democratization in 1989–2000 has thus been to serve as examples of and conduits for the newly available political, economic, and cultural options, on the one hand, and as facilitators of political, market, and cultural competition, on the other. They have clearly not evolved to the point where they serve as "dominant communication agencies" that "cultivate the dominant image patterns," even if certain news outlets have gained ascendancy in the last eleven years.[33] Indeed, there are as yet no discernible "dominant image patterns" to cultivate, and the battle still rages over which image patterns are to dominate. In Eastern Europe, dysfunctional pre-Communist and Communist cultural patterns are still present, and new cultural patterns are not yet solidly established.

Eastern European societies are works in progress and, therefore, what basic functions their media are to serve are as yet undecided. And how could it be otherwise on a journey of transformation without a well-defined map, without all the means necessary to reach, and certainly without any guarantee of actually reaching, the often articulated destination: a working liberal democracy? For the present, the region's media serve to express and reinforce their political cultures, while at the same time facilitating change by virtue of the new ideas and the debates and fights over them they present their readers, listeners, and viewers. That is all that can reasonably be expected of them.

Whatever their shortcomings, Eastern Europe's media successfully engaged their audiences in 1989–2000. These audiences have played varied, sometimes conflicting, and often less than democratically oriented roles, whether as political partisans, followers, monitors, pupils, critics, or spectators. But they have played, and continue to play, an additional role within the confines of the region's politics, quasi-market economies, and cultures: as judges and juries of media excesses. The most impressive demonstration of the power of this role involved the party press. No matter their political persuasion and the kinship felt with newspapers representing their particular politics and ideologies, readers of the party press "voted" it virtually out

of existence and forced the media, print and broadcast alike, to at least consider being less partisan, even if retaining their overpoliticized approach to
news reporting. In this instance, audiences appear to have defined themselves as active media users rather than as passive media "consumers."[34]

Thus, even though partisan, politicized, unprofessional media may not
be useful in established democracies or even directly in a period of transformation, it was inevitable that Eastern Europe's post-Communist media
would retain these characteristics at least through their first decade, characteristics that have in fact proved useful in the transformation process, however indirectly and unwittingly. These media have given voice to the turmoil
associated with the central question to be definitively answered: transformation to what? As such, they engaged in an ongoing tug-of-war between
the friends and foes of liberal values, between nationalists versus interna-
tionalists, indeed, between Western and anti-Western approaches to an-
swering the question.

The Future of the Media and Journalism in Democratization

Attempts were made in the 1989–2000 period to outline typologies for the
Eastern European media during transition and transformation and to prog-
nosticate about their future evolution.[35] Such typologies and prognostica-
tions are all reasonable and predicated on particular visions of political, social, legal, and economic evolution. Not surprisingly, they are also all
derived from Western experiences. They generally characterize the region's
media systems as a hodgepodge of different, sometimes competing, even
mutually annulling systems, modes of journalism, media roles, audience
roles, and sources of control and influence. There is justification for such a
characterization. However, if one considers the type of unprofessional journalism practiced throughout the region, the varied functions it serves, and
the lost and won battles to control or influence the media, or both, another,
more specific, clearer, and appropriate characterization emerges. The Eastern European media are essentially libertarian, perhaps more so than in the
West, despite their having to function in societies with very strong, lingering tendencies to control, influence, and overregulate them. They lack a
well-defined sense of their roles vis-à-vis society, as well as standards of responsibility and professional parameters; they have little respect for their audiences, all of which may contribute to their libertarian status. Many of the
region's media outlets serve as models of antidemocratic values, beliefs, at-

titudes, and behaviors, whereas many others (unitentionally) serve as models of democratization, facilitating the liberalization of their societies and helping to create some of the preconditions necessary for democracy. The region's media outlets are owned by a fairly wide range of indigenous and foreign groups and individuals. They are not purposeful purveyors of information, yet they inform. They are not agenda setters in the mode of Western media, yet they contribute indirectly and often unwittingly to that function.

The small yet significant signs that some news outlets and some journalists, editors, and news directors are willing and able to formulate professional standards bode well for the future. Karol Jakubowicz posits a course of the media and journalism evolution that is endogenous to the institution, one based on the desire to satisfy material needs, achieve social equilibrium, attain political stability, and achieve professional fulfillment.[36] Ultimately, the region's media may prove to follow such a course, but there is another possible scenario. With small alterations, the media and their journalism may remain in their present stage of evolution given that material needs may be satisfied even without the kind of media evolution seen as salutary to democracy, and given that the realization of professional fulfillment depends on how "professionalism" is defined in broad strokes, either in a Lippmann mode or in a Dewey mode, which is closer to the traditional European journalism.

Whether the region's journalists, editors, news directors, and media owners acquire a deeply felt need for achieving social equilibrium and attaining political stability remains to be seen. What was clear in the 1989–2000 period was that the media and their journalists could neither act nor initiate the journey in that direction. Their evolution in this period appears to have been a function of other institutions, their respective cultures, and, only in a small way, their own willingness and ability to change themselves and their journalism. Thus far, the region's media evolution, as with its social, political, cultural, and economic evolution, has been and will remain the only way it can possibly be: "unperfect."[37] The idea of a perfect society, inclusive of "perfect" media, with the purest of autonomy, unlimited pluralism, diversity, and "citizen participation" serving them, will forever remain "an enormous intellectual fallacy."[38]

The argument is often advanced in the United States that decisions on the nature, role, and practice of journalism by the media and journalists tend to insulate them from their audiences. Whether these decisions will be so made and whether this "insulation" from audiences will occur in Eastern Europe are difficult to predict. The size of the region's nations, their cultures, and the nature of their democracies and of their "citizenship" are quite different from those of the United States. There is no reason to think Eastern European societies will become Americanized and, therefore, that their audiences will react in the same manner as those in the United States.

What, then, does the future hold? When dealing with Eastern Europe, it is dangerous if not impossible to prophesy how societies and their media will ultimately evolve. What we are left with is the hope that liberal democracies will take solid root in the region and that the appropriate media, practicing a professional journalism, will sustain and nurture them. The main impediment to establishing such liberal democracies and media comes from the countries' nondemocratic political cultures and the inability or refusal of their political and media leaders to provide the necessary leadership. Although the political and commercial media have contributed to a less-than-salutary journalism, they do not represent a principal danger either to the professionalization of journalism or to the establishment of liberal democracy.[39] The principal such dangers lies elsewhere, in

1. political, economic, and cultural inertia and stagnation, especially in countries such as Albania and Romania, but potentially also in the region's other nations;
2. the underdevelopment of liberalism as an applied philosophy and the small number of truly liberal groups and individuals, and their tenuous standing and influence in Eastern European societies;
3. a resurgence of the Right, with its penchant for authoritarianism, ethnic nationalism, and xenophobia, should economic, social, and political conditions take a decided turn for the worse, allowing the well-organized right-wing parties to broaden their currently marginal following;[40]
4. a resurgence of the Left, particularly its Communist wing, now a relatively small and largely discredited movement in the region, should the lingering delusions of Marxism, neo-Marxism, and utopian Socialism, encouraged by leftist groups in the West, rekindle Socialistic dreams, and should its followers be joined by liberals with idealistic visions of a new world who succumb to leftist illiberal policies to achieve these visions.[41]

The public sphere and system of communication suggested by some scholars for the region are related, if not outright to leftist philosophy, then to a "Third Way" philosophy, which would involve "democratization of the media as well as democratization through the media."[42] Yet other institutions and factors are proving far more central to democratization than the media, which will continue to serve as important adjuncts to the transition from Communism and the transformation to democracy, aiding the process even while they remain unprofessional, provided they have the freedom to be diverse and pluralist. Drawing on the region's recent history and on media experiences elsewhere, we can speculate that democratization *through* the media is highly improbable, if not outright impossible. Nor is democratization *of* the media, entailing "participatory and alternative media forms and democratic uses of information technologies," a more probable eventuality.[43]

First, given the presence of media outlets espousing the full range of ideologies from Marxist to Fascist, presenting a wide variety of civic issues from the environment to education and health care, and reflecting an extensive range of cultural and ethnic interests, it is hard to imagine what viable "alternative" media forms might be missing from the current mix. Second, it is unclear to what extent and purpose nonjournalists might participate in the media, what effect the nonparticipation of others might have on the "participatory media," and even who might decide what "democratic use" of the media means. Third, participatory, Deweyan media forms, their efficacy questionable even in the established democracies of the West, are clearly not viable in the unconsolidated democracies of Eastern Europe. In particular, the widespread presence of computer technologies and the equally widespread, multiple uses of the Internet suggest a participatory media form may in principle be possible in the West, although it is far too early to assess the long-range role the Internet might play in democracy and increased civic participation.[44] But, in any event, these new technologies are not yet sufficiently established in Eastern Europe to be relevant. Access to the Internet is too limited to allow it to contribute to greater media participation and the democratization of civic culture. The region's poor telecommunications infrastructure and the "uncertain legal framework" handicapped the development of the new electronic media in 1990–2000.[45] For instance, the number of fixed telephone lines per 100 inhabitants ranges from a high of nearly 35 in Bulgaria to a low of fewer than 4 in Albania.[46] The estimated number of personal computers per 100 citizens ranges from a high of 12 in the Czech Republic to a low of fewer that 1 in Albania.[47] The International Telecommunications Union (ITU) estimates that, out of every 10,000 inhabitants, more than 976 and 1,202 use the Internet in the Czech and Slovak Republics respectively; 722 in Poland, 699 in Hungary, fewer than 523 in Bulgaria, 358 in Romania, and 6 in Albania.[48] Although in most countries of the region, daily and weekly publications, as well as television and radio programs and news agency reports, are available on the Internet, as the above-mentioned data suggest, access to these Internet offerings is restricted; indeed, for the foreseeable future, they will be of greatest benefit to interested foreign Internet users.[49]

Granted that the ability of the Internet to contribute to greater media participation is likely to increase over time, particularly in those countries whose economies continue to grow, where the middle class expands, and the educational system puts greater emphasis on computer literacy and computer availability, whether it will truly allow for "participatory" media forms, even in the West, remains to be seen. Once again, the question of how many individuals will choose to participate, at what level of discourse, and with what knowledge, goals, and capabilities, remains unanswered and perhaps unanswerable. Most important, neither the culture nor the necessary time, interest, and competence for participatory media forms is present in Eastern Europe, nor is it likely to be for years, perhaps decades to come. Furthermore, such an approach to journalism, in the context of the often touted "plurality of voices" ideal, cannot be the mainstay of public discourse and sociopolitical decision making because democracy is not and cannot be a "steambath of popular opinion."[50] Indeed, participatory journalism may be little more than a recipe for chaos.

The proposition that democratization through the media can be achieved only by way of "media strategies of various social movements and groups devoted to progressive issues and social change" suggests a sort of hegemonic journalistic class, one that exclusively pursues leftist or Third Way "progressive" policies.[51] The media in this "slightly contrived, almost elitist" concept "[attract] wider attention only if coupled with evangelistic methods of communication. Spin doctors are therefore essential for the Third Way."[52] Such an approach, traditionally taken by both the Right and the Left, defines the philosophy of Eastern European journalism during transformation. In disputing the very possibility, let alone the value, of objective, verifiable truth, it allows for the kind of journalistic relativism that liberally mixes fact and fiction, and that replaces reporting and analysis with evangelism, advocacy, and opinion driven by ideology, politics, or studied ignorance.

One of the supreme benefits of the twentieth century is that it has unmistakably and unambiguously taught us some crucial lessons about certain ideologies, political ideas, and practices, sociocultural mentalities, and, I suggest, the types of journalism that can and cannot contribute to an informed public and to public dialogue, discussions, and debates in a democracy. To be useful to democratic society, news reporting and analysis have to be fact-based, objective, and undistorted by personal beliefs or by sociopolitical and ideological goals. Even opinion writing, in the form of commentaries, editorials, or outright polemics, is useful and "interesting only when it is a form of information," that is, only when it is comprehensively documented, multisided, and analyzed in a balanced way.[53]

While the practices of journalism are clearly affected by the cultural milieu in which they are learned and applied, journalistic professionalism is not simply defined by culture; indeed, with increasing globalization, any support for the claim that it is culture specific may vanish.[54] More important, because democracies share certain basic characteristics, values, and processes, it is reasonable to expect that the institutions serving and making them possible, to include the media, also share fundamental characteristics, values, and processes.

Here it is instructive to review the underlying causes of the media's loss of credibility and their negative impact on democracy in both Eastern Europe and United States. These include the tabloid like sensationalizing and trivializing of public affairs by journalists who are all too often cynical, judgmental, and careless in their reporting, and who increasingly approach the selection and presentation of news stories from a political or ideological perspective.[55] Indeed, both U.S. and Eastern European journalists are seen as too opinionated, biased, and arrogant; self-appointed media "pundits" and "analysts" all too often turn out to have no particular expertise.[56] The Zola-like journalism, so characteristic of the contemporary Eastern European media, harks back to the American Progressive Era, and the apogee of muckraking and investigative journalism. It should be remembered that, even though such journalism achieved positive results, it was accompanied by a decline in overall political participation, "an age of voter apathy."[57] There are suggestive parallels in post-Communist Eastern Europe and the present-day United States.

Rejecting Western-style journalism, Slavko Splichal called for Eastern European nations to develop "an indigenous pluralistic model of journalism that would enable different conceptions to compete in practice."[58] His call has been more than answered. By the end of the 1990s, not just one but several "indigenous pluralistic" models of journalism had emerged. But which of these models will actually facilitate the transformation to democracy remains unclear. Absent a widespread, informed sense among media audiences of how and why they should digest news, and what they should demand of the news media, the "winning" journalistic model could well be inimical to liberal democracy and a free and open society.

In short, the Eastern European media do not need to be "democratized," most certainly not by the Left, nor even by the "Third Way." They need to professionalize. They need universally agreed upon standards and some combination of review boards, ombudsmen, media critics, and professional journalistic associations, as well as publications to publicly assess their work and to discuss major professional issues. They need to become morally and professionally accountable to their audiences. They need to supply accurate, balanced, complete, and verifiable information that allows citizens to debate issues, come to conclusions, and make decisions. And they need to educate their audiences both in the uses of objective, verifiable information and in the standards that make news gathering and reporting useful to them as citizens. Only by doing so can the media directly facilitate the process of democratization.

In other words, the region's media need to be professional information gatekeepers instead of sociopolitical and cultural partisans and activists, propagandists, and polemicists. Unquestionably, they also need to avoid having their journalism driven strictly by the market, which would compromise their contribution to liberal democracy and the freedoms it guarantees. The media should reflect and serve their "unperfect" democracies, animated by idealism but without illusions, prizing individual and societal freedom above all else.[59]

Where the entangled, "unperfect" evolutions of Eastern Europe's post-Communist media will take them no one knows. Thus far, their progress has been slow and often tentative, although increasingly fueled from within the media institution and journalistic profession. Only time will tell whether it will continue and where it will lead.

Notes

Chapter 1

1. See Andrew Arato, "The Rise, Decline and Reconstruction of the Concept of Civil Society, and Directions for Future Research," in Adolf Bibic and Gigi Graziano, eds., *Civil Society, Political Society* (Ljubljana, Slovenia: Slovenian Political Science Association, 1994), 3–16; Ernest Gellner, *Conditions of Liberty: Civil Society and Its Rivals* (New York: Penguin, 1994); Adam B. Seligman, *The Idea of Civil Society* (Princeton, N.J.: Princeton University Press, 1992).

2. See Gabriel A. Almond, "Introduction," in Larry Diamond, ed., *Political Culture and Democracy in Developing Countries* (Boulder, Colo.: Rienner, 1994), ix–xiii; see also Harry Eckstein, "A Culturalist Theory of Political Change," *American Political Science Review* 82 (Sept. 1988): 796–804; Gabriel A. Almond, "The Study of Political Culture," in Almond, ed., *A Divided Discipline: Schools and Sects in Political Science* (Newbury Park, Calif.: Sage, 1990), 153–6; Michael Thompson, Richard Ellis, and Aaron Wildavsky, *Cultural Theory* (Boulder, Colo.: Westview Press, 1990); Larry Diamond, Juan J. Linz, and Seymour Martin Lipset, "Democracy in Developing Countries: Facilitating and Obstructing Factors," in Raymond D. Gastil, ed., *Freedom in the World: Political Rights and Civil Liberties, 1987–1988* (New York: Freedom House, 1988), 229–60, to mention but a few.

3. Vladimir Tismaneanu, *Reinventing Politics* (New York: Free Press, 1992), 36; see also Vladimir Tismaneanu, *Fantasies of Salvation: Democracy, Nationalism and Myth in Post-Communist Europe* (Princeton, N.J.: Princeton University Press, 1998).

4. See Robert Bideleux and Ian Jeffries, *A History of Eastern Europe: Crisis and Change* (New York: Routledge, 1998).

5. For the purposes of this text, "Eastern Europe" comprises the following seven countries: Albania, Bulgaria, the Czech Republic, Hungary, Poland, Romania, and the Slovak Republic. Traditionally, Albania, Bulgaria, and Romania have been assigned to the Balkans; Hungary, Poland, and the former Czechslovakia, to East Central Europe. On the assignment of countries to a particular region, see Timothy Garton Ash, "The Puzzle of Central Europe," *New York Review of Books,* Mar. 18, 1999, 18–23.

6. See, most notably, Hannah Arendt, *The Origins of Totalitarianism* (New York: Harcourt Brace Jovanovich, 1973); Zbigniew Brzezinski, *The Soviet Bloc: Unity and*

Conflict (Cambridge, Mass.: Harvard University Press, 1967); Milovan Djilas, *The Unperfect Society: Beyond the New Class* (New York: Harcourt Brace Jovanovich, 1969); Milovan Djilas, *Land without Justice* (New York: Harcourt Brace Jovanovich, 1958); Bernard Henry Levy, *Barbarism with a Human Face* (New York: Harper and Row, 1979); F. A. Hayek, *The Fatal Conceit: The Errors of Socialism* (Chicago: University of Chicago Press, 1989); Adam Michnik, *Letters from Prison and Other Essays* (Berkeley: University of California Press, 1985); Václav Havel, *Living in Truth* (London: Faber and Faber, 1987); Leszek Kolakowski, *Main Currents of Marxism,* vol. 3, *The Breakdown* (Oxford: Oxford University Press, 1978); Raymond Aron, *The Opium of the Intellectuals* (New York: Norton, 1962); Ferenc Feher, Agnes Heller, and Gyorgy Markus, *Dictatorship over Needs* (New York: St. Martin's Press, 1983).

7. See, for example, Hilaire Belloc, *The Servile State* (London: Foulis, 1913); Jacob Burckhardt, *Reflections on History* (London: George Allen and Unwin, 1943); Ludwig von Mises, *Socialism* (New Haven, Conn.: Yale University Press, 1951); Wilhelm von Humboldt, *The Limits of State Action* (Cambridge: Cambridge University Press, 1969).

8. See Max Weber, *Economy and Society* (New York: Bedminster Press, 1968), vol. 1; Max Weber, *Selections from His Work* (New York: Crowell, 1963); on Weber's critique of Socialism, see also Daniel Bell, "The Post-Industrial Society: The Evolution of an Idea," *Survey* 79 (Spring 1971): 117–29.

9. One of the most comprehensive works is Stephane Courtois et al., *The Black Book of Communism: Crimes, Terror, Repression* (Cambridge, Mass.: Harvard University Press, 1999).

10. The phrase "sultanistic regimes" is borrowed from Weber, *Economy and Society;* "ghettoized" is borrowed from Ken Jowitt, "The Leninist Legacy," in Ivo Banac, ed., *Eastern Europe in Revolution* (Ithaca, N.Y.: Cornell University Press), 207–24; see also Ken Jowitt, *New World Disorder: The Leninist Extinction* (Berkeley: University of California Press, 1992).

11. See especially Valerie Bunce, *Subversive Institutions: The Design and the Destruction of Socialism and the State* (New York: Cambridge University Press, 1999).

12. Larry Diamond, Juan J. Linz, and Seymour Martin Lipset, "Introduction: Comparing Experiences in Democracy," in Diamond, Linz, and Lipset, eds., *Politics in Developing Countries: Comparing Experiences with Democracy* (Boulder, Colo.: Rienner, 1990), 17.

13. See Karl Popper, *The Poverty of Historicism* (New York: Routledge, 1991).

14. Diamond, Linz, and Lipset, "Introduction," 16–17; see also Howard Wiarda, ed., *Politics and Social Change in Latin America: The Distinct Tradition* (Amherst: University of Massachusetts Press, 1974); Diamond, ed., *Political Culture and Democracy,* parts 4 and 5.

15. In the context of analyzing media, "freedom" has other senses (to be discussed later), such as autonomy and differentiation, both being assigned more or less the same meaning.

16. Jeffrey C. Alexander, "The Mass Media in a Systemic, Historical and Comparative Perspective," in Elihu Katz and Tamas Szecsko, eds., *Mass Media and Social Change* (London: Sage, 1981), 33, 27.

17. Jean-François Revel, *The Flight from Truth: The Reign of Deceit in the Age of Information* (New York: Random House, 1991), 247.

18. Alexis de Tocqueville, *Democracy in America* (New York: New American Library, 1956), 203.

19. Tismaneanu, *Fantasies of Salvation,* 40.

20. For a few of the many examples of disagreements, see J. F. Brown, *Hopes and Shadows: Eastern Europe after Communism* (Durham, N.C.: Duke University Press, 1994); Tismaneanu, *Reinventing Politics;* Michael Mandelbaum, ed., *Post-Communism: Four Perspectives* (New York: Council on Foreign Relations, 1996).

21. See, for example, Leszek Balcerowicz, *Socialism, Capitalism, Transformation* (Budapest: Central European University, 1995); Robert Skidelsky, "The State and Economy: Reflections on the Transition from Communism to Capitalism in Russia," in Mandelbaum, ed., *Post-Communism,* 22–76; M. Steven Fish, *Democracy from Scratch* (Princeton, N.J.: Princeton University Press, 1995); Adam Przeworski, *Democracy and the Market* (Cambridge: Cambridge University Press, 1991); Attila Agh, *Politics of Central Europe* (London: Sage, 1998); Jon Elster, Claus Offe, and Ulrich K. Preuss, *Institutional Design in Post-Communist Societies: Rebuilding the Ship at Sea* (New York: Cambridge University Press, 1999); Stephen Holmes, "Cultural Legacies or State Collapse? Probing the Post-Communist Dilemma," in Mandelbaum, ed., *Post-Communism,* 1–21.

22. See Francis Fukuyama, *The End of History and the Last Man* (New York: Free Press 1992), 220.

23. Agh, *Politics of Central Europe,* 16–18. Agh follows the three stages of democratization suggested by Rustow: (1) pretransition or initial crisis, (2) democratic transition, and (3) consolidation. See Dankwart Rustow, "Transitions to Democracy: Toward a Dynamic Model," *Comparative Politics* 2, no. 3 (Apr. 1970): 337–65.

24. Fukuyama, *End of History,* 222.

25. See, to mention only a few, Tismaneanu, *Reinventing Politics* and *Fantasies of Salvation;* Zbigniew Brzezinski, *The Grand Failure: The Birth and Death of Communism in the Twentieth Century* (New York: Collier, 1990); Jowittt, *New World Disorder;* Katherine Verdery, *What Was Socialism, and What Comes Next?* (Princeton, N.J.: Princeton University Press, 1996).

26. See Robert D. Putnam, *Making Democracy Work* (Princeton, N.J.: Princeton University Press, 1993); Ronald Inglehart, "The Renaissance of Political Culture," *American Political Science Review* 82, no. 4 (Dec. 1988): 1203–30; see also Ronald Inglehart, *Culture Shift in Advanced Industrial Society* (Princeton, N.J.: Princeton University Press, 1990).

27. Tismaneanu, *Fantasies of Salvation,* 5.

28. Holmes, "Cultural Legacies," 7.

29. See Robert W. Jackman and Ross A. Miller, "A Renaissance of Political Culture?" *American Journal of Political Science* 40, no. 3 (Aug. 1996): 632–59.

30. See Beverly Crawford and Arend Lijphart, "Explaining Political and Economic Change in Post-Communist Eastern Europe: Old Legacies, New Institutions, Hegemonic Norms, and International Pressures," *Comparative Political Studies* 28 (July 1995): 177–99.

31. See for example, the extensive discussion of divergent explanations of post-Communist evolution in ibid.

32. See Bruce Parrott, "Perspectives on Post-communist Democratization," in Karen Dawisha and Parrott, eds., *Politics, Power, and the Struggle for Democracy in South-East Europe.* (Cambridge: Cambridge University Press, 1997), 1–40.

33. Almond, "Political Culture," 144; see also Eckstein, "Culturalist Theory," 796–804.

34. Parrott, "Perspectives," 22.

35. See, for example, Samuel P. Huntington, *The Third Wave: Democratization in the Late Twentieth Century* (Norman: University of Oklahoma Press, 1991); Daniel Chirot, *How Societies Change* (Thousand Oaks, Calif.: Pine Forge Press, 1994); see also Daniel Chirot, ed., *The Origins of Backwardness in Eastern Europe: Economics and Politics from the Middle Ages until the Early Twentieth Century* (Berkeley: University of California Press, 1989).

36. See Karen Dawisha, "Democratization and Political Participation: Research Concepts and Methodologies," in Dawisha and Bruce Parrott, eds., *The Consolidation of Democracy in East-Central Europe* (New York: Cambridge University Press, 1997), 40–65.

37. See Arato, "Rise, Decline," 3–16; see also Jean Cohen and Andrew Arato, *Civil Society and Political Theory* (Cambridge, Mass.: MIT Press, 1992); Norberto Bobbio, *The Future of Democracy* (Minneapolis: University of Minnesota Press, 1987); John Keane, *Democracy and Civil Society* (London: Verso, 1988).

38. Gellner, *Conditions of Liberty,* 12, 164.

39. See, among many others, Agh, *Politics of Central Europe;* Marcia A. Weigle and Jim Butterfield, "Civil Society in Reforming Communist Regimes: The Logic of Emergence," *Comparative Politics* 25, no. 1 (Oct. 1992): 1–23; Michael Bernhard, "Civil Society and Democratic Transition in East Central Europe," *Political Science Quarterly* 108, no. 2 (1993): 307–26; Andrzej Korbonski, "Civil Society and Democracy in Poland: Problems and Prospects," in Bibic and Graziano, eds., *Civil Society,* 215–31.

40. See Mate Szabo, "The State of Political Institutions, Political Society and Civil Society in Hungary," in Bibic and Graziano, eds., *Civil Society,* 265–86.

41. See Jeffrey C. Isaac, *Democracy in Dark Times* (Ithaca, N.Y.: Cornell University Press, 1998), 150–79.

42. Parrott, "Perspectives," 23.

43. See Seligman, *Idea of Civil Society.*

44. See Jürgen Habermas, *Between Facts and Norms: Contributions to a Discourse Theory of Law and Democracy* (Cambridge, Mass.: MIT Press, 1996).

45. See, for example, Slavko Splichal, *Media beyond Socialism* (Boulder, Colo.: Westview Press, 1994); Colin Sparks and Anna Reading, *Communism, Capitalism and the Mass Media* (London: Sage, 1998).

46. John Downing, *Internationalizing Media Theory: Transition, Power, Culture* (London: Sage, 1996), 245.

47. See Diamond, ed., *Political Culture.*

48. See Gabriel A. Almond, "The Intellectual History of the Civic Culture Concept," in Almond and Sidney Verba, eds., *The Civic Culture Revisited* (Newbury Park, Calif.: Sage, 1989), 1–36; Huntington, *Third Wave.*

49. See Gabriel A. Almond and Sidney Verba, *The Civic Culture: Political Attitudes and Democracy in Five Nations* (Princeton, N.J.: Princeton University Press, 1963).

50. See Sidney Verba, "Conclusion: Comparative Political Culture," in Lucian Pye and Verba, eds., *Political Culture and Political Development* (Princeton, N.J.: Princeton University Press, 1995), 512–60.

51. See Robert A. Dahl, *Political Oppositions in Western Democracies* (New Haven, Conn.: Yale University Press, 1966).

52. See Huntington, *Third Wave,* 258–79.

53. See Lucian W. Pye, "Introduction: Political Culture and Political Development,"

in Pye and Verba, eds., *Political Culture,* 3–26; Aaron Wildavsky, "Choosing Preferences by Constructing Institutions: A Cultural Theory of Preference Formation," *American Political Science Review* 8 (Mar. 1987): 3–21; see also Thompson, Ellis, and Wildavsky, *Cultural Theory;* Eckstein, "Culturalist Theory"; Lucian W. Pye, *Asian Power and Politics: The Cultural Dimensions of Authority* (Cambridge, Mass.: Harvard University Press, 1985), 29.

54. Pye, *Asian Power,* 20; see also ibid., 12, 24–25, 53.

55. See, for example, Russell Fitzgibbon and Julio A. Fernandez, *Latin America: Political Culture and Development* (Englewood Cliffs, N.J.: Prentice Hall, 1981); Lawrence E. Harrison, *Underdevelopment Is a State of Mind: The Latin American Case* (Lanham, Md.: Madison; Cambridge, Mass.: Center for International Affairs, Harvard University, 1985); Wiarda, ed., *Politics and Social Change;* Diamond, ed., *Political Culture;* Inglehart, "Renaissance" and *Culture Shift.* But, for a fine critique of the political cultural approach to Eastern Europe from a conceptual and methodological perspective, see Fritz Plasser and Peter Ulram, "Measuring Political Culture in East Central Europe: Political Trust and System Support," in Plasser and Andreas Pribersky, eds., *Political Culture in East Central Europe* (Brookfield, Vt.: Ashgate, 1996), 3–34.

56. See Eckstein, "Culturalist Theory"; Almond and Verba, *Civic Culture,* 15; Almond, "Intellectual History," 27–28, and "Political Culture," 153.

57. See Robert C. Tucker, *Political Culture and Leadership in Soviet Russian: From Lenin to Gobachev* (New York: Norton, 1987), 4–6.

58. Ibid., 5.

59. See Joseph Schumpeter, *Capitalism, Socialism and Democracy,* 2d ed. (New York: Harper and Brothers, 1947). I offer an elaboration of the various models of democracy in chapter 5.

60. See Robert A. Dahl, *Polyarchy: Participation and Opposition* (New Haven, Conn.: Yale University Press, 1971).

61. Huntington, *Third Wave,* 9.

62. See Edmund Burke, *Reflections on the Revolution in France* (New York: Penguin, 1986); James Madison, Alexander Hamilton, and John Jay, *The Federalist Papers* (New York: Penguin, 1987). For a "biography" of civil society, see John Ehrenberg, *Civil Society: The Critical History of an Idea* (New York: New York University Press, 1999).

63. John Keane, ed., *Civil Society and the State: New European Perspectives* (London: Verso, 1988), 364.

64. Seligman, *Idea of Civil Society,* 206.

65. Gellner, *Conditions of Liberty,* 193.

66. See Ralf Dahrendorf, *Reflections on the Revolution in Europe* (New York: Random House, 1990); Karl Popper, *The Open Society and Its Enemies* (London: Routledge, 1945).

67. Dahrendorf, *Reflections,* 41.

68. See Cohen and Arato, *Civil Society* ; see also Norberto Bobbio, *Stato, governo, societa: Per una teoria generale della politica* (Turin: Einaudi, 1985).

69. Parrott, "Perspectives," 22.

70. Revel, *Flight from Truth,* 6.

71. See Jürgen Habermas, *Structural Transformation of the Public Sphere* (Cambridge, Mass.: Polity Press, 1989), and *Between Facts;* Peter Dahlgren, "Ideology and Information in the Public Sphere," in Jennifer Daryl Slack and Fred Fejes, eds., *The Ideology of the Information Age* (Norwood, N.J.: Ablex, 1987); Nicholas Garnham, "The

Media and the Public Sphere," in Peter Golding, Graham Murdock, and Philip Schlesinger, eds., *Communication Politics: Mass Communications and the Political Process* (Leicester, England: Leicester University Press, 1986), 37–54.

72. See Jürgen Habermas, *Theorie des kommunikativen Handelns* (Frankfurt: Suhrkamp, 1985), vols. 1 and 2.

73. See Richard Rose, William Mishler, and Christian Haerpfer, *Democracy and Its Alternatives: Understanding Post-Communist Societies* (Baltimore: Johns Hopkins University Press, 1998), 34.

74. See Gellner, *Conditions of Liberty*, chaps. 17–19, 22, 24–25; see also Ralph Dahrendorf, *After 1989: Morals, Revolution and Civil Society* (New York: St. Martin's Press, 1997).

75. Rose, Mishler, and Haerpfer, *Democracy and Its Alternatives*, 34. In arguing that political parties represent civil society, the authors see the institutions of civil society missing in Eastern Europe.

76. See Cohen and Arato, *Civil Society*.

77. See Jiri Pehe, "After the Soviet Empire: Civil Society in Democratizing States," *Current*, (Mar.–Apr. 1996): 27–31.

78. Seligman, *Idea of Civil Society*, 202. Seligman traces the evolution of the concept of civil society in the context of ethics and morality in his chapter 2, "The Sources of Civil Society." See also Wilhelm Roepke, *The Moral Foundations of Civil Society* (New Brunswick, N.J.: Transaction, 1996). Roepke deals with questions fundamental to both human and humane society.

79. Seligman, *Idea of Civil Society*, 179.

80. See James Fishkin, *Democracy and Deliberation: New Directions for Democratic Reform* (New Haven, Conn.: Yale University Press, 1991); see also Amy Gutmann and Dennis Thompson, *Deliberative Democracy* (Cambridge, Mass.: Harvard University Press, 1996).

81. See Barry Holden, *Understanding Liberal Democracy* (Oxford: Allen, 1988).

82. See Jacques Attali, *Millennium* (New York: Times Books, 1991).

83. Brzezinski, *Grand Failure*, 255, suggests two types of post-Communism: authoritarian and plural.

84. Havel, *Living in Truth*, 153.

85. Isaacs, *Democracy*, 162.

86. Descriptions and explanations of this phenomenon can be found in, among other works, Stephen Fischer-Galati, ed., *The Communist Parties of Eastern Europe* (New York: Columbia University Press, 1979); Jan. F. Triska and Paul M. Cocks, eds., *Political Development in Eastern Europe* (New York: Praeger, 1977); Brzezinski, *Soviet Bloc;* Jowitt, "Leninist Legacy," 207–24. Personal testimonies of the duality in the political culture that existed in Eastern Europe until 1989 can be found in Milovan Djilas, *Fall of the New Class: A History of Communism's Self-Destruction* (New York: Alfred A. Knopf, 1998), and *Unperfect Society;* Michnik, *Letters from Prison;* Havel, *Living in Truth;* Mihai Botez, *Intelectualii din Europa de Est* (Bucharest: Romanian Cultural Foundation, 1993); and in the works of other intellectuals and former members of the various Communist parties in the region.

87. See, for example, Archie Brown and Jack Gray, *Political Culture and Political Change in Communist States* (New York: Holmes and Meier, 1977).

88. Gale Stokes, *The Walls Came Tumbling Down: The Collapse of Communism in Eastern Europe* (New York: Oxford University Press, 1993), 256.

89. Jean-François Revel, *Revirimentul democratiei* (Bucharest: Humanitas, 1993), 137. Originally published as *Le regain démocratique* (France: Editions Fayard, 1992).

90. Stjepan G. Mestrovic, *Habits of the Balkan Heart* (College Station: Texas A and M University Press, 1993), 18.

91. Bideleux and Jeffries, *History of Eastern Europe,* 27.

92. Tismaneanu, *Fantasies of Salvation,* 44.

93. See Jowitt, *New World Disorder;* see also Jowitt, "Leninist Legacy," 210.

94. See Leszek Kolakowski, "The Myth of Human Self-Identity," in Kolakowski and Stuart Hampshire, eds., *The Socialist Idea* (New York: Basic Books, 1975), 18–35.

95. Jowitt, "Leninist Legacy," 211; see also Jacques Rupnik, *The Other Europe: The Rise and Fall of Communism in East-Central Europe* (New York: Schocken, 1989).

96. Jowitt, *New World Disorder,* 78; for additional descriptions of post-Communist political culture, see Revel, *Revirementul.*

97. Tismaneanu, *Fantasies of Salvation,* 21.

98. Ibid., 46.

99. Zbigniew Brzezinski, "Post-Communist Nationalism," *Foreign Affairs* 68, no. 5 (Winter 1989–90): 2.

100. Jowitt, *New World Disorder,* 288.

101. For a detailed description of the anti-Communist civil society, see George Schopflin, *Politics in Eastern Europe, 1945–1992* (Oxford: Blackwell, 1993); see also Isaac, *Democracy,* chap. 7. It should not be forgotten that there were few politically active individuals even in Hungary and the Czech Republic; there were practically none in Albania, Bulgaria, and Romania. Only in Poland did a substantial number of politically active actors play an oppositional role vis-à-vis the Communist state.

102. Paul Lendvai, *The Bureaucracy of Truth: How Communist Governments Manage the News* (London: Burnett, 1981), 25.

103. See Paul Kecskemeti, "Totalitarian Communication as a Means of Control," *Public Opinion Quarterly* 14 (1950): 224–34.

104. For a detailed account of censorship and self-censorship in Poland and Romania, see Jane Leftwich Curry, *Black Book of Polish Censorship* (New York: Vintage Press, 1984); Ion Manea, "Does the Romanian Press Exist in Today's Romania?" *ARA Journal* 10 (1985): 142–7; Anneli Ute Gabanyi, "Das Zensursystem in Rumanien," *Wissenschaftlischer Dienst Sudosteuropa* 5 (1978): 270–3; and Marian Petcu, *Puterea si Cultura: O istorie a cenzurii* (Iasi, Romania: Polirom, 1999). On censorship in other Eastern European countries, see George Schopflin, ed., *Censorship and Political Communication: Examples from Eastern Europe* (New York: St. Martin's Press, 1983).

105. For example, it is argued that Hungary's media system was deliberately less controlled than Poland's or Czechoslovakia's in order to co-opt Hungarian intellectuals. See Schopflin, *Censorship;* see also Anthony Buzek, *How the Communist Press Works* (New York: Praeger, 1964); Wilbur Schramm, "The Soviet Communist Theory of the Press," in Fred S. Siebert, Theodore Peterson, and Schramm, eds., *Four Theories of the Press: The Authoritarian, Libertarian, Social Responsibility and Soviet Communist Concepts of What the Press Should Be and Do* (Urbana: University of Illinois Press, 1956), 105–46.

106. See Karol Jakubowicz, "Media as Agents of Change," in David L. Paletz, Jakubowicz, and Pavao Novosel, *Glasnost and After: Media and Change in Central and Eastern Europe.* (Cresskill, N.J.: Hampton Press, 1996), 19–48.

107. See Havel, *Living in Truth,* part 1, chaps. 1–2.

108. See Czeslaw Milosz, *The Captive Mind* (New York: Vintage, 1981); see also Tomasz Goban-Klas, *The Orchestration of the Media: The Politics of Mass Communications in Communist Poland and Its Aftermath* (Boulder, Colo.: Westview Press, 1994); Dean Mills, "Mass Media as Vehicles of Education, Persuasion, and Opinion Making . . . in the Communist World," in L. John Martin and Anju Grover Chaudhary, eds., *Comparative Mass Media Systems* (New York: Longman, 1983), 167–86; Romulus Boila, "Press and Radio," in Alexander Cretzianu, ed., *Captive Romania* (New York: Praeger, 1956), 257–84; Kecskemeti, "Totalitarian Communication"; Madeleine Korbel Albright, *Poland: The Role of the Press in Political Change* (New York: Praeger, 1983). There are many other works, too many to list here, specifically focusing on the media of each Eastern European country during the Communist era.

109. See Françoise Thom, *Newspeak: The Language of Soviet Communism* (London: Claridge Press, 1989).

110. Havel, *Living in Truth,* 47; for a comprehensive discussion of language and information manipulation through the media, see Milosz, *Captive Mind;* Leszek Kolakowski, "On Total Control and Its Contradictions: The Power of Information," *Encounter* 2 (1989): 65–71; Leszek Kolakowski, "Totalitarianism and the Virtue of the Lie," in Irving Howe, ed., *1984 Revisited* (New York: Harper and Row, 1983), 123–35.

111. For a discussion of the underground presses of Eastern Europe, see H. Gordon Skilling, *Samizdat and an Independent Society in Central and Eastern Europe* (Columbus: Ohio State University Press, 1989). For an overview of the foreign media's penetration and effects after 1989, see J. Semelin, "The Reshaping of East-West Communications in Europe," in Jörg Becker and A. Butrimenko, eds., *Europe Speaks to Europe: Telecommunications in a Common European House* (Frankfurt: Haag and Herchen, 1993), 53–60; Zoltan Jakab and Mihaly Galik, *Survival, Efficiency and Independence: The Presence of Foreign Capital in the Hungarian Media Market* (Manchester, England: European Institute for the Media, 1991); Karol Jakubowicz, *Conquest or Partnership? East-West European Intergration in the Media Field* (Düsseldorf: European Institute for the Media, 1996); Tom Fenton, *Betting on the Media: Foreigners in for Low-Ante, High-Stakes Central European Game* (Arlington, Va.: Freedom Forum, Dec. 1995).

112. Brzezinski, *Grand Failure,* 254.

113. Bronislaw Geremek as quoted in Ravel, *Revirimentul,* 182. A Polish historian, Geremek was for a time the head of the Solidarity parliamentary faction.

114. See Holmes, "Cultural Legacies," 22–76; see, for example, Jowitt, "Leninist Legacy."

115. For a succinct description of the cultural legacies of Communism, see Jane Leftwich Curry, "The Sociological Legacies of Communism," in Zoltan Barany and Ivan Volgyes, eds., *The Legacies of Communism in Eastern Europe* (Baltimore: Johns Hopkins University Press, 1995), 67.

116. Umberto Eco, "Ur-Fascism," *New York Review of Books,* June 22, 1995, 12; Tismaneanu, *Fantasies of Salvation,* 30; see also Barany and Volgyes, eds., *Legacies of Communism.*

117. Tismaneanu, *Fantasies of Salvation,* 163.

118. For a full explanation of the nationalist, racist, and anti-Semitic legacies of Communism and pre-Communism, see Tismaneanu, *Fantasies of Salvation.*

119. Jowitt, "Leninist Legacy," 215.

120. See Adam Michnik, *Letters from Freedom: Post-Cold War Realities and Per-*

spectives, ed. Irena Grudzinska Gross (Berkeley: University of California Press, 1998), 178–83.

121. Charles Gati, "The Mirage of Democracy," *Transition* 2, no. 6 (Mar. 22, 1996): 6–12, 62.

122. See Jonathan Schell, "Three Kinds of Fundamentalism," in Michnik, *Letters from Freedom.*

123. See *Eurobarometer Survey* (Brussels: Commission of the European Communities, 1994); see also the poll or survey results published in Plasser and Pribesrsky, eds., *Political Culture,* chap. 1, and those regarding Romania in *Barometrul de Opinie Publica* (Bucharest: Romanian Center for Urban and Regional Sociology, Oct. 9–15, 1996).

124. See *New Democracies Barometer IV* (Vienna: Paul Lazarsfeld Society, 1996); Gati, "Mirage of Democracy."

125. Tismaneanu, *Fantasies of Salvation,* 30.

126. See Richard Rose, *What is Europe?* (New York: HarperCollins, 1996).

127. Isaac, *Democracy,* 159; see also Dahl, *Polyarchy,* 129–162.

128. See George Schopflin, "Post-Communism: A Profile," *Public* 2, no. 1 (1995): 63–74; see also Stephen Fischer-Galati, "Political Culture in Eastern Europe: Romania as a Case Study of a General Phenomenon," in Joan Serafin, ed., *East Central Europe in the 1990s* (Boulder, Colo.: Westview Press, 1994), 137–60; Trond Gilberg, "Romanians and Democratic Values: Socialization after Communism," in Daniel N. Nelson, ed., *Romania after Tyranny* (Boulder, Colo.: Westview Press, 1992), 83–94.

129. Zoltan Barany, "Hungary," in Barany and Volgyes, eds., *Legacies of Communism,* 182.

130. See Schumpeter, *Capitalism, Socialism.*

131. For one of the best discussions of the rule of man versus the rule of law issue, see Bobbio, *Future of Democracy,* 138–56.

132. See Wojciech Lamentowicz as paraphrased by Karol Jakubowicz, "Television and Elections in Post-1989 Poland: How Powerful Is the Medium?" in David L. Swanson and Paolo Mancini, eds. *Politics, Media and Modern Democracy* (Westport, Conn.: Praeger, 1996), 139–54.

133. See, for example, Barany and Volgyes, eds., *Legacies of Communism,* chaps. 7–12, 13, 15.

134. Wojciech Lamentowicz as quoted by Jakubowicz, "Television and Elections," 150.

135. See *Eurobarometer Survey;* Jane Leftwich Curry, "A Reconsideration of the Realities of 'Civil Society' in the Light of Postcommunist Society," in Bibic and Graziano, eds., *Civil Society,* 231–48.

136. See T. H. Marshall, *Class, Citizenship and Social Development* (Westport, Conn.: Greenwood Press, 1972), 71–72.

137. Gellner, *Conditions of Liberty,* 206.

138. Curry, "Reconsideration," 242.

139. Ibid.

140. Seligman, *Idea of Civil Society,* 114, 203.

141. See Dina Iordanova, "Bulgaria: Provisional Rules and Directorial Changes: Restructuring of National TV," *Public* 2, no. 3 (1995): 19–32; see also Rose, Mishler, and Haerpfer, *Democracy and Its Alternatives,* 66.

142. See Jiri Pehe, "Czech Crisis Deepens," *New Presence,* Jan. 1999 <www.new-presence.cz>; see also Brown, *Hopes and Shadows;* Michael Bernhard, "Civil Society

after the First Transition: Dilemmas of Post-Communist Democratization in Poland and Beyond," *Communist and Post-Communist Studies* 29, no. 3 (Sept. 1996): 309–31; Mate Szabo, "Repertoires of Contention in Post-Communist Protest Cultures: An East Central European Comparative Survey (Hungary, Slovakia, Slovenia)," *Social Research* 63, no. 4 (Winter 1996): 1155–83; Daniel Chirot, "Why East Central Europe Is Not Quite Ready for Peron, but May Be One Day," *East European Politics and Society* 10, no. 2 (Fall 1996): 536–42; Aleksander Smolar, "From Opposition to Atomization: Civil Society after Communism," *Journal of Democracy* 7, no. 1 (Jan. 1996): 24–39; Bronislaw Geremek, "Civil Society Then and Now," *Journal of Democracy* 2 (1992): 3–12; Korbonski, "Civil Society," 215–30; Szabo, "State of Political Institutions," 265–86; Dahrendorf, *After 1989;* Habermas, *Between Facts;* Peter Dahlgren, *Television and the Public Sphere: Citizenship, Democracy and the Media* (London: Sage, 1995); Garnham, "Media," 359–76; John Keane, *The Media and Democracy* (Cambridge: Polity Press, 1991), and *Democracy.*

143. See Curry, "Reconsideration," 231–48. The existence or nonexistence of civil society serves not only to characterize a particular nation but also to distinguish one nation from another.

144. Agh, *Politics of Central Europe,* 215; see also Larry Diamond, "Economic Development and Democracy Reconsidered," in Gary Marks and Larry Diamond, eds., *Reexamining Democracy: Essays in Honor of Seymour Martin Lipset* (Newbury Park, Calif.: Sage, 1992), 93–139.

145. See Cohen and Arato, *Civil Society,* chap. 1.

146. Agh, *Politics of Central Europe,* 215.

147. See, for example, Daniel N. Nelson, "Civil Society Endangered: The Perils of Post-Communism" Occasional paper no. 42, Woodrow Wilson International Center for Scholars, Washington, D.C., Sept. 1995.

148. See Grzegorz Ekiert and Jan Kubik, *Rebellious Civil Society: Popular Protest and Democratic Consolidation in Poland* (Ann Arbor: University of Michigan Press, 2000).

149. Brown, *Hopes and Shadows,* 26.

150. Habermas, *Between Facts,* 371.

151. Seligman, *Idea of Civil Society,* 203.

152. Ibid., 115–6.

153. See Pehe, "After the Soviet Empire"; Bibic, "Democracy and Civil Society," 62.

154. Schopflin, *Politics in Eastern Europe,* 284.

155. For a concise explication of the debate, see Pehe, "After the Soviet Empire"; for additional views of civil society's development in Eastern Europe, see Bernhard, "Civil Society after the First Transition."

156. Václav Klaus as quoted by Pehe, "After the Soviet Empire," 29.

157. Schopflin, "Post-Communism," 63.

158. See Oleg Manaev, "Rethinking the Social Role of the Media in a Society in Transition," *Canadian Journal of Communication* 20 (1995): 45–65.

159. Dahlgren, *Television and the Public Sphere,* 12.

160. Ibid., 2.

161. For descriptions of post-1989 media in Eastern Europe, see, among many other works, Oleg Manaev and Yuri Pryluk, eds., *Media in Transition from Totalitarianism to Democracy* (Kiev: ABRIS, 1993); Johanna Neuman, "The Media: Partners in the Revolution of 1989," working paper, Atlantic Council of the United States, June

1991. Scores of other works were published between 1990 and 1999; some are listed elsewhere in these notes.

162. See Janos Horvat, "The East European Journalist," *Journal of International Affairs* 45 (1991): 191–200.

163. See Siebert, Peterson, and Schramm, eds., *Four Theories of the Press.*

164. See Albert Namurois, *Problems of Structure and Organization of Broadcasting in the Framework of Radio Communications* (Geneva: European Broadcasting Union, 1964); see also John C. Merrill and Ralph Lowenstein, *Media, Messages and Men: New Perspective in Communication* (New York: McKay, 1979); J. Herbert Altschull, *Agents of Power: The Role of News Media in Human Affairs* (White Plains, N.Y.: Longman, 1984).

165. The former media system types were advanced by Raymond Williams, *Communications* (Harmondsworth, England: Penguin, 1968); the latter by William A. Hachten, *The World News Prism: Changing Media, Clashing Ideologies* (Ames: Iowa State University Press, 1987), and *The World News Prism: Changing Media of International Communication* (Ames: Iowa State University Press, 1992).

166. See, for example, John C. Merrill, "A Conceptual Overview of World Journalism," in Merrill and Heinz-Dietrich Fischer, eds., *International and Intercultural Communication* (New York: Hastings House, 1976), 18–28.

167. See Richard Picard, "Revisions of the Four Theories Press Model," *Mass Comm Review* (Winter–Spring 1982–83): 83, 27.

168. See Merrill and Lowenstein, *Media, Messages and Men,* chap. 10; Altschull, *Agents of Power.*

169. See Michael Gurevitch and Jay G. Blumler, "Linkages between the Mass Media and Politics: A Model for Analysis of Political Communication Systems," in James Curran, Gurevitch, and Janet Woollacott, eds., *Mass Communication and Society* (London: Arnold, 1983), 270–90.

170. Theodore Peterson, Jay Walbourne Jensen, and William L. Rivers, *The Mass Media and Modern Society* (New York: Holt, Rinehart and Winston, 1966).

171. See Karl Erik Rosengren, "Mass Media and Social Change: Some Current Approaches," in Katz and Szecsko, eds., *Mass Media,* 247–64.

172. See Walter Lippmann, *The Phantom Public* (New York: Macmillan, 1927); Walter Lippmann, *The Public Philosophy* (New York: Mentor, 1955).

173. See George Donohue, Clarice Olien, and Phillip Tichenor, "A 'Guard Dog' Conception of Mass Media," paper presented at the Association for Education in Journalism and Mass Communication Conference, held in San Antonio, Aug. 1987.

174. Melvin DeFleur and Sandra Ball-Rokeach, *Theories of Mass Communication,* 5th ed. (New York: Longman, 1990), 315–6.

175. See Merrill and Lowenstein, *Media, Messages, and Men,* chaps. 9 and 12.

176. Hachten, *World News Prism* (1987), 70.

177. For a good discussion of the four theories of the events of 1989, see Sparks and Reading, *Communism, Capitalism,* chap. 4.

178. Hachten, *World News Prism* (1987), 73.

179. See, among others, Wilbur Schramm, "Communication Development and the Development Process," in Lucian W. Pye, ed., *Communications and Political Development* (Princeton, N.J.: Princeton University Press, 1963), 30–57; Daniel Lerner, *The Passing of Traditional Society: Modernizing the Middle East* (Glencoe, Ill.: Free Press, 1958); Daniel Lerner, "Toward a Communication Theory of Modernization," in Pye, ed., *Communications,* 327–50; Karl Deutsch, "The Growth of Nations: Some Recurrent Pat-

terns of Political and Social Integrations," *World Politics* 5 (Jan. 1953): 168–95; Ithiel de Sola Pool, *Technologies of Freedom* (Cambridge, Mass.: Harvard University Press, 1983).

180. See Ekaterina Ognianova, *The Transitional Media of Post-Communist Bulgaria* (Columbia, S.C.: Association for Education in Journalism and Mass Communication, June 1997), Journalism and Mass Communication Monographs, no. 162.

181. See Slavko Splichal, "The 'Civil Society Paradox' and the Media in Central and Eastern Europe," in *Research on Democracy and Society* (Greenwich, Conn.: JAI Press, 1993), vol. 1, pp. 85–109. Splichal further developed his arguments in his *Media beyond Socialism;* see also Paolo Mancini, "The Public Sphere and the Use of News in a 'Coalition' System of Government," in Peter Dahlgren and Colin Sparks, eds., *Communication and Citizenship* (London: Routledge, 1991), 137–54.

182. Sparks and Reading, *Communism, Capitalism,* 180.

183. See Karol Jakubowicz, "Lovebirds? The Media, the State and Politics in Central and Eastern Europe," *Public* 2, no. 1 (1995): 75–91; see also Brzezinski, *Grand Failure.*

184. See Michael Gurevitch and Jay G. Blumler, "Political Communication System and Democratic Values," in Judith Lichtenberg, ed., *Democracy and the Mass Media* (New York: Cambridge University Press, 1990), 269–89.

185. Habermas, *Between Facts,* 378.

186. Keane, *Media and Democracy,* 126. On media democratization, see, for example, Janet Wasco and Vincent Mosco, eds., *Democratic Communications in the Information Age* (Toronto: Garamond Press; Norwood, N.J.: Ablex, 1992); see also Slavko Splichal and Janet Wasco, *Communication and Democracy* (Norwood, N.J.: Ablex, 1993).

187. Todd Gitlin, *The World Is Watching* (Berkeley: University of California Press, 1980), 7. For works examining the nature of news, see also Herbert Gans, *Deciding What's News* (New York: Pantheon, 1979); Gaye Tuchman, *Making News: A Study in the Construction of Reality* (New York: Free Press, 1978).

188. See Michael Schudson, "How News Becomes News," *Forbes Media Critic* (Summer 1995), 76–85.

189. See, for example, Joseph Man Chan and Chin-Chuan Lee, *Mass Media and Political Transition: The Hong Kong Press in China's Orbit* (London: Guilford Press, 1991).

190. Denis McQuail, *Mass Communication Theory: An Introduction* (London: Sage, 1987), 269.

Chapter 2

1. Small, local, mostly short-lived print and radio outlets were established in Eastern Europe during the first post-Communist year.

2. Liviu Antonesei aptly characterizes political discourse under Communism as a combination of "indoctrination and training" (as in animal training: *"dresaj"*). See Antonesei, "Cultura Politica si Terapie Sociala in Romania Post-Comunista," *Revista de Cercetari Sociale* 1 (1994): 118–23.

3. Lucian W. Pye, "Communications and Civic Training in Transitional Societies" (introduction to chap. 7), in Pye, ed., *Communications,* 124–7.

4. See, for example, Liana Giorgi, *The Post-Socialist Media: What Power the*

West: The Changing Media Landscape in Poland, Hungary, and the Czech Republic (Aldershot, England: Avebury, 1995), chaps. 2–4.

5. Ibid.; see also Oleg Manaev, "Rethinking the Social Role of the Media in a Society in Transition," *Canadian Journal of Communication* 20 (1995): 45–65.

6. Giorgi, *Post-Socialist Media,* 33; Oleg Manaev, "Media Autonomy and the State in Post-Communist Society: Diversity vs. Unity (the Case of Belarus)" (Belorussian State University, Minsk, n.d., photocopy). See see also Alexander, "Mass Media," 17–52.

7. Bruce Parrott, "Perspectives," 17. Political scientists make clear distinctions between political parties and political systems; the type, nature, origins, and problems encountered in forming and reforming political parties are comprehensively described by Agh, *Politics of Central Europe,* chap. 5.

8. Agh, *Politics of Central Europe,* 106.

9. Habermas, *Between Facts,* 379; see also Keane, *Media and Democracy.*

10. Agh, *Politics of Central Europe,* 108.

11. Ibid., 106.

12. Ibid., 109.

13. See Brzezinski, *Grand Failure,* 225.

14. See A. Lanczi and Patrick H. O'Neil, "Pluralization and the Politics of Central Europe: Media Change in Hungary," in O'Neil, ed., *Post-Communism and the Media in Eastern Europe* (London: Cass, 1997), 82–101.

15. Tomasz Goban-Klas, "Politics versus the Media in Poland: A Game without Rules," in O'Neil, ed., *Post-Communism and the Media,* 32.

16. See, for example, *NDB-Neue Demokratien Barometer* (Vienna: Fessel and Paul Lazarsfeld, 1994); U.S. Information Agency, "Romanians' Confidence in Media Steadily Declining," research memorandum, Feb. 1992.

17. See Mihai Coman, "Romanian Journalism in a Transition Period, 1990–1992," in Gerd Hallemberger and Michael Krzeminski, eds., *Osten Europa Medienlandschaft im Umbruch* (Berlin: Vistas, 1994), 81–98.

18. There were differences between the opposition media of Czechoslovakia, Hungary, and Poland. Furthermore, the opposition media in these countries were themselves divided into the "underground" media and the "aboveground" media, tolerated by the Communist regimes. In all countries of the region, with or without opposition media, there were also "alternative" media (which, though not oppositional in nature, offered an alternative to the politically engaged official media) and foreign media. See Karol Jakubowicz, "Musical Chairs: The Three Public Spheres in Poland," in Dahlgren and Sparks, eds., *Communication and Citizenship,* 155–75; see also Skilling, *Samizdat.*

19. By "civil society," I mean small groups of people getting together for other than political reasons and organizing small, informal or formal associations, mostly local, with varied interests.

20. See Peter Gross, "Small Signs of Great Changes . . . at a Romanian TV Station," *Columbia Journalism Review* 29, no. 1 (May–June 1990): 37–39.

21. Interviews with journalists in Bulgaria (1992), Poland (1994 and 1995), Albania (1994), the Czech Republic (1995, 1996, 1997), Romania (1990, 1991, 1992, 1993, 1994, 1995, 1996, and 1997), and Hungary (1990 and 1996).

22. For a discussion of different types of post-Communist political parties, see Agh, *Politics of Central Europe,* chap. 5, pp. 126–63.

23. See Karol Jakubowicz, "Media Concentrations and Foreign Media Presence in

Central and Eastern Europe" (University of Warsaw, n.d., photocopy), 13–8, 22–6, 31–49.

24. Ognianova, *Transitional Media,* 18.

25. Janos Horvat, "Media Democracy and Media Freedom in Eastern Europe," paper presented at the annual meeting of the International Communication Association, held in Miami, June 1992.

26. See Ildiko Kovats and Gordon Whiting, "Hungary," in Paletz, Jakobowicz, and Novosel, eds., *Glasnost and After,* 97–129.

27. See Lanczi and O'Neil, "Pluralization," 96, for the Hungarian version of this complaint, which was also expressed to me by journalists in Albania, Bulgaria, the Czech Republic, and Romania.

28. Goban-Klas, "Politics versus the media," 24–41.

29. Splichal, *Media beyond Socialism,* 147.

30. That all newspapers in Albania had been politicized was made clear to me in Jan. 1994 in numerous interviews with Albanian editors and journalists during a weeklong visit to Tirana. See also Nicholas Pano, "The Process of Democratization in Albania," in Dawisha and Parrott, eds., *Politics, Power,* 285–352.

31. Ibid., 332. See also Al Hester, "The Albanian Press: Battling for More Freedom," in Hester, L. Earle Reybold, and Kimberly Conger, eds., *The Post-Communist Press in Eastern and Central Europe: New Studies* (Athens: University of Georgia, James M. Cox, Jr., Center for International Mass Communication Training and Research, 1992), 5–26.

32. Interview with Prec Zogaj in Tirana, Jan. 1994.

33. Owen Johnson, "East Central and Southeastern Europe and Russia and the Newly Independent States" (Indiana University, Bloomington, n.d., photocopy).

34. Prec Zogaj as quoted in Cathy Packer, "The Emergence of the Free Press in Albania," in Al Hester and Kristina White, eds. *Creating a Free Press in Eastern Europe* (Athens: University of Georgia, James M. Corx, Jr. Center for International Mass Communication Training and Research, 1993), 96.

35. Ognianova, *Transitional Media,* 20.

36. See R. Kolakova and D. Dimitriov, "Postcommunist Media in Bulgaria," 1995 <www.soc.culture.bulgaria>.

37. See Ivan Nikolchev, "Polarization and Diversification in the Bulgarian Press," in 'ONeil, ed., *Post-Communism and the Media,* 124–44; cites "1,705"; Ekaterina Ognianova and Byron Scott, "Milton's Paradox: The Market-place of Ideas in Post-Communist Bulgaria," *European Journal of Communication* 12, no. 3 (Sept. 1997): 369–90; cite "2,664."

38. See Peter Gross, *Mass Media in Revolution and National Development: The Romanian Laboratory* (Ames: Iowa State University Press, 1996).

39. Cornel Nistorescu, "Libertatea amara," *Expres* (Bucharest), July 27, 1990, 6. Translations of material quoted from foreign-language sources throughout this work are mine, unless otherwise noted.

40. The relationship between Solidarity and Solidarity journalists was a strained one even before it took power. Specifically, the union's heavy hand in attempting to control freedom of the press was continued after 1989. See Karol Jakubowicz, "Solidarity and the Media," *European Journal of Communications* 2–3 (1990): 333–54. For a discussion of the relationship between Walesa, Solidarity, and *Gazeta Wyborcza,* see Adam Michnik, "My Vote against Walesa," in Michnik, *Letters from Freedom,* 156–66.

41. See Goban-Klas, *Orchestration of the Media,* 222; see also Goban-Klas, "Politics versus the Media," 24–41.

42. Karol Jakubowicz, "Is 'Solidarity' the Sorcerer's Apprentice? Reconstructing Public or Corporate Communication?" (University of Warsaw, 1991).

43. Karol Jakubowicz, "Poland," in Paletz, Jakubowicz, and Novosel, eds., *Glasnost and After,* 140.

44. Ibid., 144–7.

45. Goban-Klas, *Orchestration of the Media,* 223.

46. See Giorgi, *Post-Socialist Media,* 90; Johnson, "East Central," estimates there were 2,500 Polish publications in Poland in 1993–94.

47. Owen V. Johnson, "The Czech Republic," in Maurice Fliess, ed., *Looking for the Future: A Survey of Journalism Education in Central and Eastern Europe and the former Soviet Union* (Reston, Va.: Freedom Forum, Aug. 1994), 22–26. As is the case in the rest of Eastern Europe, the party press system in what used to be Czechoslovakia has strong roots in the region's political traditions and was part and parcel of the media system in the 1918–39 period, when the country was recognized and applauded as a parliamentary democracy.

48. See Rudolf Prevratil, "Czechoslovakia," in Paletz, Jakubowicz, and Novosel, eds., *Glasnost and After,* 149–71.

49. Michael J. Jordan, "Stumbling toward Press Freedom," *International Press Institute Report* (1998, 2d quarter): 23, 31.

50. Giorgi, *Post-Socialist Media,* 112.

51. Ibid.; see Barbara Kopplova, Jan Jirak and Frank L. Kaplan, "Major Trends in the Czech Mass Media after November 1989," in Hester and White, eds., *Creating a Free Press,* 193–256.

52. Prevratil, "Czechoslovakia," 168.

53. See Andrej Skolkay, "Journalists, Political Elites and the Post-Communist Public: The Case of Slovakia," in O'Neil, ed., *Post-Communism and the Media,* 61–81; see also Juraj Vojtek, "Journalism and Journalism Education in Slovakia since 1989" (Comenius University, Bratislava, 1996).

54. See Lanczi and O'Neil, "Pluralization," 82–101.

55. Kovats and Whitting, "Hungary," 116; see also Peter Gross, "Hungary's New Tabloid Media," *Christian Science Monitor,* Feb. 27, 1990, 19.

56. Giorgi, *Post-Socialist Media,* 54.

57. Curry, "Sociological Legacies," 72.

58. See Schramm, "Communication Development," 30–57.

59. Ibid., 34.

60. See, for example, Yudit Kiss, "Privatization in Hungary—Two Years Later," *Soviet Studies* 44, no. 6 (1992): 1015–38; Teresa Kuczynska, "The Capitalists among Us," *Telos* 92 (1992): 159–63; Kazimierz Z. Poznanski, "Privatization of the Polish Economy: Problems of Transition," *Soviet Studies* 44, no. 4 (1992): 641–64; Ernest Gellner, "The Price of Velvet: On Thomas Masaryk and Vaclav Havel," *Telos* 94 (1993): 183–92.

61. Ognianova and Scott, "Milton's Paradox," 382.

62. See Giorgi, *Post-Socialist Media,* 57.

63. Nikolchev, "Polarization and Diversification," 129.

64. See Coman, "Romanian Journalism," 81–98.

65. See Mihai Coman, "1996—Starea Mass Media in Romania" (University of Bucharest, n.d., photocopy).

66. See Karol Jakubowicz, "Media Autonomization in Central and Eastern Europe: Some Remarks on the Polish Case" (University of Warsaw, 1998).

67. "Albania," *Post-Soviet Media Law and Policy Newsletter,* May 15, 1998, 26.

68. See Nikolchev, "Polarization and Diversification," 129.

69. See Colin Seymour-Ure, *The Political Impact of Mass Media* (Beverly Hills, Calif.: Sage, 1974), chap. 6.

70. Ognianova, *Transitional Media,* 24. There is little proof that such a drastic change occurred. Bulgarian journalists still "frequently color their reports to conform with the views of the political parties or economic groups that own their respective newspapers." "Bulgaria," *Post-Soviet Media Law and Policy Newsletter,* May 15, 1998, 27.

71. See Goban-Klas, "Politics versus the Media," 24–41.

72. France Vreg, "Political, National, and Media Crisis," in Paletz, Jakubowicz, and Novosel, eds., *Glasnost and After,* 52.

73. Dean E. Murphy, "A Slow Transition," *International Press Institute Report* (1997, 1st quarter): 13–5.

74. Adam Michnik, "Samizdat Goes Public," *Media Studies Journal* 5, no. 3 (Summer 1995): 77.

75. Pye, "Communications," 126.

76. Denis McQuail, " The Influence and Effects of Mass Media," in Doris A. Graber, ed., *Media Power in Politics,* 3d ed. (Washington, D.C.: CQ, 1994), 21.

77. See John Dewey, *The Public and Its Problems* (New York: Holt, 1927), 168–9, 177, 180–2.

78. Christopher Lasch, *The Revolt of the Elites and the Betrayal of Democracy* (New York: Norton, 1995), 174.

79. Agh, *Politics of Central Europe,* 112.

80. Rustow, "Transitions to Democracy," 337.

81. Klaus von Beyme, *Systemwechsel in Osteuropa* (Frankfurt: Suhrkamp, 1994), 13.

82. Agh, *Politics of Central Europe,* 69–72.

83. Ibid.; see also Jowitt, *New World Disorder,* 294–9.

84. See Elemer Hankiss, "In Search of a Paradigm," *Daedalus* 119, no. 1 (Winter 1990): 183–215.

85. See, for example, Agh, *Politics of Central Europe,* parts 3 and 4.

86. Jowitt, *New World Disorder,* 296.

87. Splichal, *Media beyond Socialism,* 107; see also Schopflin, *Politics in Eastern Europe,* 287.

88. See Colin Sparks and Anna Reading, "Understanding Media Change in East Central Europe," *Media, Culture and Society* 16, no. 2 (1994): 243–70.

89. Lerner, "Toward a Communication Theory," 342.

90. Downing, *Internationalizing,* 148.

91. Lanczi and O'Neil, "Pluralization," 89.

92. Colin Sparks, "Is There Such a Thing as a 'Post-Communist Media System'?" *Sfera Politicii,* no. 64 (Dec. 1998): 23–26.

93. Johnson, "East Central," 161.

94. Suskosd, "Media War," 69.

95. Interview with Ylli Rakipi, editor-in-chief of *Republika,* in Tirana, Jan. 1994.

96. Goban-Klas, *Orchestration of the Media,* 244.

97. Skolkay, "Journalists, Political Elites," 73.

98. See Johnson, "East Central."

99. See Tom Nicholson, "Slovak Television Abandons Public Media Norms," *New Presence,* July 1998 <www.new-presence.cz>.

100. See Jan Culik, "Spectacular Failure of Reform," *New Presence,* Aug. 1998 <www.new-presence.cz>.

101. Goban-Klas, *Orchestration of the Media,* 244.

102. See Kovats and Whiting, "Hungary," 112.

103. See, for example, Elemer Hankiss, *The Hungarian Media's War of Independence: Analysis* (Budapest: Center for Social Studies, 1993).

104. Andrew K. Milton, "News Media Reform in Eastern Europe: A Cross-National Comparison," in O'Neil, ed., *Post-Communism and the Media,* 12.

105. Prevratil, "Czechoslovakia," 169.

106. Goban-Klas, *Orchestration of the Media,* 225.

107. For example, Dinu Patriciu, a leader of the Liberal Party is also owner of the daily *Ziua,* and Ion Ratiu, a leader of the National Christian Democratic Peasant Party, owns *Cotidianul.* See also Virgil Stefan Nitulescu, "Media Transparency in Romania: Current Situation and Possible Problems," *Post-Soviet Media Law and Policy Newsletter,* June 15, 1998, 45–48.

108. Richard A. Hall, "The Dynamics of Media Independence in Post-Ceausescu Romania," in O'Neil, ed., *Post-Communism and the Media,* 103. The extent of direct or indirect influence exerted by former Securitate members is difficult to ascertain. Some media outlets are in the hands of former Securitate officers. For example, the television station Antena 1, Radio Romantic, and the newspaper *Jurnalul National* are all owned by Dan Voiculescu, a former Securitate officer turned businessman; the newspaper *Curierul National* is owned by George Constantin Paunescu, another former Securitate officer, who is now a businessman with financial interest in the daily *Evenimentul Zilei.*

109. See Splichal, "'Civil Service Paradox,'" 85–109; Mancini, "Public Sphere," 133–54.

110. Eric Hobsbawm, *The Age of Extremes: A History of the World, 1914–1991* (New York: Vintage, 1996), 581.

111. Henry F. Carey, "From Big Lie to Small Lies: State Mass Media Dominance in Post-Communist Romania," *East European Politics and Society* 10, no. 1 (Winter 1996): 17.

112. See Lanczi and O'Neil, "Pluralization," 98.

113. See Dawisha, "Democratization," 40–68.

114. For a good description of the "enmity" factor and personalization in East European politics, see Schopflin, *Politics in Eastern Europe,* 276–77.

115. Brown, *Hope and Shadows,* 32–34. On opposition to the party or parties in power viewed through the political lens of extreme antagonism—the "friend-foe" concept of politics—see Carl Schmitt, *Der Begriff des Politischen: Mit einer Rede über das Zeitalter der Neutralisierungen und Entpolitisierungen neu heraugegeben von Carl Schmitt* (Munich: Duncker and Humblot, 1932).

116. Bideleux and Jeffries, *History of Eastern Europe,* 604.

117. See Herbert Passin, "Writer and Journalist in the Transitional Society," in Pye, ed., *Communications,* 82–123.

118. See Elizabeth Fox, ed., *Media and Politics in Latin America: The Struggle for Democracy.* (London: Sage, 1988).

119. Passin, "Writer and Journalist," 123.
120. Teresa Sasinska-Klas as quoted by Karol Jakubowicz, "Normative Models of Media and Journalism in Central and Eastern Europe," paper presented at the "Profession of Journalism in a Democratic Society: East-West Perspective" conference, held at Napier University, Edinburgh, Sept. 4–5, 1998, 10.
121. Patricia Clough, as quoted in Bideleux and Jeffries, *History of Eastern Europe,* 603.
122. Agh, *Politics of Central Europe,* 96; see also Sabrina P. Ramet, *Whose Democracy? Nationalism, Religion, and the Doctrine of Collective Rights in Post-1989 Eastern Europe.* (Lanham, Md.: Rowman and Littlefield, 1997).
123. Hobsbawm, *Age of Extremes,* 581.
124. See, for example, David L. Swanson, "Political Institutions in Media-Centered Democracy," as quoted in Ralph Negrine, *The Communication of Politics* (London: Sage, 1996), 158; see also Negrine, *Communication of Politics,* 180.
125. For the Romanian case, see Gross, *Mass Media,* chaps. 4 and 5.
126. See Jerome Aumente et al., *Eastern European Journalism: Before, during and after Communism* (Cresskill, N.J.: Hampton Press, 1999), 142.
127. Christina Spolar, "Albania Reverts to One-Party Government," *Washington Post,* June 22, 1996, A19, A 21.
128. Linnet Myers, "Hungary Leaders Succumb to Media's Lack of Balance," *Chicago Tribune,* June 12, 1994, sec. 4, 1, 7.
129. Ibid.
130. See Gross, *Mass Media,* 133–40; Carey, "From Big Lie"; Peter Gross, *Colosul cu picioare de lut* (Iasi, Romania: Polirom, 1999).
131. Myers, "Hungary Leaders Succumb," 1.
132. See, for example, European Institute for the Media, *Monitoring Media Coverage of Local Elections in Albania: Final Report,* Jan. 1997, and *Monitoring the Media Coverage of the 1996 Romanian Parliamentary and Presidential Elections: Final Report,* Mar. 1997.
133. Jan Culik, "News and Current Affairs in Czech Television," paper presented at "The Profession of Journalism in a Democratic Society: East-West Perspectives" conference, held at Napier University, Edinburgh, Sept. 4–5, 1998, 4.
134. Ibid., 3; see also Culik, "Spectacular Failure."
135. J. Bralczyk and M. Mrozowski, "The Presidential Election Campaign on Television: Construing the (Self-) Portrayals of the Candidates," as quoted in Jakubowicz, "Television and Elections," 129–54.
136. See Václav Havel, "Anti-Political Politics," in Keane, ed., *Civil Society and the State,* 381–98.
137. None of the suggestions made by scholars are implementable in the context of the transition's reality. For instance, Vreg's fourteen normative guidelines for preventing political communication from working against democratic development are not applicable because they are based on unrealistic assumptions. See Vreg, "Political, National," 49–64, esp. 60–61.
138. The rapidity with which the media divorced themselves from political parties varied from country to country during the period 1992–99, the only exception being Albania, where the party press persisted into the latter half of the 1990s.
139. See "Deputatii vor publicitate pe TVR," *Telegrama* (Bucharest), Sept. 10, 1998.
140. In the early 1990s, before market economies were sufficiently established, one

way parties in government could gain influence over the media was to manipulate advertising contracts between state-owned enterprises and media outlets. This happened most glaringly in Hungary. See U.S. Department of State, *Human Rights Report for 1999— Country Reports* <www.state.gov/global/human_rights/1999.hrpreport/hungary.html>.

141. See Gurevitch and Blumler, "Linkages," 270–290.

142. See Barbara Geddes, *Politician's Dilemma: Building State Capacity in Latin America.* Berkeley: University of California Press, 1994. Schumpeter made the same observation in the context of the United States. See Schumpeter, *Capitalism.*

143. See, for example, Victor M. Perez-Diaz, *The Return of Civil Society: The Emergence of Democratic Spain* (Cambridge, Mass.: Harvard University Press, 1993).

Chapter 3

1. For in-depth descriptions of the Hungarian "media wars," see Hankiss, *Hungarian Media's War;* Patrick H. O'Neil, "Communication and Democracy: The Hungarian Experience" (1998, photocopy).

2. Sukosd, "Media War," 69.

3. Splichal, *Media beyond Socialism,* 144.

4. See Brown, *Hopes and Shadows,* 34.

5. Curry, "Sociological Legacies," 72; see also Hankiss, *Hungarian Media's War;* Ognianova, *Transitional Media;* Downing, *Internationalizing Media Theory;* O'Neil, ed., *Post-Communism and the Media.*

6. Dahlgren, *Television and the Public Sphere,* 6; see also Jakubowicz, "Media Autonomization"; Splichal, *Media beyond Socialism,* 136.

7. Patrick H. O'Neil, "Introduction: Media Reform and Democratization," in O'Neil, ed., *Post Communism and the Media,* 2.

8. Splichal, *Media beyond Socialism,* 135.

9. For a good description of such media models, see Splichal, *Media beyond Socialism,* 138–43; Keane, *Media and Democracy* (Cambridge: Polity Press, 1991), 51–92, 115–62.

10. See Peter Gross, "(Imperfect) Work in Progress," in David L. Paletz, Karol Jakubowicz, and Pavao Novosel, eds., *Business as Usual? Continuity and Change in Central and Eastern European Media* (Cresskill, N.J.: Hampton Press, forthcoming), 243–80.

11. Michael J. Jordan, "Apathy in Central Europe," *International Press Institute Report* (Aug.–Sept. 1996): 29.

12. See for example, Splichal, *Media beyond Socialism;* Sparks and Reading, *Communism, Capitalism;* Jakubowicz, "Media Autonomization." Depending on those concerned, fears about state control of the media are tied to politics, the role of the state, or the market.

13. See Gross, *Mass Media,* chap. 3.

14. Giorgi, *Post-Socialist Media,* 27.

15. Ibid., 74–77.

16. Kolarova and Dimitrov, " Postcommunist Media in Bulgaria," 130–1.

17. "Eastern Europe's Ailing Press," *New York Times,* Aug. 6, 1996, A16.

18. Aumente et al., *Eastern European Journalism,* 94.

19. Lanczi and O'Neil, "Pluralization," 88; József Antall's Hungarian Democratic

Forum (MDF) government managed to block the sale of newspapers to companies seen as hostile to it and to place two state publishing houses off limits to privatization. See Cynthia Wilson, "Freedom Tests the Press in Eastern Europe," *Presstime* 13, no. 3 (Mar. 1991): 20–27; see also Sukosd, "Media War."

20. R. Frydman, J. Murphy, and A. Rapaczynski, "Capitalism with a Comrade's Face," *Transitions,* Jan. 26, 1996, 5.

21. See Giorgi, *Post-Socialist Media,* 59.

22. "Hungary," *Post-Soviet Media Law and Policy Newsletter,* Sept. 15, 1998, 19.

23. "Albania," *Post-Soviet Media Law and Policy Newsletter,* May 15, 1998, 15.

24. "Albania," *Post-Soviet Media Law and Policy Newsletter,* Apr. 15, 1998, 14.

25. See Rossen Milev, "Fernsehen in Bulgarien: Die Entwicklung des dualen Modells in medienrechtlichen Vakuum," in R. Milev, ed., *TV auf dem Balkan* (Hamburg: Hans-Bredow Institut, 1996), 27–60.

26. Tom Fenton, *Quiet Revolution: Cable Television Comes to Central Europe* (New York: Columbia University, Freedom Forum Media Studies Center, 1994), 9.

27. For the best summation of foreign investments in Eastern European broadcasting, see Jakubowicz, *Conquest or Partnership?;* see also Fenton, *Betting on the Media.*

28. See Semelin, "Reshaping," 53–60.

29. See, for example, Jakab and Galik, *Survival, Efficiency.*

30. Giorgi, *Post-Socialist Media,* 118–9.

31. Ibid., 119.

32. Ibid., 58.

33. The fund invested more than $500,000 in printing and other equipment. A number of other Romanian newspapers also benefited from Western European and American grants to equip their operations.

34. At this writing, the Polish government proposed to Parliament that the limit to foreign interests in terrestrial broadcasting be raised from 33 percent to 49 percent and that majority foreign ownership be permitted when Poland joins the European Union. See International Journalists' Network, Oct. 19, 1999 <http://www.ijnet.org/Archive>.

35. See Normandy Madden, "Foreign Investors Find Success, and Frustration, in Terrestrial Television Broadcasting," *Transitions,* Apr. 19, 1996, 10–12.

36. Giorgi, *Post-Socialist Media,* 29. A private commercial television license was granted to a joint Czech-Italian venture in 1992.

37. For a relatively comprehensive list of foreign investors see Jakubowicz, *Conquest or Partnership?* 33, 37–42. Since 1996, foreign investments have continued to be made in the region at a modest pace.

38. For a description of various aspects of Eastern European economies, see Jacek Rostowski, *Macroeconomic Instability in Post-Communist Countries* (New York: Oxford University Press, 1998); Olivier Blanchard, *The Economics of Post-Communist Transition* (New York: Oxford University Press, 1997); Ronald W. Anderson and Chantal Kegels, *Transition Banking: Financial Development of Central and Eastern Europe* (New York: Oxford University Press, 1998).

39. See Mihai Coman, "Ten Years After: Development in Theories of Media Transitions in East/Central Europe," *Journalism Studies* 1 (2000): 35–56.

40. "Albania," *Post-Soviet Media Law and Policy Newsletter,* May 15, 1998, 25–27.

41. See Alison Smale, "Governments Clamp Down on Freewheeling Media," Associated Press, Dec. 20, 1993.

42. Nikolchev, "Polarization and Diversification," 133.

43. "Slovakia," *International Press Institute Report* (Dec.–Jan. 1996–97): 85–86.

44. Among banks owning media enterprises in Eastern Europe are the Hungarian Credit Bank, Postabank (Hungary), the Invetnici Bank (the Czech Republic), and Bancorex (Romania). See also Splichal, *Media beyond Socialism,* chaps. 3 and 4.

45. Nowhere is this benefit of privatization implied more clearly than in Jakubowicz, "Media Concentrations."

46. By the mid-1990s, there had already been a slight exodus of Western media companies and investments from some countries. See Milton, "News Media Reform," 7–23. One of the latest examples is the sale of Central Media Enterprises (CME) shares to Russian businessman Vladimir Guzinsky. CME owned the major commercial television stations in a number of Eastern European nations. See Lusitania Iacob and Mona Velcu, "Un rus a cumparat actiuni la CME, proprietara Pro TV," *National* (Bucharest), Oct. 7, 1999, 3. On the other hand, in Hungary foreign ownership of the print and broadcast media increased by the end of the 1990s. See Agnes Gulyas, "Mediamorphosis: The Political Economy of the Print Media in the Czech Republic, Hungary and Poland during the First Decade of the Post-Communist Era," Ph.D. diss., Napier University, Edinburgh, 2001.

47. For varied views on media monopolization and globalization, see Ithiel de Sola Pool, *Politics in Wired Nations: Selected Writings of Ithiel de Sola Pool* (Somerset, N.J.: Transaction, 1998); Dean Alger, *Megamedia: How Giant Corporations Dominate Mass Media, Distort Competition, and Endanger Democracy* (Lanham, Md.: Rowman and Littlefield, 1998); Edward S. Herman and Robert W. McChesney, *The Global Media: The New Missionaries of Corporate Capitalism* (London: Cassell, 1997).

48. For examples, see Peter Gross, "Restricting the Free Press in Romania," *Orbis* 35, no. 3 (Summer 1991): 265–75.

49. See Marvin Stone, "A Magyar Mélange," *Nieman Reports* 50, no. 2 (Summer 1996): 64–69.

50. See Charles Hornberger, "Publishers Strike Blow to the Middleman," *New World Publications KFT: Budapest Business Journal,* May 26, 1995; Charles Hornberger, "Publishers Make Play for Distribution," *New World Publications KFT: Budapest Business Journal,* May 12, 1995.

51. Goban-Klas, *Orchestration of the Media,* 223.

52. "Poland," *Post-Soviet Media Law and Policy Newsletter,* May 15, 1998, 35–37.

53. See Johnston Mitchell, "Print Media Privatization: Ownership, Distribution and Production, The Baltic States and Bulgaria," in Hester and White, eds., *Creating a Free Press,* 449–64.

54. Ognianova, *Transitional Media,* 16.

55. "Slovak Republic," *Post-Soviet Media Law and Policy Newsletter,* May 15, 1998, 38–40; Skolkay, "Journalists, Political Elites," 71.

56. Complaints about media distribution were a major issue during the 1990 and 1992 general elections. See Peter Gross, "Restricting the Free Press."

57. "Albania," *International Press Institute Report* (Nov.–Dec. 1995): 6–7.

58. "Albania," *International Press Institute Report* (Dec.–Jan. 1996–97): 8; see also *World Press Freedom Review 1996.*

59. See also "Albania," *Post-Soviet Media Law and Policy Newsletter,* May 15, 1998, 26.

60. Skolkay, "Journalists, Political Elites," 71.

61. Nikolchev, "Polarization and Diversification," 132.

62. See Peter Gross, "Rollercoaster Media Role in Post-Communist Romania" (1996).

63. "Romania," *International Press Institute Report* (Nov.–Dec. 1995): 84–85.

64. Hester, "Albanian Press," 5.

65. Giorgi, *Post-Socialist Media,* 77.

66. Goban-Klas, *Orchestration of the Media,* 223.

67. Skolkay, "Journalists, Political Elites," 71.

68. Aumente et al., *Eastern European Journalism,* 84.

69. Packer, "Emergence," 102.

70. Nikolchev, "Polarization and Diversification," 132–3; Ognianova, *Transitional Media,* 15.

71. "Albania," *International Press Institute Report* (Nov.–Dec. 1995): 6–7.

72. "Czech Republic," *Post-Soviet Media Law and Policy Newsletter,* May 15, 1998, 28; Jeremy Drucker, "The Ongoing Struggle for Freedom of Information," *New Presence,* August 1998 <www.new-transitions.cz>.

73. "Slovak Republic," *Post-Soviet Media Law and Policy Newsletter,* May 15, 1998, 38–40.

74. For a good, all-around explication of the legal aspects of the protection of journalists, access to information, and other media-related issues in Romania, see Gabriel Andreescu, Manuela Stefanescu, and Renate Weber, *Access to Information in Romania* (Bucharest: Center for Human Rights, 1996).

75. Adrian Ursu, "Puterea se ascunde de cetateni," *Adevarul* (Bucharest), Feb. 5, 1998, 1.

76. See Drucker, "Ongoing Struggle."

77. Ibid.

78. See Freedom House, *Media Responses to Corruption in the Emerging Democracies: Bulgaria, Hungary, Romania, Ukraine,* Jan. 19, 2000 <www.freedomhouse.org/reports/mediatxt.html>.

79. Steve Kettle, "The Development of the Czech Media Since the Fall of Communism," in O'Neil, ed., *Post-Communism and the Media,* 56.

80. See "Poland," *International Press Institute Report* (Nov.–Dec. 1995): 83–84; see also Wojciech Sadurski, "Freedom of the Press in Postcommunist Poland," *East European Politics and Society* 10, no. 3 (1996): 439–56.

81. See "Poland," *Post-Soviet Media Law and Policy Newsletter,* May 15, 1998, 35–37.

82. Albania, alone of the seven Eastern European states, has failed to enact a new constitution, after abrogating the Communist one in 1991.

83. See, for example, Ronald Koven, "Media Laws in Eastern Europe: The Meddler's Itch," *CSCE/ODIHR Bulletin* 2, no. 1 (Winter 1994): 9–15.

84. In Hungary, Imre Pozsgay's "proposals on how to reform the press" were rejected by both conservatives and liberals. See Giorgi, *Post-Socialist Media,* 48–50.

85. See "Albania," *Post-Soviet Media Law and Policy Newsletter,* Mar. 31, 1996, 20–21.

86. See "Albania," *Post-Soviet Media Law and Policy Newsletter,* May 15, 1998, 25–26.

87. See "Albania," *Post-Soviet Media Law and Policy Newsletter,* Apr. 15, 1998, 14–15.

88. See International Journalists' Network, "Albanian Parliament Scraps Media Punishment Clause from State Secrets Law," 1999 <www.ijnet.org/Archive>.

89. For a discussion of journalistic practices and the nature of the independent media, see chapters 2 and 4.

90. See Andras Sajo, "Hate Speech for Hostile Hungarians," *East European Constitutional Review* 3, no. 2 (Spring 1994): 82–87.

91. Nikolchev, "Polarization and Diversification," 135.

92. See Gross, *Mass Media,* chap. 3.

93. Conversations with Hungarian journalists in Budapest in fall 1989.

94. Victor Ciorbea as quoted in "Victor Ciorbea considera ca legea presei nu e nici necesara, nici oportuna." *Telegrama* (Bucharest), Apr. 24, 1997.

95. Declaration of the Rights of Man and the Citizen as quoted in Koven, "Media Laws in Eastern Europe," 10.

96. "Czech Republic," *Post-Soviet Media Law and Policy Newsletter,* May 15, 1998, 28.

97. "Poland," *Post-Soviet Media Law and Policy Newsletter,* May 15, 1998, 35–36.

98. For examples, see Ruth Walden, *Insult Laws: An Insult to Press Freedom: A World Press Freedom Committee Study of More than 90 Countries and Territories* (Reston, Va.: World Press Freedom Committee, 2000).

99. "Bulgaria," *Post-Soviet Media Law and Policy Newsletter,* July 15, 1999, 30–31.

100. Walden, *Insult Laws,* 69.

101. Lech Walesa, speech given at the Freedom Forum World Center, Reston, Va., Apr. 21, 1993.

102. Post-Communist Media Law and Policy, December 1998 <www.pcmlp@socio-legal-strolies.oxford.ac.uk>.

103. "Poland," *Post-Soviet Media Law and Policy Newsletter,* May 1, 1999, 18. There was no mention of the specific points of incompatibility.

104. Kathleen Imholz, "Note on the Albanian Private Media Law," *Post-Soviet Media Law and Policy Newsletter,* Nov. 1, 1998, 51–52.

105. "Romania," *Post-Soviet Media Law and Policy Newsletter,* May 1, 1999, 18.

106. Owen V. Johnson, "Whose Voice? Freedom of Speech and the Media in Central Europe," in Hester and White, eds., *Creating a Free Press,* 3.

107. "Law on Radio and Television Broadcasting," *Romanian Legislation,* vol. 3, 5, Parliament of Romania, Bucharest, 1992. It should be acknowledged that such a rule also exists in Western countries such as Britain.

108. "Hungary," *Post-Soviet Media Law and Policy Newsletter,* Dec. 15, 1998, 25–26.

109. "Bulgaria," *Post-Soviet Media Law and Policy Newsletter,* June 15, 1998, 23–25.

110. "Albania," *Post-Soviet Media Law and Policy Newsletter,* Feb. 15, 1999, 21–22.

111. For example, in Romania, the Media Monitoring Agency established by the Freedom of Expression Project in July 1999 monitors and publicizes threats and abuses aimed at journalists in Bulgaria, Romania, Hungary, and Ukraine. To that end, it launched a Web site on Dec. 7, 1999. See International Journalists' Network, "Romanian Agency to Monitor Abuses of Region's Journalists" and "Journalists' Protection Web Site Launched in Romania" <www.ijnet.org/Archive>.

112. Thus, despite strong political and cultural resistance, progressive changes to public broadcast laws, as well as progressive interpretations and applications of these laws by the responsible boards and councils, continue to be made. See, for example, "Slovakia," *Post-Soviet Media Law and Policy Newsletter,* May 15, 1998, 27–29.

113. In Hungary, the head of the HNRTB is appointed by the president and the prime minister.

114. "Slovakia," *Post-Soviet Media Law and Policy Newsletter,* May 15, 1998, 28–29; see also April Orcutt, "Optimism, Pessimism, and Paradox: Broadcast Freedom in Slovakia," in Hester and White, eds., *Creating a Free Press,* 311–39. Broadcasting

in the Slovak Republic is actually overseen by three councils, each appointed by the Parliament: two that establish policy and one that issues licenses.

115. "Poland," *Post-Soviet Media Law and Policy Newsletter,* May 15, 1998, 35–37; see also "Country Reports from Central and Eastern Europe—Poland," *Post-Soviet Media Law and Policy Newsletter,* Mar. 31, 1996, 25.

116. See Downing, *Internationalizing,* 149. The PNRTC supervises programming, assigns frequencies and licenses, and allocates the revenue from licenses; the controversies surrounding the PNRTC continued into 1998. See "Poland," *Post-Soviet Media Law and Policy Newsletter,* June 15, 1998, 25–28.

117. Kettle, "Development of the Czech Media," 51.

118. See Milan Smid, "Broadcasting Law in the Czech Republic" (1995).

119. See Gross, *Mass Media,* 75–82.

120. See, for example, Nitulescu, "Media Transparency in Romania," 45–48.

121. "Slovakia," *Post-Soviet Media Law and Policy Newsletter,* Nov. 1, 1998, 18–19.

122. "Slovakia, VI: Journalists' Union to Boycott Radio, TV Councils," *Post-Soviet Media Law and Policy Newsletter,* Dec. 15, 1998, 27.

123. "Bulgaria," *Post-Soviet Media Law and Policy Newsletter,* July 15, 1999, 30–31.

124. See, for example, Karol Jakubowicz, "Civil Society and Public Service Broadcasting in Central and Eastern Europe," *Public* 3, no. 2 (1996): 51–69.

125. See Paddy Scannell, "Public Service Broadcasting and Modern Life," *Media, Culture and Society* 11, no. 2 (1989): 135–66.

126. Keane, *Media and Democracy,* 167. Keane's normative view, shared by most media scholars, is central to the concepts of the public sphere and civil society, discussed in greater detail in chapter 5.

127. See "Miazek Shakes Up Polish Television; Consequences for Broadcasting Licenses," *Post-Soviet Media Law and Policy Newsletter,* Apr. 30, 1996, 5–7; see also chapters 2 and 4 of this book.

128. See Culik, "Spectacular Failure."

129. Ibid.

130. "Hungary," *Post-Soviet Media Law and Policy Newsletter,* Nov. 1, 1998, 16–17.

131. "Romania," *Post-Soviet Media Law and Policy Newsletter,* May 15, 1998, 38.

132. See Nicholson, "Slovak Television."

133. See "Poland," *Post-Soviet Media Law and Policy Newsletter,* Nov. 1, 1998, 17–18.

134. See "On Public and Private Radio and Television in the Republic of Albania" (Law no. 8410, Sept. 30, 1998), Article 66.

135. See Elsa Ballauri, "Albanian Television," in Milev, ed., *TV auf dem Balkan,* 11–16; "Albania," *Post-Soviet Media Law and Policy Newsletter,* July 15, 1999, 29–30.

136. See Rossen Milev, "Fernsehen in den Balkan-Landern: Die schwierige Emanzipation eines Mediums in der Welt des staatlichen Dirigismus," in Milev, ed., *TV auf dem Balkan,* 147–73; 158.

137. Sparks and Reading, *Communism, Capitalism,* 157.

138. See Isaiah Berlin, "Two Concepts of Liberty," in *Four Essays on Liberty* (Oxford: Oxford University Press, 1969), 118–73. Berlin differentiates between "negative" and "positive" freedom.

139. Keane, *Media and Democracy,* 158.

140. Ibid., 167.

141. See O'Neil, "Introduction: Media Reform," 2; Jakubowicz, "Media Autonomization"; Splichal, *Media beyond Socialism,* chaps. 2 and 3. I will deal with the issues of market, civil society, and politicization in chapters 5 and 6.

142. Peter Molnar, "Transforming Hungarian Broadcasting," *Media Studies Journal* 13, no. 3 (Fall 1999): 96.

143. Monroe Price, "Free Media Depends on Laws, Institutions, and Culture," in *Democracy Dialogue: Technical Notes from U.S. AID's Global Center for Democracy and Governance,* July 1998, 4.

Chapter 4

1. See Leo Bogart, "Media and Democracy," *Media Studies Journal* 9, no. 3 (Summer 1995): 1–10.

2. See Lendvai, *Bureaucracy,* chaps. 1 and 2; Thom, *Newspeak.* 14.

3. Michael Schudson, "Creating Public Knowledge," *Media Studies Journal* 9, no. 3 (Summer 1995): 28.

4. One of the cornerstones of U.S. policy in post-Communist Eastern Europe was the establishment of independent media. The investment took the form of equipment, training, and financial support for individual media outlets. See Aumente et al., *Eastern Europe Journalism,* chap. 5.

5. See Denis McQuail, "New Role for New Times?" *Media Studies Journal* 9, no, 3 (Summer 1995): 11–19.

6. See Alina Mungiu, *Romanii dupa '89: Istoria unei neintelegeri* (Bucharest: Humanitas, 1995).

7. Karol Jakubowicz, "From Party Propaganda to Corporate Speech? Polish Journalism in Search of a New Identity," *Journal of Communication* 42, no. 3 (Summer 1992): 70.

8. The phrase "'soft' dictatorship" was coined by Kovats and Whiting in "Hungary."

9. Jakubowicz, "From Party Propaganda," 70–71.

10. Goban-Klas, *Orchestration of the Media,* 241.

11. Mario Plenkovic and Vlasta Kucis, "Structuring Media Elite in Croatia," *Global Network,* no. 2 (May 1995): 26–27.

12. J. Zakowski, "Etyka mediow," as quoted in Jakubowicz, "Media Autonomization," 5.

13. See Zoltan A. Biro and Julianna Bodo, "Hungarian Media Elite in Romania: On Social Context of Recruiting Practices," *Global Network,* no. 2 (May 1995): 29–36.

14. Zyhdi Dervishi, "Mass Media Elites within the Spectrum of the Albanian Elites," *Global Network,* no. 2 (May 1995): 33–34.

15. Lucian W. Pye, "The Emergence of Professional Communicators," in Pye, ed., *Communications,* 79.

16. Throughout the period 1989–99, Eastern European journalists explained to me that fact-based journalism could not be practiced and that, in any case, they had to "explain" matters to their audience, which was incapable of digesting information on its own.

17. Mihai Coman, "1996—Concluzii si confuzii," *Curierul Romanesc,* no. 1 (Jan. 1997): 6.

18. Ibid.

19. See Horvat, "East European Journalist."

20. Among that handful are Adam Michnik in Poland, Elemer Hankiss in Hungary, and H.-R. Patapievici in Romania.

21. See Raymond Aron, *La lutte de classes: Nouvelles leçons sur les sociétés industrielles* (Paris: Editions Gallimard, 1964). Aron categorizes societal elites as follows: (1) the spiritual aristocracy, which includes clergy and intellectuals; (2) the political leadership, aided by the upper echelons of the army and police; (3) managers; and (4) mass leaders.

22. See Kenneth Starck, "Media Elitism: A Contradiction in a Democratic Society?" *Global Network*, no. 2 (May 1995): 17–24.

23. Goban-Klas, *Orchestration of the Media*, 243.

24. Karl Deutsch, *The Analysis of International Relations* (Englewood Cliffs, N.J.: Prentice Hall, 1968), 107.

25. Jan Culik as quoted in Jeremy Drucker, "Naked Bodies, Runaway Ratings: TV Nova and the Czech Republic," *Media Studies Journal* 13, no. 3 (Fall 1999): 70–77. Zelezny left TV Nova in 1999.

26. Culik, "News and Current Affairs," 3.

27. For a study of the significant differences between U.S. and Western European journalists, see Wolfgang Donsbach, "Lapdogs, Watchdogs, and Junkyard dogs," *Media Studies Journal* 9, no. 4 (Fall 1995): 17–30.

28. See Skolkay, "Journalists, Political Elites," 77–78.

29. See Jerzy Oledzki, "Polish Journalists: Professionals or Not?" in David H. Weaver, ed., *The Global Journalists: News People around the World* (Cresskill, N.J.: Hampton Press, 1998), 277–98.

30. See Ivan Klima, *Waiting for the Dark, Waiting for the Light* (New York: Grove Press, 1995).

31. "Professionalism" as used in this work is defined in the second section of this chapter, "Journalists and Political and Professional Cultures."

32. See Nadia Rybarova, "Director of Czech TV to Be Sued," Associated Press, Jan. 4, 2001.

33. Skolkay, "Journalists, Political Elites," 77.

34. Owen V. Johnson, "Czechs and Balances: Mass Media and the Velvet Revolution," in Jeremy Popkin, ed., *Media and Revolution* (Lexington: University Press of Kentucky, 1995), 228.

35. Skolkay, "Journalists, Political Elites," 77.

36. See Rybarova, "Director of Czech TV."

37. See "Miazek Shakes Up Polish Television; Consequences for Broadcast Licenses," *Post-Soviet Media Law and Policy Newsletter,* Apr. 30, 1996, 5–7.

38. See Peter Gross, "Limping to Nowhere: Romania's Media under Constantinescu," in *Romania: One Year into the Constantinescu Presidency,* Occasional paper no. 51, Woodrow Wilson International Center for Scholars, Jan. 1999, 9–20. Mungiu-Pippidi lost her job in a leadership reshuffle in 1999.

39. Lanczi and O'Neil, "Pluralization," 98.

40. "Bulgaria," *International Press Institute Report* (Dec.–Jan. 1996–97): 22.

41. "Media Watch . . . Elsewhere," *Transitions* 5, no. 3 (Mar. 1998): 88.

42. African leaders such as Julius Nyerere (Tanzania), Jomo Kenyatta (Kenya), Hastings Banda (Malawi), Kwame Nkrumah (Ghana), Felix Houphouet-Boigny (Ivory Coast), Leopold Sedar-Senghor (Senegal), and Mobutu Sese Seko (Zaire) began their public career as newspaper owners, publishers, editors, or reporters.

43. Dervishi, "Mass Media Elites," 34.

44. See Mihai Coman, "Fabricare si metamorfoza," *Sfera Politicii* 5, no. 35 (Feb. 1996): 8–12.

45. See Biro and Bodo, "Hungarian Media Elite."

46. Bogart, "Media and Democracy," 10.

47. My conversations with many members of Eastern Europe's media elite in the 1990s suggested their understanding of a working democracy was at best limited.

48. By 1997, with 100 points being the maximum attainable, press freedom was rated at 81 for the Czech Republic, 79 for Poland, 66 for Hungary, 59 for the Slovak Republic, 51 for Romania, 29 for Albania. See Boris Shor, "Nations in Transit: 1997 Freedom House Rankings," May–June 1997, 2–4 <www.world-bank.org/html/trans /mayjune97>.

49. Goban-Klas, "Politics versus the Media," 37.

50. Ibid.

51. A number of Eastern European editors told me they wanted greater autonomy so they would be able to pursue coverage of their communities and an editorial line consonant to their own political views and not have to follow the political dictates of their publishers or station owners.

52. Ithiel de Sola Pool, "The Mass Media and Politics in the Modernization Process," in Pye, ed., *Communications*, 244–5.

53. Cornel Nistorescu, "Inamicul public numarul unu," *Evenimentul Zilei*, Apr. 2, 1998, 6.

54. Ibid.

55. Goban-Klas, "Politics versus the Media in Poland," 37.

56. Kovats and Whiting, "Hungary," 112.

57. See Christopher Lasch, "Journalism, Publicity and the Lost Art of Argument," *Media Studies Journal* 9, no. 1 (Winter 1995): 81–91.

58. Chan and Lee, *Mass Media*, 26.

59. See suggestions and amplifications in Deutsch, *Analysis of International Relations*, 107.

60. For a view of this issue in the United States, see Howard Kurtz, *Media Circus: The Trouble with American Newspapers* (New York: Times Books, 1993).

61. John C. Merrill, *Global Journalism: A Survey of the World's Mass Media* (New York: Longman, 1983), 39–40.

62. See Aumente et al., *Eastern European Journalism*, chap. 5.

63. In the first few post-1989 years, most of the new journalists had engineering or liberal arts degrees, whereas, by the end of the 1990s, many entering journalism were graduates of the new journalism programs established at state and private universities or by professional associations.

64. There is a continuous call to "democratize" the newsroom, from some academic quarters, as a way of having each segment of civil society represented (an issue addressed in chapter 5). See, for example, Janet Wasco, "Introduction: Go Tell It to the Spartans," in Wasco and Mosco, eds., *Democratic Communications*, 1–27.

65. Goban-Klas, *Orchestration of the Media*, 242.

66. See Aumente et al., *Eastern European Journalism*, chaps. 1 and 5.

67. See Sandor Szerdahelyi, ed., *A magyar bohemvilag: A Budapesti ujsagirok almanachja 1908–ra* (Budapest: A Budapesti Ujsagirok Egyesulete, 1908), 63–64.

68. Mircea Eliade, *Despre Eminescu si Hasdeu* (Iasi, Romania: Junimea, 1987), 80.

69. Goban-Klas, *Orchestration of the Media*, 242.

70. Ibid.

71. Michnik, "Samizdat Goes Public," 74.

72. Passin, "Writer and Journalist," 109.

73. Ibid.

74. Kettle, "Development of the Czech Media," 59.

75. Ibid.

76. Jakubowicz, "From Party Propaganda," 71.

77. Goban-Klas, "Politics versus the Media," 33.

78. See Oledzki, "Polish Journalists," 290.

79. See Coman, "Romanian Journalism."

80. Interview with Ylli Rakipi, editor in chief of *Republika* (Tirana), Jan. 1994.

81. Interview with Gyorgyi Kocsis, editor of the *World Economic Review* and a reformer in the Association of Hungarian Journalists, Sept. 1989; see also Gati, "Mirage of Democracy," 62.

82. See "Intre Deontoligia Profesiei—Interviu cu Nestor Rates," *Dilema* (Bucharest), Feb. 6–12, 1998, 8.

83. See Ildiko Kovats, "Hungarian Journalists," in Weaver, ed., *Global Journalists,* 257–76.

84. Goban-Klas, *Orchestration of the Media,* 241.

85. Ognianova, *Transitional Media,* 15.

86. Such a situation was repeatedly reported to me by journalists in Bulgaria, Poland, Hungary, Romania, and the Czech Republic in 1990–98.

87. Conversations with Romanian journalists, Nov. 1996.

88. Owen V. Johnson, "Media" (University of Indiana, Bloomington, 1992), 13.

89. Skolkay, "Journalists, Political Elites," 67.

90. See Ray Hiebert, "Hungary" (University of Maryland, College Park, 1995).

91. Dean Mills, "Post-1989 Journalism in the Absence of Democratic Traditions," in Aumente et al., *Eastern European Journalism,* 140.

92. Sparks and Reading, *Communism, Capitalism,* 141.

93. Skolkay, "Journalists, Political Elites," 77; Kettle, "Development of the Czech Media," 52; and as related to me by Romanian journalists in 1997.

94. Kettle, "Development of the Czech Media," 42.

95. See Sukosd, "Media War."

96. Ognianova, *Transitional Media,* 32.

97. Goban-Klas, *Orchestration of the Media,* 242.

98. With great fanfare, the Romanian Press Club made public a ten-article ethics code in Feb. 1998. Within a few weeks, it was forgotten. See "A fost lansat un nou cod etic al presei din Romania," *Ziua* (Bucharest), Feb. 20, 1998, 1.

99. Goban-Klas, *Orchestration of the Media,* 241.

100. Ognianova, *Transitional Media,* 32.

101. Goban-Klas, "Politics versus the Media," 39.

102. As related to me by Romanian journalists in 1996 and 1997.

103. Kettle, "Development of the Czech Media," 55.

104. See Hans Mathias Kepplinger and Renate Kocher, "Professionalism in the Media World?" *European Journal of Communication* 5, nos. 2–3 (June 1990): 285–311.

105. Jakubowicz, "Media Autonomization," 10.

106. Although young journalists from Albania, Bulgaria, the Czech Republic, Hungary, Poland, and Romania all expressed their desire to practice "American" journalism,

few displayed any knowledge of how journalism is practiced in the United States beyond the notion that it is "fact-based."

107. Jakubowicz, "Media Autonomization," 10.

108. Kepplinger and Kocher, "Professionalism in the Media World?" 307.

109. Schudson, "How News Becomes News"; Chan and Lee, *Mass Media,* 31.

110. For a description of the nature of pre-Communist journalism, see Horvat, "East European Journalist"; Aumente et al., *Eastern European Journalism,* chaps. 1 and 2.

111. Such a claim is pandemic throughout the region. See, for example, Peter S. Green, "The End of Easy Targets," *New Presence,* Jan. 1999 <www.new-presence.cz>.

112. Oledzki, "Polish Journalists," 290.

113. See J. Zakowski, "Etyka mediow," as quoted in Jakubowicz, "Normative Models of Media," 15.

114. Mungiu, *Romanii dupa '89,* 254.

115. Three classifications are suggested in the evolution of media, in step with the evolution of society: elitist, popular, and specialized. See Merrill and Lowenstein, *Media, Messages,* 33. The post-1989 Eastern Europe media began largely in the specialized phase—that is, they were mostly organs of political parties or of elite intellectual groups. Private, commercial television was to become national or quasi-national by the end of the 1990s in almost all Eastern European countries.

116. See Everett M. Rogers and James W. Dearing, "Agenda-Setting Research: Where Has It Been, Where Is It Going?" in Doris A. Graber, ed., *Media Power in Politics* (Washington, D.C.: CQ Press, 1984), 77–95; but see also Kettle, "Development of the Czech Media," 43: "Opinion polls show that more respondents have faith in the media than in institutions such as the presidency, political parties, trade unions or the Catholic Church." *New Democracies Barometer III* (Vienna: Paul Lazarsfeld Society, 1994) shows that the media are trusted by only 15 percent (mean) of Czechs, Slovaks, Hungarians, Poles, Slovenians, Belorussians, and Ukrainians. See Rose, Mishler, and Haerpfer, *Democracy and Its Alternatives,* 87; for Romania see, for example, U.S. Information Agency, "Romanians' Confidence in Media Steadily Declining," research memorandum, Washington, D.C., Feb. 1992. Other studies show that more than 39 percent of Bulgarians, more than 55 percent of Hungarians, 62 percent of Poles, and 68 percent of Romanians distrust the media in their respective countries. Data collected between Mar. 1998 and Mar. 2000, as cited in Slavko Splichal, "Imitative Revolutions: Changes in the Media and Journalism in East-Central Europe," paper presented at the "Democratization and the Mass Media: Comparative Perspectives from Europe and Asia" conference, held at the Rockefeller Bellagio Center, Italy, Apr. 9–13, 2001.

117. See McQuail, "New Role?" 17.

118. Walter Lippmann, *Public Opinion* (New York: Free Press, 1965), 229.

119. Swanson and Mancini, eds., *Politics, Media,* 15–16.

120. See James E. Fletcher, "Eastern Europe: Public Opinion Polling Practices and Organizations," in Al Hester and L. Earle Reybold, eds., *Revolutions for Freedom: The Mass Media in Eastern and Central Europe* (Athens: University of Georgia , James M. Cox, Jr. Center for International Mass Communication Training and Research, 1993), 63–83. The increased use of polls and surveys to gauge public opinion and the dissemination of their findings through the mass media suggest the slow ascendancy of public opinion in importance.

121. Lawrence K. Grossman, *The Electronic Republic: Reshaping Democracy in the Information Age* (New York: Penguin, 1995), 6.

122. Revel, *Flight from Truth,* 237.

123. Tuchman, *Making News,* 87.

124. Curry, "Sociological Legacies," 72.

125. Aumente et al., *Eastern European Journalism,* 141.

126. Journalists throughout Eastern Europe have repeatedly made this point to me since 1990.

127. See Kovats and Whiting, "Hungary," 112.

128. W. Lance Bennett, *News: The Politics of Illusion* (New York: Longman, 1983), 84.

129. See Dan Schiller, *Objectivity and the News: The Public and the Rise of Commercial Journalism* (Philadelphia: University of Pennsylvania Press, 1981).

130. Journalists in Poland, for example, are seen as having low ethical norms. See Oledzki, "Polish Journalists," 294; the same is true in Romania. See Coman, "Romanian Journalism," 291, 294; see also Kenneth Starck, "Groping toward Ethics in Transitioning Press Systems: The Case of Romania," *Journal of Mass Media Ethics* 14, no. 1(1999): 28–41; Ognianova, *Transitional Media.* By contrast, the journalists' status in the brief transition phase seems to have been uniformly high.

131. In each Eastern European country, journalists have been instrumental in affecting the nature or passage of media laws. In almost all cases, they have successfully defeated attempts to enact press laws they viewed as restrictive to the practice of journalism. In Bulgaria, they even have had a direct hand in lawmaking. See Ivan Nikolchev, "Journalists as Lawmakers: Grassroots Initiatives for Media Regulation in Bulgaria, 1996–1998," paper presented at the "Profession of Journalism in a Democratic Society: East-West Perspectives" conference, held at Napier University, Edinburgh, Sept. 4–5, 1998.

132. Andrej Bartosiewicz, director of the Independent Media Monitoring '98 Project, as quoted in Green, "End of Easy Targets," 2.

133. See Adam Michnik, *"Gazeta Wyborcza* at 10: The Progress of Poland since Communism," *Media Studies Journal* 13, no. 3 (Fall 1999): 80–89.

134. See, for example, Jakubowicz, "Normative Models of Media," 15–17.

135. See Drucker, "Naked Bodies," 75.

136. Discussions with ten Albanian journalists, each representing different newspapers, Apr. 1996.

137. See Roumiana Deltcheva, "New Tendencies in Post-Totalitarian Bulgaria: Mass Culture and the Media," *Europe-Asia Studies* 48, no. 2 (Mar. 1996): 305–16.

138. See Herbert Gans, "Bystanders as Opinion Makers," *Media Studies Journal* 9, no. 1 (Winter 1995): 93–100.

139. James W. Dearing and Everett M. Rogers, *Agenda-Setting* (London: Sage), 7.

140. Ibid., 2.

141. See Harold Lasswell, "The Structure and Function of Communication in Society," in Lyman Bryson, ed., *The Communication of Ideas* (New York: Harper and Row, 1948), 37–52; see also David H. Weaver and G. Cleveland Wilhoit, "The American Journalist in the 1990s," in Shanto Iyengar and Richard Reeves, eds., *Do the Media Govern? Politicians, Voters, and Reporters in America* (Thousand Oaks, Calif.: Sage, 1997), 18–28; Passin, "Writer and Journalist."

142. See Chan and Lee, *Mass Media,* 35.

143. For an outline of these media roles, see McQuail, *Mass Communication Theory;* Gurevitch and Blumler, "Linkages."

144. See Schudson, "How News Becomes News"; Gitlin, *Whole World Is Watching.*

145. See Peterson, Jensen, and Rivers, *Mass Media in Modern Society.*

146. See Gans, *Deciding What's News.*

147. See Michnik, "After Communism, Journalism," *Media Studies Journal* 12, no. 2 (Spring–Summer 1998): 104–13.

148. Kytka lost his job shortly thereafter. See Culik, "News and Current Affairs," 3, 4.

149. See, for example, James Fallows, *Breaking the News: How the Media Undermine American Democracy* (New York: Pantheon, 1996).

150. Donsbach, "Lapdogs, Watchdogs," 21.

151. See, for example, Armand Mattelart, *Mass Media, Ideologies, and the Revolutionary Movement* (Atlantic Highlands, N.J.: Humanities Press, 1980); and Stephanie Gutmann, "The Breeding Ground," *National Review,* June 21, 1993.

152. Schudson, "How News Becomes News," 81.

153. See ibid.

154. See Tuchman, *Making News;* see also Jay G. Blumler and Michael Gurevitch, "Politicians and the Press: An Essay in Role Relationship," in Dan Nimmo and Keith R. Sanders, eds., *Handbook of Political Communication* (Beverly Hills, Calif.: Sage, 1981), 467–93.

155. See Tuchman, *Making News.*

156. See Gans, *Deciding What's News;* Schudson, "How News Becomes News." Rawls has taken this point one step further by suggesting that the "tradition of objectivity in journalism has favored official views, making journalists mere stenographers for the official transcript of social reality." See John Rawls, *A Theory of Justice* (Cambridge, Mass.: Harvard University Press, 1971), 185.

157. See Schudson, "How News Becomes News."

158. David S. Broder, *Behind the Front Page: A Candid Look at How the News Is Made* (New York: Simon and Schuster, 1988), 300.

159. See Thomas E. Patterson, *Out of Order* (New York: Knopf, 1993).

160. See Ben Bagdikian, *The Media Monopoly,* 4th ed. (Boston: Beacon, 1992).

161. Goban-Klas, "Politics versus the Media," 32, and *Orchestration of the Media,* 244.

162. Goban-Klas, "Politics versus the Media," 38.

163. Kettle, "Development of the Czech Media," 54.

164. Stefan Stanciugelu, "Gazetaria ca forma de donjuanism," *Dilema* (Bucharest), Feb. 6–12, 1998, 7.

165. C. Gombar, head of Hungarian Radio, "Introductory Address," in Anthony Pragnell and Ildiko Gergely, eds., *The Political Content of Broadcasting* (Manchester, England: European Institute for Media, 1992), Media Monograph no. 15, pp. 4–6.

166. Goban-Klas, *Orchestration of the Media,* 241.

167. Milton, "News Media Reform," 12.

168. Coman, "1996–Concluzii," 6.

169. See Green, "End of Easy Targets."

170. Jakubowicz, "From Party Propaganda," 16.

171. See Thomas E. Patterson, Bradlee Professor of Government and the Press at Harvard University, as quoted in Judith Sheppard, "Playing Defense," *American Journalism Review* 20, no. 7 (Sept. 1998): 48–56.

172. Jakubowicz, "Normative Models of Media," 16; Gabriel Andreescu, "Political Manipulation at Its Best," *Transitions,* Dec. 1, 1995, 46.

173. See Antonesei, "Cultura Politica," 118.

174. See Peter Rutland, "Television, Politics, Money," *Transitions,* Apr. 19, 1996, 5.

175. See Culik, "News and Current Affairs."

176. See Schudson, "How News Becomes News."

177. Milton, "News Media Reform," 15.

178. See Bogart, "Media and Democracy."

179. See the claims made by, among others, C. Klein, "Fernsehen und andere Massenmedien in Osteuropa: Gemeinsamkeiten und Unterschiede der Medienentwicklung, 1989–1993," in G. Hallenberger and M. Krzeminski, eds., *Osteuropa: Medienlandschaft im Umbruch: Berichte und Analysen aus neun Landern* (Berlin: Vistas, 1994), 13–26.

180. See, for example, John H. McManus, *Market-Driven Journalism: Let the Citizen Beware?* (Thousand Oaks, Calif.: Sage, 1994).

181. On journalists and journalism in Sweden, see S. Hadenius and L. Weibull as quoted by Kent Asp and Peter Esaiasson, "The Modernization of Swedish Campaigns: Individualization, Professionalization, and Medialization," in Swanson and Mancini, eds., *Politics, Media,* 73–90.

182. Sparks and Reading, *Communism, Capitalism,* 176.

183. "Social responsibility" for journalists is here defined as bringing to the public verifiable, complete, accurate, and sourced information—judged according to its impact on the community as a whole and the number of people in a community being affected.

184. Revel, *Flight from Truth,* 236.

185. Eastern European journalism education is uneven at best. In most instances, it is a case of the "blind leading the blind." See Aumente et al., *Eastern European Journalism,* chap. 5.

186. See, for example, European Institute for the Media, *Monitoring Media Coverage of Local Elections in Albania: Final Report,* Jan. 1997, and *Monitoring the Media Coverage of the 1996 Romanian Parliamentary and Presidential Elections: Final Report,* Mar. 1997. For an explanation of Czech journalism's role in the collapse of the Václav Klaus government in November 1997, which may have represented the ideological "decompression" of Czech journalism and the assertion of at least a measure of autonomy, see also Jonathan Stein, "Still in Bed Together: Czech Journalism and Party Politics," *New Presence,* Jan. 1998 <www.new-presence.cz>.

187. Lanczi and O'Neil, "Pluralization," 99.

Chapter 5

1. The "public sphere" used here refers to the one defined by Habermas and Garnham as the network of knowledge- and opinion-forming institutions. See Habermas, *Between Facts;* see also Jürgen Habermas, *The Inclusion of the Other: Studies in Political Theory* (Cambridge, Mass.: MIT Press, 1998); Garnham, "Media and the Public Sphere," 28–33. Dahlgren argues that the public sphere "'takes place' when citizens, exercising the rights of assembly and association, gather as public bodies to discuss issues of the day, specifically those of political concern." Dahlgren, *Television and the Public Sphere,* 7–8.

2. Dahlgren, *Television and the Public Sphere,* 7–8.

3. See Elemer Hankiss, *East European Alternatives* (Oxford: Oxford University Press, 1990), chap. 3.

4. Of course, one can argue with some justification that the broad range of political and ideological views that came together to oppose Communism represented a reflection of a civil society. Underground or alternative media were also established by singular elements of a would-be civil society, such as ethnic minority groups, for example, in Romania. Although there were no underground media and no organized groups that brought together all the disparate elements opposing Communism, from time to time attempts at communicating anti-Communist messages were made. The Hungarian minority was better organized in its opposition to Communism and periodically published an underground press. See, for example, Skilling, *Samizdat;* Michael Shafir, *Romania: Politics, Economics and Society* (Boulder, Colo.: Rienner, 1985).

5. Jakubowicz, "Media as Agents," 34.

6. Curry, "Reconsideration," 242.

7. See Habermas, *Between Facts,* chaps. 7 and 8; Garnham, "Media," 28–33; Dahlgren, *Television and the Public Sphere,* 7–8.

8. For Cohen and Arato, civil society consists of (1) the intimate sphere, (2) the sphere of voluntary associations, (3) social movements, and (4) many forms of public communication. See Cohen and Arato, *Civil Society.*

9. See Slavko Splichal, Andrew Calabrese, and Colin Sparks, "Introduction," in Splichal, Calabrese, and Sparks, eds., *Information Society and Civil Society: Contemporary Perspectives on the Changing World Order* (West Lafayette, Ind.: Purdue University Press, 1994), 1–20.

10. See Adam Michnik's statement in Martin Krygier, "The Character of Civil Society," paper presented at the "1989–1999: Ten Years After: The Countries of Eastern and Central Europe between Project and Reality" conference, held in Bucharest, Sept. 15–19, 1999.

11. Tismaneanu, *Fantasies of Salvation,* 3.

12. Brown, *Hopes and Shadows,* 9.

13. See, for example, Dahrendorf, *Reflections,* 6–12.

14. See, for example, Bernhard, "Civil Society and Democratic Transition."

15. See Curry, "Reconsideration," 240; see also Larry Diamond, "Economic Development and Democracy Reconsidered," in Marks and Diamond, eds., *Reexamining Democracy,* 93–139.

16. Dahrendorf, *Reflections,* 105.

17. These crucial elements are defined in Larry Diamond, Juan J. Linz, and Seymour Martin, eds., *Democracy in Developing Countries,* vol. 2 (Boulder, Colo.: Rienner, 1988), xvi; see also Rustow, "Transitions to Democracy," 337–65.

18. See Dietrich Rueschemeyer, "The Self-Organization of Society and Democratic Rule: Specifying the Relationship," in Rueschemeyer, Marilyn Rueschemeyer, and Bjorn Wittrock, eds., *Participation and Democracy East and West: Comparisons and Interpretations* (Armonk, N.Y.: Sharpe, 1998), 9–25.

19. Ibid., 20.

20. See C. B. Macpherson, *The Life and Times of Liberal Democracy* (Oxford: Oxford University Press, 1977).

21. See, for example, Terry Lynn Karl, "Dilemmas of Democratization in Latin

America," *Comparative Politics* 23, no. 1 (1990): 1–21; Frances Hagopian, "Democracy by Undemocratic Means? Elites, Political Pacts, and Regime Transition in Brazil," *Comparative Political Studies* 23, no. 2 (1990): 154–7; Robert Jackson and Carl G. Rosberg, "Democracy in Tropical Africa: Democracy versus Autocracy in African Politics," *Journal of International Affairs* 38, no. 2 (1985): 293–306 ; see also Juan J. Linz, "Transitions to Democracy," *Washington Quarterly* 13, no. 3 (1990): 143–64.

22. See Dahl, *Polyarchy,* chap. 1; see also Robert A. Dahl, "Democracy and Free Speech," in *Toward Democracy: A Journey,* vol. 1, *Reflections: 1940–1997* (Berkeley: Institute of Governmental Studies Press, University of California, 1997), 153–65.

23. See David Held, *Prospects for Democracy: North, South, East, West* (Stanford, Calif.: Stanford University Press, 1993); see also David Held, *Democracy and the Global Order: From the Modern State to Cosmopolitan Governance* (Cambridge: Polity Press, 1995).

24. See Rustow, "Transitions to Democracy."

25. For a discussion of consolidated versus unconsolidated democracies, see Linz, "Transitions to Democracy," 158.

26. The eight conditions are (1) freedom to form and join organizations; (2) freedom of expression; (3) right to vote; (4) eligibility for public office; (5) right of political leaders to compete for support and for votes; (6) alternative sources of information; (7) free and fair elections; and (8) institutions for making government policies depend on votes and other expressions of preference. Dahl, *Polyarchy,* 3; see also Dahl, *Toward Democracy.*

27. See Tucker, *Political Culture and Leadership,* 14.

28. See Holden, *Understanding Liberal Democracy,* 55.

29. See Habermas, *Between Facts,* and *Structural Transformation;* Dahlgren, *Television and the Public Sphere,* 7–8.

30. See Lippmann, *Phantom Public* and *Public Opinion,* 248; see also Ronald Steel, *Walter Lippmann and the American Century* (London: Bodley and Head, 1980); Dewey, *Public and Its Problems,* chap. 5; see also James Carey, *Communication and Culture* (New York: Unwin Hyman, 1989); Robert B. Westbrook, *John Dewey and American Democracy* (Ithaca, N.Y.: Cornell University Press, 1991).

31. See Jakubowicz, "Media Autonomization", "Civil Society and Public Service Broadcasting," and "Normative Models of Media."

32. Slavko Splichal, "Civil Society and Media Democratization in East-Central Europe: Dilemmas in the Evolution of a New Model," in Bibic and Graziano, eds., *Civil Society,* 315.

33. Alexander, "Mass Media," 27.

34. Sparks and Reading, *Communism, Capitalism,* 116–7.

35. Djilas, *Unperfect Society,* 4–5.

36. Sparks and Reading, *Communism, Capitalism,* also discern yet another "theory," a derivative of the idealistic one that has at its heart the empowerment of only "nice associations," those "filled with good intentions." See also Jakubowicz, "Normative Models of Media."

37. See, for example, Ekiert and Kubik, *Rebellious Civil Society.*

38. Borrowing the terms from sociologist William Graham Sumner, Daniel Bell uses "enacted" and "crescive" to distinguish between process and event. See Daniel Bell, "Ten Theories in Search of Reality: The Prediction of Soviet Behavior in the Social Sciences," *World Politics* 10 (Apr. 1958): 326–65.

39. See Jakubowicz, "Media Autonomization"; see also Karol Jakubowicz, "Insti-

tutional Change: Civil Society and Communication in Central and Eastern Europe: A Polish Case Study" (n.d., photocopy); Splichal, *Media beyond Socialism,* who sees Eastern European media as having been "Italianized," that is, as having become commercial and paternalistic; Sparks and Reading, *Communism, Capitalism.*

40. Sadurski, "Freedom of the Press," 439.

41. See Jeffery Mondak, "Media and Tolerance: Empirical Evidence of Mixed Effects," in Paletz, Jakubowicz, and Novosel, eds., *Business as Usual?* 319–56.

42. Lerner, "Toward a Communication Theory," 342.

43. See Schramm, "Communication Development."

44. The first two possibilities are derived from Rosengren, "Mass Media."

45. Jakubowicz, "Media as Agents of Change," 22.

46. The partisan, political media are a case in point; the ethnic press may also fall into this category, as may the extremist press, such as *Romania Mare* in Romania, and religious media outlets, such as the more extreme (Catholic) Radio Maria in Poland.

47. Splichal, *Media beyond Socialism,* 126.

48. See U.S. Department of State, *Human Rights Reports for 1999—Country Reports;* see also International Journalists Network <www.ijnet.org>.

49. Prevratil, "Czechoslovakia," 161.

50. Gross, *Mass Media,* 53.

51. See also Nikolchev, "Polarization and Diversification."

52. Michael Gurevitch and Jay G. Blumler, "Mass Media and Political Institutions: The Systems Approach," in George Gerbner, ed., *Mass Media Policies in Changing Cultures* (London: Wiley, 1977), 263.

53. George Gerbner, "Violence in Television Drama: Trends and Social Functions," in George A. Comstock and Eli A. Rubinstein, eds., *Television and Social Behavior,* vol. 1, *Media Content and Control* (Washington, D.C.: U.S. Government Printing Office, 1972), 114.

54. Price, "Free Media Depends," 6.

55. For example, Hungarian Television is down to about 10 percent of market share. See Molnar, "Transforming Hungarian Broadcasting."

56. Keane, *Media and Democracy,* 193.

57. That is, they depend on their audiences' political culture and their perception of "citizenship." What do they demand of the media, what media do they use, and how do they use them?

58. See Michnik, "After Communism, Journalism," 106.

59. Rutland, "Television, Politics, Money," 5. The key word here is "perceived"; we have seen convincing evidence of significant gains in actual media autonomy and of substantial gains in actual media pluralism over the period 1989–2000.

60. See, for example, Robert D. Entman, *Democracy without Citizens: Media and the Decay of American Politics* (New York: Oxford University Press, 1989); Robert Hart, *Seducing America: How Television Charms the Modern Voter* (New York: Oxford University Press, 1994); Joseph N. Cappella and Kathleen Hall Jamieson, *Spiral of Cynicism: The Press and the Public Good* (New York: Oxford University Press, 1997); Stephen Ansolabehere and Shanto Iyengar, *Going Negative: How Attack Ads Shrink and Polarize the Electorate* (New York: Free Press, 1995); Shanto Iyengar, *Is Anyone Responsible? How Television Charms the Modern Voter* (New York: Oxford University Press, 1994); Shanto Iyengar and Donald R. Kinder, *News That Matters: Television and American Opinion* (Chicago: University of Chicago Press, 1987).

61. Rudolf L. Tokes, "Party Politics and Political Participation in Postcommunist Hungary," in Dawisha and Parrott, eds., *Consolidation of Democracy,* 126.

62. Dawisha, "Democratization," 54.

63. See Pippa Norris, "Does Television Erode Social Capital? A Reply to Putnam," *PS: Political Science and Politics* 29, no. 3 (1996): 474–80; see also Robert D. Putnam, "Tuning In, Tuning Out: The Strange Disappearance of Social Capital in America," *PS: Political Science and Politics* 28, no. 4 (1995): 664–83.

64. "Participation" by obedience to Communist ideals, programs, and the Communist party translated into actual nonparticipation in civic life.

65. See Nelson, *Civil Society Endangered,* 9.

66. See, for example, Ion Dragan, "Les médias roumains: La crise de crédibilité," *Global Network* 2 (May 1995): 61–66; Ognianova, *Transitional Media;* Goban-Klas, *Orchestration of the Media;* see also *New Democracies Barometer III;* Robyn S. Goodman, "The Post-Cold War Bulgarian Media: Free and Independent at Last?" *International Communication Bulletin* 35, nos. 3–4 (Fall 2000): 4–11.

67. See *New Democracies Barometer III;* see also chapter 4, note 116.

68. Jakubowicz, "Media Autonomization," 8.

69. See Nelson, *Civil Society Endangered.*

70. Andrzej Rychard, "Institutions and Actors in a New Democracy," in Rueschemeyer, Rueschemeyer, and Wittrock, eds., *Participation and Democracy,* 40.

71. See, for example, Michal Illner, "Local Democratization in the Czech Republic after 1989," in Rueschemeyer, Rueschemeyer, and Wittrock, eds., *Participation and Democracy,* 51–82.

72. Dietrich Rueschemeyer, Marilyn Rueschemeyer, and Bjorn Wittrock, "Conclusion: Contrasting Patterns of Participation and Democracy," in Rueschemeyer, Rueschemeyer, and Wittrock, eds., *Participation and Democracy,* 274.

73. See Splichal, *Media beyond Socialism;* Sparks and Reading, *Communism, Capitalism;* Jörg Becker, "D'un espace public à l'autre: de la censure à l'émergence des lois du marché dans les médias des pays de l'Est," *Réseaux* 57 (1993): 291–312; Charles De Bruyker, *Le marché des médias en Europe Centrale et Orientale* (Paris: DATAR, 1994).

74. Gellner, *Conditions of Liberty,* 80.

75. Rueschemeyer, Rueschemeyer, and Wittrock, "Conclusion," 279.

76. As partial proof of this contention, I offer the statistics found in many works on the Eastern European press showing an explosion in the number of media outlets, a steep decline in circulation for dailies since 1990 and a less steep decline for weeklies, an explosion in the number of broadcast outlets and other information and entertainment outlets, including a plethora of foreign media outlets. For instance, in Albania, circulation for dailies declined from 85,000 in 1998 to 65,000 in 1999; in Bulgaria, *Duma* sold 680,000 copies in 1990, but only 70,000 in 1995, and *Demokratsia*'s circulation shrank from 420,000 to 50,000 in the same period; in Romania, major dailies such as *Romania Libera* and *Adevarul* each enjoyed a circulation of over 1 million in 1990, but less than 80,000 by 1999. Similar declines in circulation were experienced by Polish newspapers. See Goban-Klas, *Orchestration of the Media,* 248; Gross, *Mass Media,* 55, 59–60.

77. Keane, *Media and Democracy,* 176.

78. The three classifications—elitist, popular, and specialized—were developed by Merrill and Lowenstein, *Media, Messages.*

79. Goodman, "Post–Cold War Bulgarian Media," 10.

80. Pye, "Communications," 125.

81. Deltcheva, "New Tendencies," 312–3.

82. Ibid.

83. See Alexander, "Mass Media."

84. See Scott R. Olson, "New Democratic Vistas: Demassification and the Polish Media," in Fred L. Casmir, ed., *Communication in Eastern Europe: The Role of History, Culture, and Media in Contemporary Conflicts* (Mahwah, N.J.: Erlbaum, 1995). 167–96.

85. The phrase "the great multiplier" was coined by Lerner, *Passing of Traditional Society,* chap. 2. When, after studying the media of developing nations, Herbert Hyman concluded that "as instruments of socialization, they are efficient and their sweep is vast enough to cover huge populations requiring modernization," he meant the *mass* media. Herbert Hyman, "Mass Media and Political Socialization: The Role of Patterns of Communication," in Pye, ed., *Communications,* 126.

86. For instance, Romania's Pro-TV reached nearly 60 percent of the country by the end of 1996 and more than 80 percent by 2000.

87. See Wilbur Schramm, *Mass Media and National Development: The Role of Information in the Developing Countries* (Stanford, Calif.: Stanford University Press, 1964). That mass media can promote nation building does not mean that nation building is necessarily achieved. In the present context, it is the rebuilding of nations that is to be promoted, perhaps an easier task. See also Robert Hornik, "Communication as Complement in Development," *Journal of Communication* 30 (1980): 10–24.

88. For instance, Habermas defines public sphere differently from Dewey because his different sociopolitical outlook demands it. See Habermas, *Structural Transformation;* Dewey, *Public and Its Problems.*

89. See Habermas, *Between Facts,* chap. 8.

90. Ibid., 371; see also Jakubowicz, "Musical Chairs?" 195.

91. See Sparks and Reading, *Communism, Capitalism;* Splichal, *Media beyond Socialism.*

92. Thus, in Romania in the fall of 1999, the prime minister and parliamentarians were forced to deal with the Association of Hunters and Fishermen.

93. Dahlgren, *Television and the Public Sphere,* 12.

94. See ibid., 7–12.

95. The local newspapers constituted more than 10 percent of all newspapers in Bulgaria in 1995, up from some 1 percent in 1988. See *Statistical Reference Book of the Republic of Bulgaria* (Sofia: National Statistical Institute, 1999), 173. Similar increases were registered in the other countries of the region, with even more marked increases in the number of local radio, television, and cable stations. There are radio and television programs and stations for ethnic minorities across the region. Newly launched Romany newspapers can be found in many of the region's countries. In Hungary alone, there are eleven newspapers, as well as radio and television programs, in Romany; in Romania, newspapers are published in Armenian, German, Hungarian, and Russian. The Jewish media have also been resurrected in a number of countries. See Ruth Ellen Gruber, "The Renaissance of Jewish Media," *Media Studies Journal* 13, no. 3 (Fall 1999): 158–65.

96. See Bogart, "Media and Democracy," 2.

97. See, for example, Korbonski, "Civil Society." Free markets established themselves more quickly in the Czech Republic, Hungary, and Poland than in Albania, Bulgaria, Romania, and the Slovak Republic.

98. See, for example, Splichal, *Media beyond Socialism;* Sparks and Reading, *Communism, Capitalism.*

99. See Jakubowicz, "Normative Models of Media."

100. See Ferenc Miszlivetz and Jody Jensen, "An Emerging Paradox: Civil Society from Above?" in Rueschemeyer, Rueschemeyer, and Wittrock, eds., *Participation and Democracy,* 83–98. This is not to say that all these nongovernmental entities contribute significantly to policy making, but merely that their establishment is a first step in the democratization process. See Robert Jenkins, "The Role of the Hungarian Non-Profit Sector in Post-Communist Society," *East European Studies* (May–June 1999): 9 and 12.

101. See John Mueller, "Democracy, Capitalism, and the End of Transition," in Mandelbaum, ed., *Post-Communism,* 102–67.

102. For example, throughout the region during the 1990s public relations and advertising firms sprang up, both Western and indigenous, in several Eastern European countries. Additionally, public relations programs in universities were launched, graduating hundreds of students eager to step into this line of business. See, for example, Katka Krosnar, "Hope for PR in Eastern Europe," *Marketing Magazine* 106, no. 2 (Jan. 15, 2001): 6.

103. Seymour Martin Lipset and Stein Rokkan as quoted in Rose, Mishler, and Haerpfer, *Democracy and Its Alternatives,* 34.

104. See, for example, John D. Bell, "Democratization and Political Participation in 'Postcommunist' Bulgaria," in Dawisha and Parrott, eds., *Politics, Power,* 353–402.

105. Witness, for example, the power of the Romanian miners' union and that of the Polish farmers unions, which, acting through political parties, successfully pressed for government subsidies and an end to cheap imports. See "Poland Opens Talks with Bitter Farmers," *New York Times,* Feb. 3, 1999, A10.

106. See Gellner, *Conditions of Liberty.*

107. See Scott Mainwaring and Timothy R. Scully, "Introduction: Party Systems in Latin America," in Mainwaring and Scully, eds., *Building Democratic Institutions: Party Systems in Latin America* (Stanford, Calif.: Stanford University Press, 1995), 27.

108. See "Political Scientist: SZDSZ Controls Media," *FBIS Daily Report—Eastern Europe,* Mar. 16, 1995.

109. See Michael Walzer, "The Civil Society Argument," in Chantal Mouffe, ed., *Dimensions of Radical Democracy* (London: Verso, 1992), 89–107.

110. See, for example, Skolkay, "Journalists, Political Elites," 79.

111. See Andrew Arato, "Revolution, Civil Society and Democracy," *Praxis International* 10, nos. 1–2 (1990): 24–38.

112. See, for example, European Institute for the Media, *Monitoring Media Coverage of Local Elections in Albania: Final Report,* Jan. 1997, and *Monitoring the Media Coverage of the 1996 Romanian Parliamentary and Presidential Elections: Final Report,* Mar. 1997.

113. On the political level, for example, public opinion polls may create the bandwagon effect, on the one hand, or the spiral of silence, on the other. See Bernard Berelson, Paul F. Lasarsfeld, and William N. McPhee, *Voting* (Chicago: University of Chicago Press, 1954); Thomas E. Patterson, *The Mass Media Election* (New York: Praeger, 1980); Elisabeth Noelle-Neumann, *The Spiral of Silence: Public Opinion, Our Social Skin* (Chicago: University of Chicago Press, 1984).

114. See Miszlivetz and Jensen, "Emerging Paradox," 90.

115. See Splichal, "Civil Society and Media Democratization."

116. See, for example, Drucker, "Ongoing Struggle."

117. See Kovats and Whiting, "Hungary."

118. See Splichal, *Media beyond Socialism;* see also Sparks and Reading, *Communism, Capitalism.*

119. Splichal, *Media beyond Socialism,* 126.

120. Ibid., 98.

121. Ibid.

122. See Colin Sparks, "From State to Market: What Eastern Europe Inherits from the West," *Media Development* 38, no. 3 (1991): 11–15.

123. Splichal, *Media beyond Socialism,* 71.

124. See Slavko Splichal and Colin Sparks, "Democratization of the Media from Two Perspectives: Political and Professional Orientations among Journalism Students in 22 Countries," in Splichal, John Hochheimer, and Karol Jakubowicz, eds., *Democratization and the Media: An East-West Dialogue* (Ljubljana, Slovenia: Communication and Culture Colloquia, 1990), 149–72.

125. Mueller, "Democracy, Capitalism," 107.

126. The existence of a diverse media system admittedly does not address the use of this diversity nor the possible dominance of the media scene by one or two media outlets. For example, *Chasa* and *Trud,* both owned by the German *Westdeutsche Allgemeine Zeitung,* together account for 80–90 percent of Bulgaria's total national newspaper circulation. See Freedom House, "Media Responses to Corruption in the Emerging Democracies," 1999 <www.freedomhouse.org/reports/mediatxt.html#Bulgaria>.

127. Oscar Wilde, *The Soul of Man under Socialism and Other Essays* (London: Harper Colophon, 1970), 255.

128. On the other hand, many works have decried the negative aspects of commercial media and their inability to ensure "media quality." See, for example, Claude-Jean Bertrand, *Media Ethics and Accountability Systems* (New Brunswick, N.J.: Transaction, 2000).

129. See Sparks, "From State to Market," 14; see also W. Russell Neuman, Marion R. Just, and Ann N. Crigler, *Common Knowledge: News and the Construction of Political Meaning* (Chicago: University of Chicago Press, 1992); David Gauntlett, *Moving Experiences: Understanding Television's Influences and Effects* (Luton, England: University of Luton Press, 1995); Iyengar, *Is Anyone Responsible?;* Iyengar, Peters, and Kinder, "Experimental Demonstrations"; and Iyengar and Kinder, *News That Matters.*

130. James Q. Wilson, *On Character* (Washington, D.C.: AEI Press, 1991), 148.

131. Goban-Klas, *Orchestration of the Media,* 241.

132. See Kamelia Anguelova, "Ethnic and Religious Minorities in the Bulgarian Press (April 1998–September 1998)," *Balkan Neighbours Newsletter,* 1998–99 <www.access.online.bg/gn/newsletter/bn-8/bulgaria2.htm>.

133. See Arato, "Rise, Decline."

134. See Seymour Martin Lipset, "The Social Requisites of Democracy Revisited," *American Sociological Science Review* 59 (1994): 1–22; see also Adam Przeworski and Fernando Limongi, "Modernization: Theories and Facts," *World Politics* 49, no. 2 (Jan. 1997): 155–83.

135. See Samuel Huntington, "Will More Countries Become Democratic?" *Political Science Quarterly* 99, no. 2 (1984): 199.

136. Chan and Lee, *Mass Media,* 32.

137. Splichal, "Civil Society and Media," 315.

138. See Splichal, *Media beyond Socialism,* 138–43.
139. Starck, "Media Elitism," 18.
140. See Jean Baudrillard, *Les stratégies fatales* (Paris: Editions Grasset and Fasquelle, 1983).
141. See, for example, the arguments made by Dahl, *Democracy and Its Critics;* see also Dahl, "Democracy and Free Speech."
142. Keane, *Media and Democracy,* 190.
143. Splichal, *Media beyond Socialism,* 81. Splichal borrowed the phrase "corporate speech" from Keane, *Media and Democracy,* 83–89.

Chapter 6

1. Schumpeter, *Capitalism, Socialism,* 261.
2. Nikolchev, "Polarization and Diversification," 137. Nikolchev's comments about Bulgaria's intellectual press hold for all countries in the region. On television in Eastern Europe, see *UNESCO Statistical Yearbook, 1999* (Paris: UNESCO; Bernan Press); see also <www.unesco.org/statsen/yearbook/tables>.
3. See Barbara Geddes, *Politician's Dilemma.*
4. See Lippmann, *Phantom Public* and *Public Opinion.*
5. Lippmann, *Public Philosophy,* 100.
6. Ibid.
7. See Dewey, *Public and Its Problems.*
8. Lasch, *Revolt of the Elites,* 174.
9. See Revel, *Flight from Truth,* 236.
10. Ibid.
11. See Dahrendorf, *Reflections,* 106; see also Dahrendorf, *After 1989,* 37–82.
12. Carey, "From Big Lie," 17.
13. J. Bralczyk and M. Mrozowski as quoted in Jakubowicz, "Television and Elections," 131.
14. See Asp and Esaiasson, "Modernization of Swedish Campaigns."
15. According to Diamond, Linz, and Lipset, "Introduction," 1–27, to become stable democracies, societies have to adopt a "belief in the legitimacy of democracy; tolerance for opposing parties, beliefs, and preferences; a willingness to compromise with political opponents, and underlying this, pragmatism and flexibility; some minimum of trust in the political environment, and cooperation, particularly among political competitors; moderation in political positions and partisan identifications; civility of political discourse, and political efficacy and participation." On culture and trust as the keys to economic prosperity, see also Francis Fukuyama, *Trust: The Social Virtues and the Creation of Prosperity* (London: Free Press, 1995).
16. See Stein, "Still in Bed Together."
17. See Gurevitch and Blumler, "Political Communication System," 270.
18. See Jiri Pehe, "Disappointments of Democracy"—"On the Eve of Elections, Political and Economic Reality Bursts the Czechs' Bubble," *New Presence* <www.newpresence.cz>.
19. See Jay G. Blumler, "Broadcasting Policy in a Changing Information Environ-

ment," *Bulletin of Institute of Journalism and Communication Studies* (University of Tokyo) 43 (1991): 1–13.

20. See, for example, Doris Graber, "Media and Politics: A Theme Paper," paper presented at the annual meeting of the Midwest Political Science Association, held in Chicago, Apr. 1989.

21. See Silvo Lenart, *Shaping Political Attitudes: The Impact of Interpersonal Communication and Mass Media* (London: Sage, 1994).

22. See Peter Dahlgren, "TV News and the Suppression of Reflexivity," in Katz and Szecsko, eds., *Mass Media,* 101–14; see also Dahlgren, *Television and the Public Sphere.*

23. See Neuman, Just, and Crigler, *Common Knowledge.*

24. See Hyman, "Mass Media and Political Socialization."

25. See Lenart, *Shaping Political Attitudes.*

26. See, for example, Joseph Klapper, *The Effects of Mass Communication* (New York: Free Press, 1960); Maxwell McCombs and Donald Shaw, "The Agenda-Setting Function of the Mass Media," *Public Opinion Quarterly* 36 (1972): 176–87; Maxwell McCombs and Donald Shaw, "Structuring the Unseen Environment," *Journal of Communication* 26, no. 2 (1976): 18–22; Maxwell McCombs and Donald Shaw, "Agenda-Setting and the Political Process," in Shaw and McCombs, eds., *The Emergence of American Political Issues: The Agenda-Setting Function of the Press* (Saint Paul, Minn.: West, 1977), 149–56.

27. See Russell Dalton et al., "A Test of Media-Centered Agenda Setting: Newspaper Content and Public Interests in Presidential Election," *Political Communication* 17, no. 4 (Oct. 2000): 463–82; Matthew R. Kerbel, Sumaiya Apee, and Marc Howard Ross, "PBS Ain't So Different: Public Broadcasting, Election Frames and Democratic Empowerment," *Harvard International Journal of Press Politics* 5, no. 4 (Fall 2000): 8–32; Maxwell McCombs, Esteban Lopez-Escobar, and Juan Pablo Llamas, "Setting the Agenda of Attribution in the 1996 Spanish General Election," *Journal of Communication* 50, no. 2.

28. Iyengar and Kinder, *News That Matters,* 63–64, 114–6, 94–97.

29. For example, an editor of the Hungarian *Mediakutato* (Media Researcher) reports that the Socialist Party-led coalition in power between 1994 and 1998 most likely lost the 1998 election thanks to the media's focusing on its corruption and allegedly antidemocratic practices, whereas the success of the economic stabilization measures introduced by the coalition hardly got any press.

30. See Iyengar, *Is Anyone Responsible?* chap. 2.

31. For example, only days before the 1996 Romanian presidential election, the newspaper *Ziua* published an exposé of a purported telephone operation by the then-ruling Romanian Democratic Socialist Party (PDSR). The article spoke of the PDSR's "secret service" and of the young "mercenaries" allegedly employed by the PDSR, whereas it characterized opposition Romanian Democratic Convention (CDR) members as "revolutionaries." See Razvan Savaliuc and Alin Cosoveanu, "O retea clandestina de telefonisti politici al PDSR a fost prinsa in flagrant delict," *Ziua,* Oct. 1, 1996, 1, 4. Other examples of excessive "framing" abound in Bulgarian coverage of the Rom, who are stereotyped as "lazy," "thieving," and so on, and who are repeatedly said to pose a "danger" to the demographics of the nation. See Anguelova, "Ethnic and Religious Minorities." Similar "framing" is used in Hungarian and Romanian newspapers.

32. See, for example, the Bulgarian case as described by Deltcheva, "New Tendencies."

33. See George Gerbner, "Comparative Cultural Indicators," in Gerbner, ed., *Mass Media Policies*, 205.

34. Splichal, "Civil Society and Media Democratization," 315.

35. See, for example, ibid.; see also Jakubowicz, "Lovebirds?"; Aumente et al., *Eastern European Journalism.*

36. See Karol Jakubowicz, "Media within and without the State: Press Freedom in Eastern Europe," *Journal of Communication* 45, no. 4 (1995): 125–39.

37. Djilas, *Unperfect Society,* 4.

38. See Isaiah Berlin, *The First and the Last* (New York: New York Review, 1999), 7–8. François Furet's comprehensive and, as far as I am concerned, brilliant examination of Communism in Eastern Europe and the former Soviet Union does not sufficiently emphasize that the "illusion" regarding the kind of "perfect" society driving what the Left today calls the "experiment" in those regions has not "passed." See François Furet, *The Passing of an Illusion: The Idea of Communism in the Twentieth Century* (Chicago: University of Chicago Press, 1999).

39. Although some scholars continue to argue that democracy may take many forms, I tend to agree with Thomas Carothers, "Think Again: Democracy," *Foreign Policy* 1997 (Summer): 11–12, that the basic liberal democratic model established in the West is the only credible one.

40. For a thorough analysis of the resurgence of the radical Right in Eastern Europe, see Sabrina P. Ramet, *The Radical Right in Central and Eastern Europe since 1989* (University Park: Penn State University Press, 1999). In the 2000 presidential election in Romania, the head of the xenophobic, extreme right-wing Greater Romanian Party, Corneliu Vadim Tudor, won 30 percent of the vote, although he lost the runoff election against Ion Iliescu.

41. The Left includes an array of fairly diverse groups and individuals, some Communists, others Socialists of varied stripes, and still others "liberals" with utopian visions and "the end justifies the means" mentality. Despite the existence of Social Democratic parties and Socialist parties, many of them successful in post-1989 electoral politics, as a movement, the Left has been neither strongly ideological nor radical in Eastern Europe in 1990–2000. That may change. For a good review of leftist politics in post-Communist Eastern Europe, see Linda Cook, Mitchell Orenstein, and Marilyn Rueschemeyer, eds., *Left Parties and Social Policy in Postcommunist Europe* (Boulder, Colo.: Westview Press, 1999).

42. Gorbachev first introduced the "Third Way" in an attempt to save Communism by marrying Marxism-Leninism with capitalism and some elements of liberal democracy. Many Western leftists and some liberals who share the Left's dreams of a utopian society and disregard the Left's illiberal ways and antiliberal inclinations, continue to hold on to a vision of a highly socially minded and highly controlled capitalist society in which individual liberties are dictated by the needs of society. One of the best examples of this thinking is exemplified in the paper authored by British Prime Minister Tony Blair and German Chancellor Gerhard Schroder, "Europe: The Third Way/Die Neue Mitte, 1999." It was widely published in Europe. See, for example, "The Blair/Schroeder Manifesto. Europe: The Third Way/Die Neue Mitte," *Amsterdam Post,* June 11, 1999. But the "mirage" of a Third Way, as Dahrendorf, *Reflections,* 66, says, is "wrong in theory because it arouses the totalitarian potential of all Utopias" and also "wrong in

practice" because it replaces an open, free society with a system that inhibits individual and societal freedoms. See also Wasco, "Introduction," 1–15.

43. See Wasco, "Introduction," 1–13.

44. For an interesting discussion of the concerns and challenges regarding the Internet in Eastern Europe, see Laura Lengal, ed., *Culture and Technology in the New Europe: Civic Discourse in Transformation in Post-Socialist Nations* (Stamford, Conn.: JAI Press; Ablex, 1999). On the Internet's contributions to democratization, see, for example, Peter Dahlgren, "The Internet and the Democratization of Civic Culture," *Political Communication* 17, no. 4 (Oct. 2000): 335–40; Margaret Scammell, "The Internet and Civic Engagement: The Age of the Citizen Consumer," *Political Communication* 17, no. 4 (Oct. 2000): 351–56.

45. See UN/UNESCO, *Information Society: Background Document* (Brussels: International Federation of Journalists, 1997).

46. See ITU, *World Telecommunication Indicators,* 2000. <www.itu.int/ITU-D /ict/statistics>.

47. Ibid.

48. Ibid.

49. Some of the Internet addresses include Albania: <www.hri.org/news/balkans/ ata>; <www.albanian.com/main/news>; Bulgaria: <www.hri.org/news/agencies/bta/>; <www.nationalradio.bg>; Czech Republic: <www.muselik.com/czech/news.html>; <www. omicron.felk.cvut.cz/springier/czpress/html>; <www.lolumbiaedu/js332/czech. html>; Hungary: <www.lib.klte.hu/start/media/news>; <www.hungary.com/dunatv>; Poland: <www.pap.com.pl>; <www.gazeta.pl>; <www.radiopol.com>; <www.tvpol. com>; Romania: <www.romlinkinternational.com/ziare>; Slovak Republic: <www. slovakradio.sk>; <www. omicron.felk.cvut.cz/springier/czpress/html>.

50. See Dahrendorf, *Reflections,* 13.

51. Wasko, "Introduction," 7.

52. Ralf Dahrendorf, "The Third Way and Liberty: An Authoritarian Streak in Europe's New Center," *Foreign Affairs* 78, no. 5 (Sept.–Oct. 1999): 13–17.

53. Revel, *Flight from Truth,* 284.

54. On the influence of the cultural milieu, see, for example, Schudson, "How News Becomes News," 76–85.

55. See, for example, William A. Hachten, *The Troubles of Journalism: A Critical Look at What's Right and Wrong with the Press* (London: Erlbaum, 1998).

56. For an informative and amusing account of American "opinion-meisters," see Eric Alterman, *Sound and Fury: The Making of Punditocracy* (Ithaca, N.Y.: Cornell University Press, 1999).

57. See Thomas C. Leonard, *The Power of the Press: The Birth of American Political Reporting* (Oxford: Oxford University Press, 1986), chap. 4, p. 94.

58. Splichal, *Media beyond Socialism,* 78.

59. In his articulate defense of "the vital center," the liberal alternative to the Right and the Left, Arthur Schlesinger Jr., asserts, with good reason, that both the Right and the Left "faced by problems they cannot understand and fear to meet, tend to compound their own failure by delivering free society to its totalitarian foe." See Arthur M. Schlesinger Jr., *The Vital Center: The Politics of Freedom* (New Brunswick, N.J.: Transaction, 1998), 50.

Index